WRITING LABOR'S EMANCIPATION

WRITING LABOR'S EMANCIPATION

The Anarchist Life and Times of Jay Fox

GREG HALL

UNIVERSITY OF WASHINGTON PRESS

Seattle

WRITING LABOR'S EMANCIPATION WAS MADE POSSIBLE IN PART BY A GRANT FROM THE SAMUEL AND ALTHEA STROUM ENDOWED BOOK FUND.

26   25   24   23   22   5   4   3   2   1

Printed and bound in the United States of America

UNIVERSITY OF WASHINGTON PRESS
uwapress.uw.edu

LIBRARY OF CONGRESS CATALOGING-IN-PUBLICATION DATA
Names: Hall, Greg, 1961– author.
Title: Writing labor's emancipation : the anarchist life and times of Jay Fox / Greg Hall.
Description: Seattle : University of Washington Press, 2022. | Includes bibliographical references and index.
Identifiers: LCCN 2021056905 (print) | LCCN 2021056906 (ebook) | ISBN 9780295750576 (hardcover) | ISBN 9780295750583 (paperback) | ISBN 9780295750590 (ebook)
Subjects: LCSH: Fox, Jay, 1870–1961. | Anarchists—United States—Biography. | Political activists—United States—Biography. | Journalists—United States—Biography. | Labor movement—United States—History. | Anarchism—United States—History.
Classification: LCC HX843.7.F69 H35 2022 (print) | LCC HX843.7.F69 (ebook) | DDC 335/.83092 [B]—dc23/eng/20211119
LC record available at https://lccn.loc.gov/2021056905
LC ebook record available at https://lccn.loc.gov/2021056906

♾ This paper meets the requirements of ANSI/NISO Z39.48-1992 (Permanence of Paper).

For my mother and father, who taught me the value of biography and memoir

CONTENTS

ACKNOWLEDGMENTS

My first encounter with Jay Fox was as a graduate student while working on my master's degree. I wrote a study on the anarchism of Home Colony and found the anarchist editor of *The Agitator* to be a fascinating historical character. He came up again while I was researching my dissertation that became my book *Harvest Wobblies*. Over the years, I thought that a study of this anarchist in the labor movement would be a good way to examine American radicalism in the late nineteenth and early twentieth centuries. Researching and writing this book took much longer than I ever anticipated, but it has been an interesting journey and I have a number of people and institutions to thank.

Over ten years ago, I presented a paper at the Pacific Northwest Labor History Association conference on Fox and anarchism in the Pacific Northwest. I spoke with association president Ross K. Rieder and told him that I was considering a book-length study of Fox but I was not sure if enough primary sources existed for such a study. Ross smiled and told me he had a personal collection of Fox's unpublished writings that he would loan me. It really made all the difference in taking on this study. Thanks, Ross. I would also like to thank Joy Werlink (retired) and Ed Nolan at the Washington State History Research Center, the archivists, librarians, and their assistants at the University of Washington, Washington State University, Gonzaga University, the Washington State Archives, University of Michigan, and the Newberry Library, as well as Aaron Lisec at Southern Illinois University and Danielle Nista at New York University. In addition, I would like to thank Marcel van der Linden and the good people at the International Institute of Social History in Amsterdam.

I want to thank Western Illinois University for awarding me a University Research Grant, for it made the travel and other expenses possible while I did my research at special collections, archives, and libraries. The library and archives staff at WIU's Malpass Library were also extremely helpful with my research. In addition, my 2020–21 sabbatical provided me with enough time to complete my draft of the entire manuscript. Also, I wish to thank Andrew Berzanskis, Neecole Bostick, Joeth Zucco, Nicholas Taylor, and the staff at the University of Washington Press. Andrew provided insightful council about the manuscript and was especially helpful in transitioning the manuscript into a published book.

A number of my colleagues at several history conferences assessed my research on Fox and anarchism in the American labor movement. Their constructive criticism was quite helpful. I published an overview of Fox's intellectual life and labor movement activism in *Left History*. Not only did the anonymous reviewers and staff at the journal assist in making my article publishable, but the article set the scope and themes for the eventual book.

I have been working at the project for such a long period that I am sure I will forget to thank some people. Several graduate assistants, among them David Sprung, Nathan Schmidt, Adam Moss, Harrison Schulte, and Riley Gober, performed a number of tasks that made my job as a researcher much easier. Colleagues and friends such as Mary Carr, Peter Cole, Jeff Johnson, Jason Knirck, David Collins, and Mike Kilroy discussed my research and writing on this project. I appreciate their support and encouragement. Several read my article manuscript or draft chapters of the present book and offered insightful criticism. The anonymous reviewers of my manuscript at the University of Washington Press were extremely important in helping me fine-tune my analysis as well as trim down my manuscript into a more manageable length. Thanks to you all.

ABBREVIATIONS

AFL	American Federation of Labor
ARU	American Railway Union
AWIU	Amalgamated Wood Workers International Union of America
BCC	Brotherhood of the Cooperative Commonwealth
BSIW	Bridge and Structural Iron Workers' Union
BWU	Brewery Workers Union
CFL	Chicago Federation of Labor
CGT	Confédération Générale du Travail
CIO	Congress of Industrial Organizations
CLU	Central Labor Union
FLU	Federation of Labor Unions
GMA	General Managers Association
IAM	International Association of Machinists
ILGWU	International Ladies' Garment Workers' Union
ISEL	Industrial Syndicalist Education League
ISWU	International Shingle Weavers' Union
ITUEL	International Trade Union Educational League
IUT	International Union of Timber Workers
IWA	International Woodworkers of America'
IWPA	International Working People's Association
IWW	Industrial Workers of the World
MHA	Mutual Home Association
NPL	Non-Partisan League
PLM	Partido Liberal Mexicano
RILU	Red International of Labor Unions
SDA	Social Democracy of America
SLNA	Syndicalist League of North America

SLP   Socialist Labor Party
SPA   Socialist Party of America
TUEL   Trade Union Education League
UBCJA   United Brotherhood of Carpenters and Joiners
UMW   United Mine Workers
WFM   Western Federation of Miners
WMP   Workingmen's Party of the United States
WWP   Wage Workers Party

WRITING LABOR'S EMANCIPATION

Introduction

Jay Fox, the Agitator

I N SPRING 1886, A SIXTEEN-YEAR-OLD JAY FOX WAS EMPLOYED AT the Malleable Iron Works in Chicago, working in the trimming room for seventy-five cents a day, sixty hours a week, the standard workweek for most wageworkers in the United States. Labor unions and other worker organizations had been agitating for years that the eight-hour day should be the standard workday, which culminated in a call on 1 May for the shorter shift to begin. In the foundry where he worked, many of the workers, including Fox, had secretly joined the Knights of Labor, most assemblies of which advocated for the eight-hour day. The Knights' assembly at the iron works, along with workers across the country, supported the demand. When management refused the ultimatum of the foundry workers, they voted to strike, closing "the shop down tight." Thousands of workers in Chicago went on strike for the eight-hour day as well when employers would not accept the demand for the shorter workday. As many as sixty thousand workers in Chicago may have gone on strike. They were joined by several hundred thousand workers nationwide who struck when employers did not meet their demand. A general strike for the eight-hour day had begun. Fox, along with many of his fellow striking workers, picketed the foundry. He recalled many years later that this was his "first active participation in the class struggle." He grew restless on the picket line on 3 May because little was taking place at the iron works. The picket line was quiet and uneventful, for the employers did not attempt to bring in scab labor. Out of curiosity that day, he left his workers' picket line and went over to the picket line near the McCormick Reaper Works that was just a couple of blocks away, where laborers were also on strike. Fox found far more "excitement" than he had thought possible. Years later he remarked that he soon gained "a practical lesson in capitalism's murderous brutality." He continued, "There I got my first practical experience in the class war."[1]

The strike situation at the McCormick works was much more intense. There, union iron molders had been locked out for weeks and had harassed the replacement labor brought in to keep the factory running. The eight-hour-day strike wave, however, even affected the McCormick scabs, half of whom joined the strike. When Fox arrived at the McCormick picket line, the first thing he noticed was a huge bonfire. Moments earlier, the striking workers had upset three vehicles that transported strike breakers, sending the scabs fleeing in all directions. The strikers allowed the drivers to take away their horses; once the horses were clear, the strikers torched the busses. The column of police that had been there to escort the scabs was outnumbered and had backed up to the gates of the plant. They waited for reinforcements before attempting to escort out the remaining workers inside the factory. During the standoff that lasted for several hours, striking workers threw rocks and other debris at the police, which only increased the tension. Heading up Blue Island Avenue, Fox sighted a patrol wagon, followed by two others, all filled with police. Once the reinforcements arrived, they were met with a hail of rocks. The new contingent of police dodged the projectiles and took up positions alongside their brethren.

The police, now sixty to seventy in number, drew their revolvers and batons and proceeded to move against the pickets. The striking workers began to retreat, some turning away and running to leave the scene and avoid arrest. It is not clear when or for exactly what reason, but police began to fire into the crowd of retreating and fleeing workers. Fox had turned to run when the police advanced, and he felt the whizzing of bullets flying by him. A bullet grazed his arm as it struck a worker in front of him in the back. Before the worker fell to the ground, Fox was able to grab him and hold him up with the help of others. They carried him from the street to safety, but he died soon thereafter. They carried his body to his home, which Fox characterized as a "shack." He was deeply moved as the dead man's wife and children gathered around his body, weeping with shock and grief. Fox left the heartrending scene and returned to his foundry's picket line to relate his story to his fellow striking workers. As he told his story, he received treatment for his wound.[2]

Fox's life took a dramatic turn on that fateful day when he witnessed the bloody clash between strikers and the police. Instead of staying clear of such conflicts in the future—as many workers would—Fox became a committed, radicalized union worker and would spend the next forty years fighting for the emancipation of the working class. He would work a variety of trades over the course of his life, always carrying a union card. Active in the trade and industrial unions he belonged to, he would have more impact as a writer, journalist, and editor of radical and union publications. Even though his fellow workers would elect him to positions in labor organizations, he did not seek out leadership roles. He was much more comfortable as an agitator. He wanted his readership to liberate themselves by first seeing the world around them for what it was and to then taking an active part in transforming it into something more just and equitable for all. In some respects, he was a pioneer in labor journalism. He could take complex ideas and events and distill them into digestible, short essays for his largely working-class readership. As his writing evolved, he injected humor, invented characters, and included his personal history—both actual and embellished—making his writing even more accessible. Fox was one of a small number of American men and women—native-born and immigrant—who were working-class, "organic intellectuals," to use the term of the Italian Marxist Antonio Gramsci. Of course, all workers have intellects and can use them. Nevertheless, few have a class consciousness in which they use their intellectual talents as revolutionaries in the service of their class. Fox was heavily influenced by the anarchists of Chicago, who looked to the labor movement as an indispensable factor in a social revolution that would overthrow both the capitalist system and the nation-state and inaugurate a classless society of liberty and equality.[3]

In recent years, anarchism has made a resurgence. Anarchists played a part in the World Trade Organization protests in Seattle in 1999, the Occupy Wall Street movement in the wake of the Great Recession, the emergence of Antifa, and the nationwide protests against police brutality arising from George Floyd's murder at the hands of a Minneapolis police officer. With the demise of international communism and the seeming ineffectiveness of democratic socialism, anarchism offers as a salient critique of both capitalism and the nation-state as well as a vision of an egalitarian, libertarian, cooperative, and environmentally sustainable society. In addition, the history of anarchism has experienced a renaissance in scholarship that offers innovative studies of anarchists in the United States and abroad with influences moving back and forth across the globe. Historically, anarchism had a number of influential theorists, writers, and activists in different parts of the world, and specific cities harbored affinity groups of anarchists, which were significant to anarchist theory and practice. Anarchism has always embodied several different strains. In this study, two types of anarchism are most relevant: anarchist communism and anarcho-syndicalism. Both are closely related with the major differences involving strategies and tactics; yet both strive for libertarian socialism, meaning socialism without the nation-state.

Anarchism is commonly thought of as a foreign import to the United States that came with immigrants from Europe. It is true that anarchism's most important theorists—Mikhail Bakunin, Pyotr Kropotkin, Jacques Élisée Reclus, Errico Malatesta, Jean Grave, and Gustav Landauer—were Europeans. Kropotkin, who spent a good portion of his life in exile, especially in London, was a prolific writer, with much of his work written directly in English or later translated. He was the most influential anarchist of the late nineteenth and early twentieth centuries. His essays, public speaking, and books were essential to the development of anarchist-communist theory. Nevertheless, within the American anarchist press, anarchism was continually being debated, reassessed, and defined by practicing anarchists. Two significant studies of the American history of anarchism challenge the notion that anarchism arrived with immigrants. Tom Goyens's *Beer and Revolution: The German Anarchist Movement in New York City, 1880–1914* examines small German immigrant communities of anarchists in New York City and several other cities in the Northeast. His innovative study of the "radical space"—or the geography of anarchism in saloons, lecture halls, and other areas occupied by German anarchists—demonstrates that anarchism emerged from the experience of German immigrants after they arrived in the country. Similarly, Kenyon Zimmer's *Immigrants Against the State: Yiddish and Italian Anarchism in America* underscores Goyens's argument by an analysis of Yiddish and Italian immigrant communities in different areas of the country in which anarchism developed after settling in the United States as well. Fox, of Irish descent and born in the New Jersey, became an anarchist as a young man soaking up the ideas of Albert Parsons, reading a variety of anarchist literature, and experiencing working life firsthand in Chicago, among other influences.[4]

Fox's intellectual life went through three distinct phases. The anarchism that he would come to embrace took time to develop. Even though he had radicalizing experiences as a teenager, it would take ten years before he was a self-styled anarchist. He did not hold rigidly to any dogmatic form of anarchism, though he clearly was most comfortable with anarchist communism. The means by which a new society would come into being and the contours that would shape that new society were not something Fox sought to articulate in any great detail. He thought that mass insurrection or social revolution would, at some point, take place because of the exploitive and brutal nature of capitalism and due to the oppressive actions of the nation-state. A liberated people would then be free to create an egalitarian system to meet the needs of everyone in a classless, stateless society. Militarism, colonialism, and war would no longer exist in a libertarian future. His anarchism, just as it was with most anarchists of his generation, was more than a concern over the fair production and distribution of societal wealth and opposition to the violence of governments. It also had a personal or lifestyle component in that it was a counterculture. Free love, gender equality, power-free relationships, and opposition to social control by religious institutions and governments were all important features of anarchism. Over time Fox, along with many anarchists, became more focused on anarcho-syndicalism as an actual means to bring about a social revolution through the power of organized labor. The general strike, led by a revolutionary labor movement, would bring about revolution without violence and the labor unions themselves would be the system of economic organization for a new society. Moreover, an examination of Fox's writing and activities as an anarchist communist and as an anarcho-syndicalist demonstrate how these ideas, strategies, and tactics worked on the ground level.

A final phase of Fox's intellectual development took place in the late 1910s and early 1920s. The Russian Revolution and the subsequent Bolshevik seizure of power opened a different path to a more just and equitable society for anarchists, anarcho-syndicalists, left-wing socialists, and labor militants of various stripes. It is difficult to reconcile Fox's evolution from libertarian socialism to authoritarian socialism, but an examination of the transition Fox went through, which was a journey that many of his cohort also experienced, sheds light on the course of labor radicalism in the

United States. As a communist, Fox believed that a withering away of the nation-state would take place once society was sufficiently socialized. Even though he participated in a movement that was much more ideologically rigid than anarchism, he was part of an organization that was committed to the interests of the working class, at the forefront of racial and gender equality, the self-determination of colonial peoples, and the creation of a cooperative economic system.

According to the late labor historian David Montgomery, "Both 'history from the bottom up' and the common fixation on great leaders have obscured the decisive role of those whom the twentieth-century syndicalists have called the 'militant minority': the men and women who endeavored to weld their workmates and neighbors into a self-aware and purposeful working class." Fox was a member of the militant minority and a participant in the arc of American labor radicalism from the late nineteenth century to the early twentieth century. Through the study of his intellectual life and work, a window opens to a diverse labor movement that was receptive to a variety of ideas and voices addressing the conditions of laborers—skilled and unskilled, native-born and immigrant, male and female—as they experienced industrial capitalism's transformation of the American economy. The Industrial Workers of the World (IWW) has been the subject of intense study as the premier labor federation that was both radical in its demands from employers and revolutionary in its aspirations for American society. Fox was at the founding of the IWW in 1905 and was supportive of much of the new federation's agenda, particularly its effort to organize the masses of nonunionized workers on an industrial basis. Most of Fox's labor union experience, however, was in unions affiliated with the American Federation of Labor (AFL), which has traditionally been depicted by labor historians as being overwhelmingly conservative, exclusionary, and consisting of primarily white, native-born, skilled, male trade unionists. They also emphasize the federation's practice of "business unionism" or "pure and simple trade unionism" that did not fundamentally question capitalism and sought no economic alternative. Labor historian Dorothy Sue Cobble has challenged that depiction of the AFL and has skillfully argued that the federation was far more reformist and radical, particularly during the Progressive Era. Fox's union activity, especially with the International Union of Timber Workers in the Pacific Northwest and his writing in labor periodicals, demonstrations that the AFL was far more open to alternative ideas and voices within its ranks.[5]

A key period in Fox's development as a writer was as a regular columnist for *Free Society*, an anarchist-communist newspaper edited by Abe Isaak with the assistance of his family. *Free Society*, for a time, was the most significant English-language anarchist-communist periodical in the country, which featured a variety of writers including Kropotkin, Emma Goldman, Voltairine de Cleyre, and Harry Kelly, among others. The anarchist press along with the socialist press were part of the "heyday" of radical newspapers, journals, magazines, pamphlets, and books circulating in the country during Fox's most active time as a writer. Anarchist periodicals were published in a whole host of languages, with English, German, Italian, and Yiddish being some of the most prevalent. For anarchists, the act of publishing a newspaper or a pamphlet and circulating the printed word was a collective effort that was at "the heart of anarchist communities," something that gave their lives purpose and meaning. With their own periodicals, anarchists could present their unique analysis of current events, history, and critiques of the structures and institutions of society. Through their iconoclastic print culture, they provided a counternarrative to what was published in the mainstream press.

During the same period that the radical press was at its peak, the labor press was becoming more widespread and would continue to grow as the twentieth century unfolded. Many labor newspapers, journals, and magazines were directly connected to specific trade and industrial unions, the central labor councils of cities, and federations. Part of a worker's union dues were used to support a labor union newspaper. These union newspapers could be extremely important in maintaining communication with the union membership on policies, elections, strikes, and other relevant news. With mainstream newspapers often hostile to unions and striking workers, labor advocates needed to secure their own counternarrative to what was depicted in the most common media of the age: daily city newspapers. Fox's writing appeared in a variety of union periodicals, and at one point he wrote for a labor newspaper syndicate that circulated his articles across the country. His career as a published writer demonstrates the cross-pollination of ideas, commentary, and critiques of capitalism between the radical and labor presses. In addition, his experiences as a writer underscore the battle for a free press and free speech. His own case made its way to the United States Supreme Court.[6]

Rather than a traditional biography, this study of Jay Fox offers a "biographical approach" to his intellectual life and work. Social histories and labor histories that present grand analytical narratives of the American working class are extremely important endeavors that illuminate the class, race, and gender dynamics of US history. Nevertheless, they can be abstract and impersonal, and it can be difficult with these historical genres to gain a full appreciation of the evolution individuals experienced over time. Fox's intellectual evolution can be seen in his interactions with the social, economic, political, and environmental worlds he inhabited. He associated with many men and women over the course of his life. Few of these individuals left much in the historical record. However, he left enough "traces" of his life to create a microhistory of the radicals, utopians, revolutionaries, and union men and women with whom he associated, debated, and supported over the course of many decades. They contextualize his life and work, and moreover, these symbiotic relationships had dramatic impacts on him as an intellectual and as member of the American working class. Fox's writings, which are the most significant traces he left behind, illuminate how wageworkers confronted class in American society and the barriers that they faced to achieving a secure and prosperous life for themselves and their families. A close analysis of his writing, especially his published work, provides a view of how class and to some degree labor organizing actually worked. Obviously, his own interpretations are a subjective filter. Nevertheless, his writings along with those of other radical and labor writers provide for historians precious knowledge of the lived experience of working-class Americans and, even more to the point, proof that class matters in the history of the United States.[7]

Researching Fox's intellectual life, let alone his personal history, was no easy task. Late in life, he began work on a memoir as well as a history of anarchism, neither of which were ever completed and remain as unpublished manuscripts. Typewritten chapters and pages are in collections of his personal papers at the University of Washington, Washington State University, Gonzaga University, and in the possession of Ross K. Reider, former president of the Pacific Northwest Labor History Association, who purchased Fox's personal papers from a Spokane, Washington, bookstore owner in the 1970s. Ross was kind enough to loan me his collection so that I could scan the manuscripts, letters, poems, notes for speeches, and other written records. Despite a wealth of primary sources, serious gaps still exist when trying to ascertain where he was traveling, living and working, the identities of his closest comrades, aspects of his family history, and when some of his unpublished writings were written. Therefore, it is necessary, then, to focus on distinct periods of his life, with much of his personal history left only partially examined due to the lack of sources. For example, in Hapgood Hutchins's *The Spirit of Labor*, published in 1907, the American journalist refers to Fox having been married before his relationship with Esther Abramowitz.[8] Fox, though, does not mention a first wife in his memoir. In addition, he more than likely fathered a child with Esther, but he did not reference his daughter Rebecca in the surviving pieces of his memoir either. As with many other radicals and revolutionaries, Fox may have thought it inappropriate to write about too many of his personal life experiences, whether in terms of his relationships with individuals or his family. Still, I have been able to document good portions of his life in Chicago, New York, Seattle, and most especially Home, Washington, both when it was at its peak as an anarchist colony on the banks of the Puget Sound and as it evolved into a community of progressive men and women and their families. Fox's published writings are more easily accessible through traditional research practices and access to databases of digitized newspapers and labor periodicals. Fox first appears in the historical record as a writer in 1897. He claims to have written for newspapers and for labor periodicals before that year, but I have not been able to corroborate his assertion. Despite research challenges, I have been fortunate to have found enough sources to create a compelling portrait of the intellectual life and work of a true American radical, revolutionary, and agitator.

1. Becoming an Anarchist

SOON AFTER HIS PARENTS ARRIVED AT CASTLE GARDEN IN DOWN-
town Manhattan, which at the time was the main entry port for most
European immigrants to the United States, the couple temporarily moved
to New Jersey, where Jay Fox was born on 20 August 1870. The young
family did not remain in the Northeast for long, for Fox's mother had a
brother, Martin Murphy, who had immigrated sometime earlier and resided
in Chicago. Just like Irish immigrants before them, the family sought to be
near kin and compatriots as well as to prosper in the burgeoning industrial
city of the Midwest. According to Fox, they "settled back of the stock yards
in the midst of a medley of other poor foreigners." The neighborhood,
adjacent to Bridgeport, had primarily Irish and German residents, though
a number of other European immigrants lived in the community as well. His
parents remembered their new home community as consisting of "all very
fine people and good neighbors." Amid this largely immigrant, working-
class section of Chicago, they brought up their only son to be a Catholic, a
Democrat, and an educated, working man. His parents attended mass
regularly and occasionally went to confession, though Fox could not think
of what "sin" they may have needed to admit. He admired his parents' "spot-
less life" and their innate "goodness and honesty," which as a youth and as
an adult, he believed the great mass of people possessed as a "natural impulse."
He tried to please his parents by becoming an altar boy but disappointed
them when he did not take the path to become a priest as they had hoped

that he would. However, he did please his illiterate, unschooled parents by attending school and getting educated. He wrote years later that he believed his parents' lack of education was a "shining example of the low regard the governing class of England had for the cultural welfare of its subject races." Young Fox attended grammar school and learned to read, write, and "make change," which he later came to believe was "all the bosses needed" the working class to know. He decided to drop out before finishing grammar school. Therefore, most of his education had to take place outside of the classroom.[1]

Although Fox thought of himself as "a timid soft-spoken, sensitive kid," he traveled with "a gang of rowdies" when not in school or in church. He did not think of his "gang" as violent or criminal. Their primary passion was for playing baseball. Nor were they overly rebellious when it came to the "rules and regulations" of society. They conformed, and part of that conformity was to be Democrats. Fox, as a young teenager, was proud to be a supporter of Grover Cleveland in the presidential election of 1884. With drummers keeping him and the other political parade goers in time, wrapped in a "flashy sash" and carrying a torch, he marched with other boys in an evening torchlight procession for Cleveland's campaign. After the march through the ward, they returned to the headquarters of the local boss and the "kids were rewarded with ice cream and cake while the men gathered around a keg of beer." One of his most vivid memories of that political year was taking a ride on a streetcar downtown to the Lake Front armory to listen to Henry George. Decades later, Fox remembered George's opening words: "I am for Cleveland and free trade." Although, at the time, the teenage Fox did not understand the Democratic call for free trade as a solution to high consumer prices, unemployment, and low wages, he was "highly elated at having a part in the election of the first democratic president since 1857."[2]

As a young teenager, Fox would continue to embrace his father's politics, and he also followed his father into the world of wage work. Fox's uncle Murphy, who was a switch tender for the Pennsylvania Railroad, had assisted Fox's father—soon after the family arrived in Chicago—to secure a job as a section hand with the railroad. At $1.40 for ten hours of work a day, six days a week, Fox's father could provide for his small family and seemed, according to Fox, happy with his job, family, and home "and had no thought of rising even to be section boss." Fox admired his father's work ethic and personal integrity but could not understand his father's lack of ambition.

Young Fox, like his father, also had to start at the bottom as an unskilled laborer. He did so after dropping out of school to take a job. He thought he had learned all he needed to and was prepared to earn a wage. It is not clear whether his parents approved of this action on the part of young Fox, but they may have been able to use his addition to the family income. Moreover, he had the basics of an education and to complete grammar school and move on to high school was an option open to few working-class teenagers.

His working life would begin in a Chicago cabbage patch, working for John Wentworth, "the sauerkraut king of that period," according to Fox. Near the stock yards, Wentworth had "a great stretch of black soil" where he grew his cabbage. For fifty cents a day, the teenage Fox planted cabbage plant seedlings in the spring. The work was seasonal, so Fox drifted into other employment, but was back harvesting for Wentworth in the fall. Fox worked alongside other teenage boys but also among adults. The women, he remembered, were all immigrants. He also remembered an incident that had a great effect on his view of the hardiness of the immigrant working class and their need to work under the most difficult conditions and circumstances. One day at the worksite he witnessed several women gathered around a woman who was stretched out on the ground. He, along with some other boys and men, tried to investigate but were signaled way. In his unfinished memoir he wrote, "From the distance we saw her soon rise and walk to a wagon nearby upon which she was helped, given a bundle and the wagon drove away. We were then told what we suspected, she had given birth to a child. A new wage slave was born right on the job."[3]

Fox needed more permanent work than what he found with the "sauerkraut king." He was fortunate to land an authentic factory job at the Malleable Iron Works in fall 1885. At the foundry, he worked in the trimming room for seventy-five cents a day, which was half the daily wage as the men who did the same work. With no streetcars running his way, he had to rise at 5:30 a.m. and walk two miles from his home near the stock yards and be at the foundry by 7:00. At his station, he had before him a pile of small castings. His task was to inspect each casting and break off excess metal from the molding using a hammer and tongs and an iron block for leverage. After six months on the job, he approached his foreman, Pat Conley, and asked for a raise. Conley replied in his Irish brogue, "Faith, . . . I'd be glad to do it if I had the power. All wages are fixed in the office and if I turned in your complaint they might tell me to fire you, as they say they don't want anyone on the job who is not satisfied with what he is getting." Feeling discouraged, he related his story to a man in the trimming room by the name of Hurley, with whom he had become friendly, only later did he discover that Hurley was an anarchist. His friend told him that the bosses should "fire the lot of us then . . . for none of us is satisfied with what we are getting." He proceeded to tell young Fox that workers were "organizing on the quiet" and that they planned to strike for more pay and shorter hours. The anarchist asked him if he would like to join them. He was taken aback, asking "You take in boys?" "Yes," Hurley replied, "you are a wage slave exploited even more than us men. Anyway we take in everyone that works."[4]

The workers' organization that Hurley invited Fox to join in spring 1886 was the Knights of Labor. In that year, the Knights had reached their highest membership, surging from one hundred thousand in 1885 to over seven hundred thousand by June 1886. The union was exceptional for its time because it organized men and women, immigrants and the native-born, skilled and unskilled, white and black workers. The Knights, however, were intensely hostile to Chinese immigration. Fox, though not knowing at the time how powerful the Knights were in Chicago or nationally, was delighted to be thought of as an equal to other workers. Moreover, he felt proud that they had confidence in him and shared their course of action, for if "the bosses had gotten wind of what was going on" the leaders and many members of the Knights at the iron works would be fired. Fox had many questions for Hurley, and in an effort to help to further educate him, Hurley encouraged him to attend a meeting, called by Chicago's Central Labor Union (CLU), at Lake Front Park on that coming Sunday afternoon, 25 April 1886. August Spies and several other German labor leaders along with Albert Parsons established the CLU in 1884 as an alternative city labor council to the more conservative Trades and Labor Assembly of the city. Many of the member unions affiliated with the CLU were also members of the International Working People's Association (IWPA), an international anarchist organization, also known as the Black International.

The meeting turned out to be a massive rally in support of the eight-hour day. It started first as a march of approximately fifteen thousand workers beginning on the city's West Side with perhaps fifty thousand watching the procession. The marchers eventually coalesced at the park. Parsons was the main speaker and chaired the meeting. He, along with his wife Lucy, were editors of *The Alarm*, an English-language anarchist newspaper. Other prominent labor leaders of the city spoke as well, such as Samuel Fielden, who like Parsons spoke in English and Michael Schwab and Spies, who spoke in German. Before Parsons called the meeting to order, Hurley took the opportunity to introduce Fox as his young protégé to Parsons. Hurley said to Parsons that Fox was "one of the boys who will take our places when we grow too old to fight." Fox received a warm handshake from Parsons, who said, "Fine, my lad, we need thousands like you in this grand fight for human freedom." Parsons soon took the platform to begin the meeting. Young Fox fondly remembered that "Parsons was of slender build and medium height with sparkling kindly eyes." In listening to him address the gathering, he thought that even though his voice was high-pitched it had good carrying capacity. Fox further remembered, "He had the faculty of awakening in his audience the feeling of oneness with him by giving clarified expression to its inarticulate ideas and emotions."[5]

The anarchism Parsons and Hurley introduced to Fox was firmly rooted in the American working class and in the labor movement. It had emerged, in part, from the CLU and IWPA. The Pittsburg Manifesto of 1883, a mass insurrectionary anarchist document directed at the workers, which Parsons and Spies helped to create, was distributed widely in Chicago. The manifesto appeared in *The Alarm* in late 1884 and was republished in subsequent issues of the anarchist newspaper. Moreover, the city's anarchists were deeply involved in Knights' local assemblies and worked within trade unions for immediate improvements in wages, hours, and working conditions. Radicalizing labor organizations and the working class, however, was the long-term project for anarchists, something that Bakunin and other anarchists had urged back in 1873 and perhaps earlier. Like Marxists and many socialists, anarchists saw the working class as part of the great class struggle that would culminate in a social revolution. Most anarchists accepted many aspects of Karl Marx's analysis of the historical development of capitalism, the inherent exploitation of all wageworkers, class formation, and class conflict. Unlike Marxists and state socialists, anarchists viewed direct action at the point of production as the best means to bring about the transformation of society. Political parties, though useful in the short term, were increasingly viewed by anarchists in the 1870s and 1880s as counterproductive or worse, though both Spies and Parsons belonged to the Workingmen's Party of the United States (WMP). Parsons had run for public office several times when he was a member of the Chicago Socialist

Labor Party. However, he found the electoral process corrupt, which meant that working men who labored six days a week at ten hours a day were effectively disenfranchised. Therefore, in turning to the trade union movement, anarchists saw the potential for direct action by the working class. Anarchists such as Parsons, however, had a complicated relationship with the labor movement. In mid-1885, for instance, he left the National Typographical Union due to its conservativism. Over time, though, the labor union, for anarchists, would be seen as "the vehicle of class struggle, a weapon for revolution," and a microcosm of the voluntary, egalitarian, and libertarian society to come. Fox imbibed this strain of anarchism in its embryonic stage in Chicago, which would later be termed anarcho-syndicalism.[6]

Spies, the editor of the *Chicagoer Arbeiter-Zeitung*, the German-language newspaper of the WMP and a significant voice of the eight-hour movement, had been speaking to a group of striking lumber shovers a short distance from the McCormick plant. He heard gunfire and along with a number of the lumber workers raced to the scene. Spies did not see the events unfold as young Fox did, but he witnessed the aftermath and was informed of what transpired by those who were there. Spies quickly returned to his newspaper office and wrote his momentous "Revenge" circular. The leaflet was distributed widely in the city that evening and the next day, though the second version of it had been edited to remove the words "Arm yourselves and appear in full force." A second leaflet called for a meeting on 4 May at 7:30 p.m. to be held at Haymarket Square. At the meeting, leaders of the eight-hour-day movement were to denounce the attack by the police on striking workers and to discuss the progress of the strike. Fox heard about the meeting and, given what he witnessed the previous day, without hesitation decided to attend. When he arrived that evening, he saw the wagon that speakers would use as a platform to address the crowd of about 1,500 people. Fox sat on the wooden sidewalk near the wagon, which was a good spot for clearly hearing the speakers. He was seated next to Lucy Parsons, her two children, and several other women, most notably Lizzie Holmes, a prominent anarchist of Chicago, writer for *The Alarm*, and labor organizer. This was his first encounter with Lucy and Holmes. He would come to admire these women for their intellects, their writings and speeches, and their commitment to the cause of labor. Fox was looking forward to listening to the speeches of radical labor advocates such as Parsons who were also members of the Knights of Labor.[7]

It took almost an hour for the meeting to begin. Spies had wanted Parsons to kick things off, but Parsons had not been informed until very late that he was expected to speak. While he was summoned to the meeting, Spies addressed the crowd. He was most comfortable speaking in German, though this time he spoke in English. Fox listened intently as Spies explained that the "capitalist press always misrepresented the cause of labor" and that the capitalists and the police are the sources of violence during strikes. The anarchist went on to counter charges made by Cyrus McCormick Jr., the owner of the reaper works, that Spies and other Chicago organizers of the eight-hour-day strike were responsible for the violence that occurred the day before at the plant. When Spies declared that McCormick was responsible for the killing and wounding of workers, some audience members in the crowd called out to hang McCormick. Spies—Fox remembered—cautioned them that such threats would not advance their cause and that action is what mattered. Spies urged the crowd to remain committed to the eight-hour movement and reminded them that the movement consisted of native-born Americans as well as immigrants. Parsons arrived as Spies concluded his speech and mounted the speaker's wagon. With Fox hanging on his every word, Parsons proceeded to speak to the now three thousand people in the audience. His address focused on the larger issues at stake in the strike. Shorter hours and better pay and working conditions were important, but the system itself was the problem for it was against the interests of the working class. He argued that the only long-term remedy for workers, who suffered starvation wages and poor working and living conditions the world over, was to own the tools and products of the economy themselves. In other words, own the means of production. He criticized the capitalists, such as Jay Gould, the railroad baron, who used the police force and hired gunmen to attack unarmed striking workers. When an audience member called out that Gould should be hanged, Parsons replied that this struggle was not about individuals but about replacing an economic system that created the many poor and the few rich with one that was just and equitable for all.[8]

Fox remembered that Samuel Fielden, a member of the American Group of the IWPA and a popular speaker at labor rallies, was the last to speak. He had only been talking for about twenty minutes when the weather began to threaten to rain. By this time the audience had thinned to about five hundred. He noticed a disruption to the left of the speaker's platform. Police were moving against the crowd, coming down Desplaines Street. Even though

Mayor Carter Harrison had listened to the speakers earlier in the evening and had told Inspector John Bonfield at the nearby police station that the demonstration required no intervention, Bonfield, based on information from one of his detectives, thought otherwise. Without authorization from the mayor, Bonfield persuaded Captain William Ward to move against the rally and clear Haymarket Square. Ward ordered the gathering to disperse. Fielden protested that they were peaceable, but when Ward repeated his command, Fielden, Spies, and others stepped down from the wagon. Just as they began to reach the street, a bomb was thrown into the front ranks of the police and exploded as soon as it hit the ground. One officer was killed almost instantly and six others would die of their wounds later. At first the police were stunned by the blast, but very soon they began firing into the gathering. Fox, like the rest of the crowd, took cover to avoid the gun fire and then "ran like hell."[9]

Young Fox was severely shaken by the events that momentous evening as well as by the battle at the gates of the McCormick factory the preceding day. Nevertheless, he stayed devoted to the eight-hour-day movement, continued to picket the iron works, and drew inspiration from the speeches of the Haymarket anarchists and of Albert Parsons in particular. He read some of the city's newspapers in subsequent days and found the accounts of Haymarket to be horribly distorted. The Knights' Chicago newspaper reaction to that evening's events was equally discouraging to Fox. With the foundry remaining closed and no strike fund that he could use for financial support, he needed to find work. He found employment canning beef, nearer his home, at Armour and Company in Packingtown. Following the eight-hour-day strike wave in early May that pulled skilled and unskilled workers out of the meatpacking plants, owners conceded to their workers' demand for the eight-hour day. Nine assemblies of the Knights of Labor formed that spring and summer in Packingtown. Fox joined a new assembly of the Knights as a packinghouse employee. His enjoyment of labor's victory in securing the eight-hour day did not last long. In the fall, the meatpackers imposed the ten-hour day. According to Fox, "The workers naturally refused and were locked out." Fox had high hopes that the solidarity of the workforce in opposition to the employers' autocratic imposition of the ten-hour day would be broken, for the workers had turned the lockout into a strike.

The Knights' General Assembly sent Tom Barry, a member of the executive board, to take charge of the eight-hour-day drive in Packingtown.

The owners were determined not to hire back any Knights. Nevertheless, after five weeks of a "solid front" of worker refusal to accept ten hours, employers announced that they were willing to negotiate. Then, according to Fox, "the unexpected suddenly happened." Grand Master Workman Terence Powderly, leader of the Knights, called off the strike and threatened to revoke the charter of any local that did not obey his decision. Powderly, who rarely supported strikes, did not think this particular strike was winnable in the long run, given the different labor constituencies involved. For Fox, however, this was a great betrayal of worker solidarity and the justness of the eight-hour day. Though many workers wanted to maintain the strike, he witnessed its collapse in the face of the leadership's lack of support. Fox remained a Knight, as he later noted, because of the organization's inclusiveness, industrial union nature, and its effort to create a cooperative economic system that would potentially lead to worker self-management. Nevertheless, he would remain suspicious of organizational leadership and have much more confidence in the rank and file and in those who seemed to speak the truth of the conditions and struggles of the working class.[10]

While Fox fought to make the eight-hour day a reality at the point of production and tried to make sense of the Knights as a labor organization, he followed the arrests and trial of the Haymarket anarchists. Soon after the bombing, police began arresting anarchists, socialists, labor radicals, and others thought suspicious by law enforcement. In all two hundred people were arrested, though the vast majority were released for lack of evidence. A coroner's inquest found Spies, Parsons, Fielden, and others complicit in the death of Mathias J. Degan, the first of the seven police officers who died as a result of the bombing and gunfire the night of 4 May at Haymarket. Moreover, a grand jury was impaneled to hear witness testimony regarding the incident, eventually indicting thirty-one people in connection with the death of Degan and with the other police officers killed or wounded. In the end, only eight would stand trial, including Parsons, who would return from his hiding place in Wisconsin and calmly walk into the court room after the trial had commenced.

Reading the newspapers of his day, Fox found the "capitalist press was aflame" following the bombing. The Chicago papers were quick to find Parsons, Spies, Fielden, and other anarchists, socialists, and labor radicals complicit in the bombing and deserving of as much condemnation and the severest punishment as the actual bomb thrower. The editorials also were quick to call for the indiscriminate suppression of the anarchist and socialist movements in the city and for the deportation of the members of the movements' organizations. To Fox's dismay, the *Knights of Labor*, the Knights' Chicago newspaper, was just as quick to condemn those leaders associated with the Haymarket rally and to disassociate the organization from anarchism. Later in the year, Fox was able to read more dispassionate accounts, including an autobiographical sketch of Albert Parsons published in the *Knights of Labor*. Parsons's life, work, and ideas resonated with young Fox and made a deep impression on him that he would draw from later in life. The following year Fox could read more supportive examinations of Haymarket in *The Alarm*, some of whose articles were written by Lucy. Dyer D. Lum, a prominent anarchist from Massachusetts, who was also a Knight and had contributed to *The Alarm* in the past, took over editorship of the publication, reviving it after it had suspended publication when Parsons left Chicago following the bombing—and continuing to do so while Lucy was on a tour seeking support (from labor unions in particular) for the anarchists on trial.[11]

Fox was not surprised when he read of the convictions of Parsons and most of the others for murder. From what he could gather from newspaper accounts and from discussions with his fellow Knights, he thought the accused never had a fair trial and were most likely innocent of any involvement with the bombing. He also knew from firsthand experience that the lethal shots fired that night were by the police themselves. Fox followed the appeals process, and when that came of naught he signed the petition circulated in his Knights assembly that requested clemency from Governor Richard Oglesby on behalf of the convicted. Like many at the time, Fox was not sure if Louis Lingg's death from biting down on a dynamite cap in his prison cell was suicide or murder, but later in life he wrote that he thought that Lingg "anticipated what was coming and decided to die of his own hand." Oglesby ended up only commuting the sentences of Michael Schwab and Fielden, who were willing to accept life in prison. The remaining four prisoners—Parsons, Spies, George Engel, and Adolph Fischer—faced execution on 11 November 1887. Again, writing years later, Fox commented that "four worker's lives [were] sacrificed on the alter [*sic*] of Mammon." After the executions, the bodies were turned over to family and friends. Fox paid his respects along with thousands of workers and their families, and he took part in the funeral procession the subsequent Sunday. Later, he attended the actual funeral held in Waldheim Cemetery and in summer 1888 witnessed the unveiling of the monument dedicated to the anarchist martyrs. The fate of the Haymarket anarchists would have a profound impact on him over the following years. Moreover, it would have a significant effect on an entire generation of anarchists in the United States and worldwide.[12]

After leaving packinghouse employment, Fox held a series of jobs, including as a woodworker, until he eventually became a blacksmith by trade. Over the course of these years and despite the decline of the Knights at the national level and even in Chicago, Fox continued to be an active member in his local assembly. In the early 1890s, he secured a job at the Illinois Central Railroad shop in Chicago. There he worked with other metalworkers, some affiliated with the Knights, to form the Metal Trades Council. The goal of the organization was to bring together all workers in the metal trades in order to make them less divided by craft. In May 1893, his friend Jim Finn, an engineer on the railroad, suggested that he join a new union that was just in the process of forming. Finn told him that Eugene Debs resigned as secretary of the Firemen's Brotherhood, one of the strongest trade unions in the railroad industry, to organize for the new union. Fox, at first, was a bit incredulous, asking if Finn was planning on being in both unions. Finn replied, "When the new union gets rolling the old one will shrivel up." Once Fox learned that the American Railway Union (ARU) was not just another trade or craft union but would "embrace every worker employed on the railways, from section hand up to the office staff," he decided it was worth joining. Fox wrote, "In view of my experience in the Knights of Labor the prospect of one big union on the railways appealed to me strongly, so I went along and became a charter member of local one of the American Railway Union."[13]

At the time of the ARU's formation, the railroad industry had only five trade unions or collective bargaining agents. Some, though, were still primarily fraternal societies, chiefly focused on acting as "insurance systems to protect members and their families from the hazards of the very dangerous occupation of railroading." Unskilled and semiskilled laborers such as roundhouse workers, track-men, and office workers had no union at all. Even many engineers, brakemen, firemen, and conductors were not represented by the existing trade unions, leaving them unorganized. Debs wanted to bring all these workers into one labor organization, which would

Young Jay Fox, circa 1890. Courtesy University of Washington Libraries, Special Collections, UW 891.

end the practice of unions scabbing on each other during strikes by one trade or another. With all workers in one union, a strike would bring all the workers out from the industry, thereby strengthening the strike action. This concept appealed to Finn and Fox as it did many other workers in the railroad industry who had been frustrated by the failure of strikes due to their fellow workers' actions. Fox was impressed by the simple but widely circulated manifesto of the ARU that outlined its goals, and he was equally impressed by the union membership dues of only one dollar a year. Being at the ground floor of the union, he watched it grow dramatically.[14]

The first major test of the ARU came in a conflict with the Great Northern Railroad, a transcontinental railroad that extended to the Pacific Northwest and employed nine thousand workers. Along with the rest of the country, James J. Hill, the owner of the railroad, and his management staff, faced a severe economic downturn in 1893. Like many employers, in an effort to avoid bankruptcy Hill cut wages. The first wage cut came in August. Another took place the following year in January, and yet another cut came in March. With the last wage cut, some workers were earning as little as forty dollars a month and generally Great Northern employees had become the lowest paid in the industry. In April, the railroad's workers voted to strike unless management would agree to meet with their representatives to negotiate a new wage scale. Hill refused to negotiate and ignored a letter from the ARU that explained the workers' intention to strike. Due to Hill's intransigence, the strike was on by mid-month. Debs was soon leading the action. In a brilliant feat of political maneuvering before a session of the St. Paul Chamber of Commerce with Hill in attendance, Debs was able to get support for the striking workers from the most powerful economic organization west of Chicago. Debs quickly accepted the chamber's decision for the union and Hill to settle the dispute through arbitration. In less than an hour, the arbitration board found for the strikers, who received 97 percent of their wage demands. Fox was thrilled by the solidarity and leadership of his new union, for within eighteen days the strike was over.[15]

In June, as a delegate, Fox attended the first convention of the ARU, which took place at the Haymarket Theater in Chicago. High on the agenda was the Pullman strike that had been underway since 10 May. Even though members of the ARU were participating in the strike, the union itself was not officially involved. However, that would soon change. Motivated both by a report issued to the delegates and by worker eyewitness testimony that described in detail the difficult circumstances of the striking workers and that of their families in George Pullman's company town, which lay just to the south of Chicago, the delegates passed a resolution calling for a boycott of Pullman sleeper cars. Fox voted with the delegates for a strike relief fund for the Pullman workers, for an offer by the union to arbitrate the conflict on behalf of the workers, and for an authorization to boycott if necessary. Pullman's refusal to negotiate triggered the executive board of the ARU to put the boycott in effect on all Pullman sleeper cars on any railroad in any part of the country. The railroad owners attempted to unify in support of Pullman with the General Managers Association (GMA). The leaders of the GMA employed the tactic of refusing to allow Pullman's cars to be separated from their trains. Workers on the lines then began to strike. Within days major portions of the country's railroads came to a stop. With over one hundred thousand railroad workers out on strike, the boycott quickly turned into a nearly nationwide railroad work stoppage.[16]

In order to confront the unified workforce, employers needed to bring the federal government into the dispute. The only way to do that was to accuse the strikers of disrupting the mail service. Debs repeatedly urged the strikers not in interfere with the mails. Nevertheless, that was the accusation made by Thomas Milchrist, the US attorney for Chicago, who was acting on orders from Attorney General Richard Olney, who had strong ties with the railroad industry. The application of injunction against the ARU and Debs to the federal court was made on the grounds that they were disrupting the postal system and therefore violated the Sherman Antitrust Act. Federal judges William A. Woods and Peter S. Grossup granted the injunction, which would force the union to end the strike. Despite assurances by Mayor John Hopkins of Chicago and by Governor John P. Altgeld, Olney urged President Grover Cleveland to send federal troops to the city. Violence had not been a factor before the introduction of federal troops, but their appearance created a spark that ignited conflict, which motivated General Nelson A. Miles to call for reinforcements for his troops in Chicago. Debs, knowing that the strike was likely lost, called for a general strike. On 10 July, Debs and other officials of the union were arrested "on charges of conspiracy to obstruct interstate commerce and the mails." Even more distressing for the ARU and Debs, Samuel Gompers, president of the AFL, preferred to support trade union brotherhoods in the railroad industry rather than the industrial unionism of the ARU. He declared the general strike to be "impulsive" and urged workers not to participate. Given the AFL's abstention, the depletion of union strike funds, and the federal government's direct intervention, the Pullman strike collapsed. Fox, who witnessed the events of summer 1894 firsthand, believed that the ARU had actually won the strike against the owners of the railroads. For Fox, workers' solidarity could defeat the forces of capital. However, the ARU, even as a unified industrial union, was not powerful enough to defeat the federal government. With a growing accumulation of working and labor union experience, memories of Parsons's speeches, and reading the radical and labor press of Chicago, Fox was beginning to see that the federal government along with state governments put the interests of capitalists over those of workers like himself.[17]

Fox had great admiration for Debs and his willingness to risk arrest and imprisonment in the cause of advancing the rights of labor. Fox was a member of a committee representing a number of unions that met Debs upon his release from McHenry County Jail in November 1895. The speech that he gave at Battery D, in which he spoke eloquently about freedom and the promise of the American Revolution, moved Fox along with the thousands who welcomed him back from prison. Nevertheless, with the collapse of the ARU and facing a blacklist by railroad owners, Fox, along with many other union activists, left railroad employment. He took his metalworking skills to a new field of manufacturing that seemed to be springing up in many industrial cities in the 1890s: bicycles. He was gainfully employed for a couple of years at a bike shop in Chicago. Like many of his fellow workers, he could not afford to buy any of the bikes that he built. One day, without any explanation by management, the sheriff arrived at the shop and closed it down, ordering all workers to vacate the premises. Not knowing if he would ever receive his final paycheck, Fox decided to take a bicycle from the shop in lieu of wages. Using "the confusion attending the Sheriff's visit," Fox enlisted the support to two coworkers who provided cover between the bikes and the front office. With their help, he snatched a bike off the rake. He calculated that "with a new bike that cost $50 to produce and sold for $100 retail, I would be sure of my pay and a little over as a bonus for the loss of my job." He placed his tool bag over the handlebar and quietly walked his "new iron horse out" of the shop.

Maybe not coincidently, he decided that it was a good time to leave Chicago and see some of the country and perhaps the world. Fox only had a few dollars in his pocket but thought that his transportation would be cheap and he could work "short jobs" and "offer to work for [his] meals." His decision to leave Chicago for the open road was not unusual. Since the economic depression of the mid-1870s, the tramping phenomenon of primarily young, male workers in search of temporary or seasonal labor had become more common with each passing decade and received a boost with each economic downturn. The depression of the mid-1890s was just another in a series of factors that made geographic mobility a reasonable course of action for a young man to take. Fox also thought that "tramping by bicycle" would be a novelty, and as it turned out people were interested in his adventure. He was never turned down when asking for food and some people along the way put him up overnight when the weather made sleeping under the trees impractical. Before leaving Chicago, he bought a case that fit in the frame of the bicycle that he could pack with a change of clothing and necessary tools. He strapped a blanket to the back of the seat and left the city in summer 1896. At the time, Fox was probably not conscious of the fact that his freedom, independence, and confidence to embark on this adventure had a good deal to do with his gender and race. He may have thought of himself as an oppressed and exploited wageworker; nevertheless, he had opportunities that other workers—women, African Americans, and many newly arrived immigrants—did not have.[18]

Over the last several years, Fox had made a few minor contributions to the labor press and thought of himself as somewhat of an aspiring writer. While tramping he conceived another way to make some money: he would give interviews and perhaps write a column about his bicycle journey for small-town newspapers. Fox made sure that he had a sense of the political orientation of the newspaper before he started to write, for he had to keep in mind that the presidential election campaign season was in full swing and many of the readers of the local paper may be Democrats, Republicans, or Populists. Knowing the political perspective of the editor, he could slant his writing to also include "the political prospects of either party." He felt a little uneasy about acting as a journalist hireling, but he enjoyed being able to connect with readers, especially farmers. He found that they were not too interested in the outcome of the fall election because they had doubts that any of the political parties could help with their plight. He thought of them as "the last individualists in a collectivist age." He further argued that they stood alone against "the railroads, the banks, the packers, the implement companies, and the grain elevators" as they were "all capitalist combines of men and dollars."[19]

After traveling through Indiana and into Ohio, Fox arrived in Cleveland, a city known for its bicycle industry, and sought out a bicycle club he knew existed there. He was warmly "received into the fellowship as a wandering brother." The city's bicycle enthusiasts were eager to learn of his cross-country trip and the stories he could tell. They were quite impressed by his tramping lifestyle and how he made some money along the way and slept out in the open most nights. The club members provided him with food and a place to stay. He did not linger in Cleveland, for he was determined to continue his journey east. Around fifty members of the bicycle club escorted Fox to the outskirts of the city to wish him farewell the morning he left town. The club's secretary slipped him a ten-dollar bill and hailed Fox as the first bicycle tramp. He was quite moved by the camaraderie of the cohort and thought of them as "a glowing example of the brotherhood of man" in the way that they took in a stranger and received him "as a friend and comrade." As he departed from his newfound friends he told them that they demonstrated "that innate human attribute ever growing larger in the human heart that will in time . . . evolve a form of society where no man will need to tramp the country in search of an opportunity to make a living, where work and good wages will be provided for all as a natural right."[20]

Fox resumed his journey on the less than satisfactory roads of the Midwest. Unlike those in the Northeast, the roads he had to contend with were not macadam surfaced. The "Good Roads Movement" supported by the League of American Wheelman—the first national organization of bicycle enthusiasts—had yet to bear fruit outside of major urban areas. Fox negotiated roads with "deep wagon ruts and horse hoof holes" as best as he could as he made his way through the rest of Ohio, skirted the northwest corner of Pennsylvania, and journeyed to Buffalo, New York. He found the city of no particular interest but was greatly impressed by Niagara Falls, especially how the Adams Power Plant was harnessing electricity from the natural wonder. On his journey, however, there were times when many stretches of "highway" forced him to hug the shoulder. As he neared

Syracuse, he found himself descending into a steep valley. Night was approaching, and he wanted to make it to the city to sleep in a bed for a change. The road was further darkened by large oak trees. Due to the setting sun and the obscuring shade of the trees, he did not see a sharp bend in the road. Fox could not make the turn, and his bike slammed into "a deep gutter and stopped abruptly." He did not stop and subsequently flew over the handlebar and onto the gravel road face first. Although his pride was more damaged than his body, the same could not be said for his bicycle. The front fork of the bike was severely bent backward. He could not straighten it out and was forced to turn it around and try to ride. While he attended to his situation, a couple living close by came over to offer some assistance. The best they could do for him was to give him a glass of hard cider and console him that many riders had been unable to negotiate that turn. Fox had put his bike back together as best as he could, thanked the strangers' kindness, and continued with his journey.[21]

After a restful night's sleep in a haystack by the side of the road, he awoke early and speculated as to how he would better fix his bicycle, which had become more than a machine of transportation to him but a companion that he needed to nurse back to health. He walked his bike to a village on the outskirts of Syracuse, found a blacksmith's shop, and asked the proprietor if he could use the shop to fix his bike. The blacksmith agreed and seeing that Fox knew how to work a forge and the tools of the trade asked if he would like work for him for a few days. Fox agreed and stayed on in the village working for the blacksmith. After fixing his bike and assisting the blacksmith for a week, he received ten dollars for his labor and set out east toward New England. Along the way, he offered his skills as a traveling mechanic. He worked for food and for wages. Fox found many a family in need of repairs for their "little iron horse." His skills as a mechanic and a journalist sustained him on the rest of his journey.[22]

While tramping by bicycle, Fox—city born and bred—had the opportunity to gain some insight into the experience of rural America. The people whom he met on his journey tended to be quite friendly and helpful and he sensed a cooperative ethic among them that he found encouraging. He found the unhurried pace of life to his liking, and it afforded him the chance to talk with people, who seemed to live at a leisurely pace. Fox was interested in their perspective on a variety of matters. He found that "they were not the 'hay seeds' smart [city people] thought them to be." He did note, though, that they lacked the cultural advantages found in large cities, most specifically public libraries. Rural residents had to buy books, which was not practical given the cash-poor nature of most farmers. He found them receptive to his "line of gab" and "not averse to radical ideas." He thought they seemed to enjoy meeting a person from Chicago who was willing to converse with them. His rural experience, however, was not all filled with pleasant interactions. By early autumn, Fox had entered western Massachusetts. On the side of a road he found shelter under a huge maple tree where he bedded down for the night. He was in eyeshot of a farmhouse. As he settled in, he noticed that two men were approaching him. He thought they were out to investigate and to perhaps invite him in for the night. As they got closer, he saw that one of them carried a rifle on his shoulder. The man with the rifle asked if Fox was "taking a rest." Fox replied that he was and asked, "Why are you toting a gun at this hour? What sort of game might you be hunting in the dark?" The man with the gun was taken aback by the questions and offered as a response that "some tramps around here [were] stealing my potatoes." This made Fox quite angry because he could not understand why a farmer would begrudge a poor, hungry tramp a potato. He suggested that the farmer keep his rifle on his shoulder. Fox lied and said that like most westerners he carried a revolver and was quick on the draw. He further pointed out that if the farmer lowered the rifle aimed at him, he would shoot him on the spot and the other man would be a witness that it was self-defense. After this exchange, the two men turned and left. The next morning Fox happened upon another farmer. He related his exchange of the previous evening, and the farmer was pleased to hear that Fox stood up to his uncivil neighbor. The farmer fed Fox breakfast and off he was again.[23]

When he arrived in Boston, he was eager to walk the city's streets and visit its historic sites. He was especially taken by Faneuil Hall, which he thought some call "the cradle of liberty." He reflected on the revolutionary leaders who spoke at the marketplace and wondered about the mixed motives of those who sought to break from Great Britain. There were the true patriots, of course, who wanted freedom from imperial rule, but there were also the smugglers and slave traders who simply wanted freedom from British trade restrictions. The city was also known for its circle of anarchists—both individualists such as Benjamin Tucker, who published *Liberty* for a time in the city, and communists such as Harry Kelly. Fox soon looked up Kelly, who had been the editor of *The Rebel*, a short-lived anarchist newspaper. Fox, as of 1895, was an avid reader of anarchist litera-ture, subscribing to *The Firebrand*, and probably read *The Rebel* and perhaps *Solidarity*, an anarchist newspaper published in New York by John H. Edel-mann. As with many anarchist periodicals, Kelly's journal failed for lack of funds in spring of 1896. Fox had already learned that anarchist news-papers did not benefit as socialist or labor newspapers did from dues-paying members of the party or union. Even a vibrant circle of Boston anarchists, which included Nahum Berman a Russian-born anarchist communist, whom Kelly admired and counted among those who influenced his anarchism, could not keep the paper going. Although the periodical received widespread praise among anarchists across the country and in Europe, the editors struggled to secure enough subscription-paying English-language readers to maintain *The Rebel*. Kelly, nevertheless, had a good reputation, and Fox had learned of him back in Chicago. Kelly was only a year older than Fox, but he had already attained some note as anarchist writer, editor, and publisher. Kelly, like Fox, had an interest in the working class and the labor movement, for *The Rebel* carried many stories and much commentary on the state of workers in the United States and around the world. In addition, Kelly was active in the Central Labor Union, along with the British anarchist Charles Mowbray, who also influenced Kelly's anarchism and assisted with the publication of *The Rebel*. Kelly was well-connected with anarchists nation-wide and in England, too. He had traveled there in spring 1895 when he was new to the anarchist movement. In London, he met the anarchist labor leader John Turner and others who deepened his understanding of anarchist communism.[24]

According to Fox, while roaming around Boston harbor and seeing all the ships from distant countries, he started to consider traveling to England, though this thought also could have been influenced by Kelly. Many young American anarchists were traveling to Great Britain in the 1890s. Voltairine de Cleyre, a prominent anarchist writer from Philadelphia, would go in 1897 and Kelly, likewise, would travel there again in 1898. In London, the Freedom Group published *Freedom*, the world-renowned English-language anarchist-communist newspaper originally cofounded by Kropotkin, the exiled Russian anarchist, in 1886. Along with publishing the periodical, the Freedom Group, an affinity group of anarchists, had like-minded activist circles in other parts of the country. In fact, the 1890s was the heyday of anarchism in Great Britain. French, Italian, German, and many other anarchists from different parts of Europe found sanctuary there and primarily congregated in London. Fox, though, had little money on hand to fund a trip to Europe. Therefore, he would have to work his way across the Atlantic. He found a captain of a cattle ship heading to Liverpool who offered him a job. Moreover, he would earn a shilling a day while the ship was in a British harbor. Apparently, this was a standard arrangement for British shipping companies in need of hands.[25]

After a ten-day voyage, Fox arrived in Liverpool and immediately looked for work. He noticed that "the bicycle business was booming." Answering an advertisement in a newspaper for a bicycle mechanic, he landed a job in Birmingham. Within four days of his arrival in England, he was gainfully employed. He felt very fortunate to speak the language of the country and realized that it was a clear advantage for him as an immigrant worker. He found the cost of living lower than in Chicago, but the wages were lower as well. Yet, he learned that British workers were generally paid better in comparison to other Europeans. Nevertheless, he was struck by the "large slum element" of the city, "whose living standard was very low indeed." Riding the upper level of the "trams," the double-decker streetcars, Fox was able to get "a good view of the city." He was "astounded by the number of iron and steel works" that he saw around town. The quality of the steel that went into bicycle manufacturing greatly impressed him as well. After two months of working in Birmingham, he returned to Liverpool and found other employment there. In the port city, he was overwhelmed by the extremes of wealth and poverty but thought that it was emblematic of capitalism's inability to adequately distribute the wealth it generated.[26]

While in Liverpool, he contacted the city's anarchist group and proceeded to travel in its circle for the next ten months. He attended the affinity group's meetings, most of which took place outdoors to attract listeners to their soapbox orators and buyers of the literature the anarchists sold, including their monthly paper *Freedom*. He found that "the crowds always liked the A. (anarchists') criticisms and reviews of current events. They delighted in hearing their politicians and exploiters razzed." The English, though, did not join the anarchist group in large numbers. Fox thought that they liked listening to anarchists speak but considered anarchism as something in the far-off future. He wrote, "The English are slow to take on new ideas. They don't easily change their minds. But once they do move mentally forward there is no match. They stick to their guns and become most reliable comrades in the battle for freedom." According to Fox, freedom, the essence of anarchism, "asked for nothing, nothing to 'form,' no dues to pay, no pledges to sign, nothing but a mental conception of a new life free from the imposition and restrictions imposed by their rulers and exploiters." Of the soap-boxers he met, the two who stood out to him were Mat Kavanagh, a barber, and a jewelry worker by the name of Fernand Després. Ten years later, Kavanagh would be a popular lecturer on anarchism and the Paris Commune as well as being part of the Francisco Ferrer school reform movement and the Liverpool anarchist Sunday School. Some of those who came to listen to the anarchists were socialists, whose movement also struggled for converts. One "old time socialist" in particular whom Fox got to know was John Edwards. He remarked to Fox that the anarchist movement did an important service by keeping socialists "from getting too damn fond of the state."[27]

At some point during his stay in England, he made his way to London, to the heart of the anarchist movement in Great Britain. There, he met de Cleyre along with other anarchists. During her stay in England and Scotland, she gave a series of lectures on anarchism and other topics. Fox would return on the same ship as she did and remembered her commenting on the good quality of the questions her audience members asked and the warm reception she received in the country. After spending a year in England working as a metalworker, getting to know the anarchists of Liverpool, and reading issues of *Freedom*, Fox decided that it was time to return to Chicago. He would do so as a committed anarchist, but one determined to bring the message of anarchism to the working class and by doing so assist workers in their self-emancipation. When taking into account his experiences of the last ten or so years, Fox knew that the competitive capitalist system needed to be replaced by a cooperative economic one in which workers would receive the full fruits of their labor. Fox viewed the nation-state, either through its police force or through its court system, as a servant of capital and opposed to the interests of the working class. The workers, therefore, could not turn to a government for assistance.

He further concluded that the power of the written word could enlighten and effect change. Workers, though, could not rely on the conventional press. Most newspapers were geared toward the interests of capital, and journalists could not be trusted to give a fair appraisal of events, especially strikes. He witnessed that firsthand with the McCormick shootings and Haymarket bombing and subsequent trial and conviction, in the press, of the Haymarket Martyrs. Fox, therefore, would need to find an outlet for his ideas and his observations of the events of the day. He would find that vehicle in the anarchist press, namely *Free Society*. Like his hero, Albert Parsons, Fox would dedicate himself to a journalism that would reveal the exploitation workers experienced and speak to their interests. He also would argue for an inclusive labor organization at the point of production as the best means for workers to take control of the economy and operate it in their own interests as well as those of their families and communities. This could all be achieved without violence, but it did require that workers have a dedicated core of activists to help them attain their freedom. Fox would be a member of that core of committed activists, a member of the militant minority.[28]

2. Writing Anarchy

IN SUMMER 1897, JAY FOX RETURNED TO CHICAGO AND BEGAN to actively participate in the anarchist movement of the city and to publish in the English-language anarchist press. The movement he joined had rebounded following the tragic events surrounding Haymarket. Although the city's anarchists maintained their idealism and commitment to the cause, the movement lacked the hopeful enthusiasm it had possessed in the mid-1880s. State oppression and the execution of some of the most prominent movement writers and organizers had a chilling effect that lasted almost a decade. Moreover, anarchists had to compete for recruits with socialists and labor unions, for each had a different pathway to revolutionary change or to basic improvements in the working-class quality of life. These other options, furthermore, did not have the taint of violence associated with them. Many of the immigrant anarchists had a difficult time recruiting a second generation to follow in their footsteps. Even though a movement culture continued to exist in the city, particularly in the form of club and saloon life, it needed new recruits in order to grow. Assisting in recruitment, the immigrant anarchist press revived in the late 1880s and persevered through the 1890s with several foreign-language newspapers.

The native-born anarchists, who were never a large cohort, remained small and fragmented in the wake of the Haymarket tragedy. The English-language anarchist press struggled in Chicago. Despite the efforts of Lum, *The Alarm* ceased publication in 1889. Lucy Parsons, with the assistance of

Holmes, published *Freedom* from 1890 to 1892, though it too folded. Even though Chicago hosted an international anarchist conference to coincide with the World's Fair in 1893, no English-language anarchist-communist publication was being produced in the city. Anarchism, nevertheless, was still a vibrant ideology that had a core of committed activists, which included Fox. He was a close associate of Parsons and together they helped to revive the English-speaking element of the movement along with T. Putman Quinn, an Irish American who had recently relocated from New York, Eric B. Morton, L. S. Oliver, Clemens Pfuetzner, and Sam Hammersmark. Inaugurating that late 1890s revival was the commemoration of the Haymarket Martyrs on 11 November 1897, the ten-year anniversary of the executions of Parsons, Engel, Fischer, and Spies as well as the death of Lingg. Fox and Oliver spoke at the event along with Emma Goldman, who was already a prominent anarchist.[1]

The bomb thrown at Haymarket in 1886 and the botched assassination attempt of industrialist Henry Clay Frick by the young Russian immigrant anarchist Alexander Berkman, during the 1892 Homestead lockout, disillusioned anarchists over the violence associated with the concept of "propaganda by the deed" as a means to overthrow the existing system. Whether immigrant or native-born, most anarchists never thought violence was a useful tactic anyway. At best, self-defense was as far as most would go. Even the German Lehr-und-Wehr Verein, essentially radical rifle clubs made up of socialists and anarchists in the 1870s and 1880s, were primarily defensive organizations. In addition, anarchists tended to adhere to the conviction that the means and ends needed to be one and the same. Anarchism was still a revolutionary philosophy in the 1890s and anarchists thought that a social revolution was probable at some point in the future. The people, however, had to be persuaded that they had it within their power to bring about a revolution. The spark that would ignite the revolution was not going to be a bomb or a bullet; rather, it was going to be the realization, by the masses of the working class, that individual freedom within the context of an egalitarian, cooperative society was within their grasp if only the people had the initiative to create it. Therefore, anarchists believed that the power of the written and spoken word was necessary to bring about a new society. Rhetoric consumed much of anarchist agitation in the mid- to late 1890s, which made anarchist publications extremely important for the movement. According to the anarchist-communist editors of *The Rebel*, "Our motto is: Educate, in order to understand our true value as workers in society; Agitate, in order to arouse our apathetic fellow workers; Organize, to overthrow the power of government, capitalism, and superstition, and thus pave the way for that bright future when the worker shall have free access to the means of life, and the world shall cease to know misery, poverty, and crime."[2]

Echoing that perspective in *The Rebel* was another English-language anarchist-communist periodical, which also came into existence in mid-1890s and attracted the attention of Fox and other radicals. Three anarchists—Abe Isaak, Henry Addis, and Abner J. Pope—published *The Firebrand* in Portland, Oregon, beginning in January 1894. The primary goal of the paper was to bring a discussion of anarchist-communist ideas to the English-speaking public across the United States, as well as to be a vehicle for radical thought and commentary on the West Coast that would complement the East Coast anarchist-communist newspapers *The Rebel* and *Solidarity*. *The Firebrand* was issued weekly and featured articles on topics related to labor, women's rights, the nation-state, radicalism and revolution overseas, and anarchist thought both in the United States and abroad. In summer 1895, the editors held a symposium on anarchist communism in the paper. Contributors included William Holmes, husband of Lizzie Holmes and longtime anarchist in Chicago; William C. Owen, an immigrant English radical who had traveled in socialist and anarchist circles over the years; Viroqua Daniels, a frequently published anarchist writer and poet of the 1890s and 1900s; and the paper's editor Addis, among many others. The writers sought to explain how anarchist communism was different from anarchist individualism. Although by stressing voluntarism, the primacy of the individual, and the abolition of the nation-state, the writers argued that more bound the two strains of anarchism together than divided them. Despite the radicalism of the publication, it was not anarchism that brought about the suppression of *The Firebrand*, but the editors' publication of essays on women's sexual freedom and the Walt Whitman poem "A Woman Waits for Me." Postal authorities claimed that the newspaper published material that violated federal obscenity laws and shut it down in September 1897. In the end, only the poem led to an indictment. Pope refused to accept the authority of the federal government or work within the legal system, thereby ending up in jail for four months. Addis and Isaak accepted bail and appealed their convictions, which were overturned in 1898. In the meantime, Isaak restarted the paper in San Francisco in late 1897 with the title *Free Society*.[3]

Fox began to write for *Free Society* in fall 1897. He was one of several Chicago anarchists whose work appeared in the publication. The city was a major center of union activity and radicalism, and without a local English-language anarchist paper *Free Society* became a primary literary vehicle for the city's anarchists. Fox, who had admired Debs and had attended a convention of reform clubs and trade unions with him in Chicago in September, chastised him in his first article in *Free Society*. He claimed that Debs was moving to embrace political action rather than devoting the newly formed Social Democracy of America (SDA) to colonization projects in the Far West, an effort strongly supported by anarchists and others attracted to a non-statist path to socialism. Goldman also attended the September convention, further underscoring anarchist support for the SDA. At the final convention of the ARU in June, while Fox was still in Great Britain, the Brotherhood of the Cooperative Commonwealth (BCC), members of the Ruskin Colony, Chicago Labor Exchange representatives, and Midwest socialists formed the organization. A major goal of the SDA was to create colonies in the Far West that would eventually bring about a cooperative commonwealth state by state. The peaceful, egalitarian, and nonauthoritarian path to a cooperative society had obvious appeal to anarchists.

Fox became involved with Chicago's Branch 2 of the SDA, which included Parsons, Quinn, and Morton. Fox wrote, "The practicability of common property was to be proven by large colonies located in some sparsely settled state, with the ultimate end of making such a state a co-operative commonwealth, repeating it in other states until the peaceful revolution shall have been accomplished." However, inherent within the SDA was a tension between those interested in political campaigns and those devoted to nonpolitical strategies to achieve socialism. Despite Debs's support of colonization, in a summer speech given in Milwaukee—perhaps due to the influence of one of the most significant socialists in the city, Victor Berger—he noted that "were the colonization plan to prove a failure, it would not stop the Social Democracy movement," for he insisted that the SDA was at its core a "political movement."[4]

Further alienating Fox and other anarchists was the condemnation and suspension of Branch 2 by Debs and the executive council of the SDA. The branch had passed several resolutions condemning the massacre of nineteen striking mine workers who had been gunned down while peacefully protesting conditions in Lattimer, Pennsylvania, in September 1897. The branch's incendiary rhetoric as well as the proliferation of anarchist-controlled SDA branches in Chicago together motivated the suspension of Branch 2. Anarchists and other nonpolitical action delegates at the SDA convention in June 1898 had a strong presence. In a vote as to whether colonization or political means should take precedence in the SDA, the colonizers won, fifty-three to thirty-seven. Debs, though, had already thrown his support to political action. Nevertheless, it is striking that most of the SDA delegates supported an anarchist or at least a non-statist path toward revolutionary change. With Debs's support in hand, however, Burger and the other "political actionists" left the convention and formed the Social Democratic Party, which eventually would become the Socialist Party of America (SPA) in 1901. Debs accepted election to the executive board of the Social Democratic Party, leaving the SDA without its most important leader. Undeterred, the SDA remained committed to creating colonies in the Far West. The Burley Colony was founded in western Washington in fall 1898, even though the SDA had largely evaporated as an organization before the end of the decade.[5]

Fox, like all anarchist communists, wanted the working class to choose the libertarian path to socialism. Following the practice of anarchists before him, he was not opposed to working within political organizations or even political parties, as long as they moved away from governmental solutions. This was a means to gaining converts to anarchism, which helps to explain why he, Parsons, and other anarchists worked within the SDA. Writing in *Free Society*, he sought to capitalize on what he thought was a growing revolutionary movement in Chicago by criticizing the lack of freedom within the city's two major socialist parties. He argued that there was widespread discontent with the Socialist Labor Party (SLP) and with the "political actionists" in the SDA, for each had leaders who acted with autocratic power and were supported by executive councils that sought to block the will of the rank and file. For example, he noted that the SLP would only allow speakers at meetings who had been chosen by the "upper council." Fox believed that the leadership of the SLP feared that anarchists might get to be heard at these meetings and perhaps take control of them. Party leader Daniel De Leon and the council had reason to fear anarchist influence. The party was growing in the late 1890s. It expanded from a largely German immigrant socialist party into one that native-born American radicals increasingly joined. The history of anarchists affiliated with the SLP or who had attempted to consolidate the SLP with other anarchist organizations went back to the 1870s. In fact, Albert Parsons was one of the editors of the party's newspaper *The Socialist* in 1878 and 1879. The state socialists, though committed to revolutionary unions and a stateless society in the distant future, were not going to let anarchists divert the party from current political campaigns and party politics. Fox, in addition, had just as much criticism for the SDA. He argued that Debs and many of the leaders of the organization sought votes like any other political party and refused to acknowledge the general membership, which he believed leaned libertarian.[6]

Although Fox was willing to work within socialist organizations and engage in discussions with socialists, he was committed to an uncompromising libertarianism. Therefore, cultivating his relationships with fellow anarchists and bringing the anarchist message to the public became increasingly important for him over the next several years. In spring 1899, he worked with Goldman to establish a Social Science Club in Chicago. Anarchists used the term "social science" as a rubric under which to analyze "social issues from an anarchist perspective." The club in Chicago as well as social science clubs in New York, Boston, Philadelphia, San Francisco, and other cities were important centers for anarchists, both native-born and immigrant, to establish affinity groups and to create an anarchist public space. This was similar to the anarchist club life that German immigrants established in Chicago and New York in the 1870s and 1880s. The social science clubs also bore a great similarity to liberal clubs and even had an overlap of guest speakers, who appeared at either club in a given city. The liberal clubs first came into being following the Civil War. With no specific ideology to promote, they were open to a variety of radical perspectives and commentary and perhaps more inviting than the immigrant German anarchist clubs, which were more firmly grounded ideologically.

Social science clubs had the dual purpose to be a forum for anarchist ideas and activity and to be open to recruiting from the public individuals who were either curious about anarchism or interested in a perspective different from what could be found in more mainstream forums. The social science clubs held free weekly lectures on a variety of controversial topics of the day. Goldman was one of the most popular draws to such venues as was de Cleyre and other native-born anarchists as well as anarchists from Europe. Along with sponsoring public talks, the social science clubs provided anarchist, socialist, and other radical literature for sale to audience members and club visitors. Moreover, anarchists used the clubs to socialize on holidays and Sundays, creating a space in which they could freely interact as libertarians, with no leaders, no followers, and no social divides based on gender or ethnicity. The members of the clubs frequently organized family outings, especially picnics during the spring and summer months. These outings were not exclusive to anarchists and their families but were open to the larger public, which was again an effort to recruit new members to the cause and create a welcoming anarchist space.[7]

Fox was aware of the danger that an insulated movement posed to its long-term viability. Therefore, organizing and growing the anarchist community were important elements of the ongoing educational effort. He wanted the public to understand that anarchism was a rational and practical path to changing society for the better. He went as far as to assist in creating an Anarchist Club, which sponsored meetings open to the public in downtown Chicago on the nature and goals of anarchism. He wanted to disabuse the public of the stereotype of the bomb-throwing anarchist. Fox spoke often at the Anarchist Club as well as at the Social Science Club. He also organized engagements for other speakers to come to Chicago along with promoting social gatherings for the city's anarchists, especially commemorations of Haymarket. He was quickly becoming a sought-after lecturer, for he was invited to speak to other groups and at other locations in the city. For example, he gave several talks for the Society of Anthropology at the downtown Athenaeum Building. He spoke on labor issues, some from a historical perspective, which he then connected to current struggles. From Fox's perspective, there had always been a "labor question" from ancient times to the present. In 1901, he gave a talk to the society on the US Steel strike in which workers were fighting for union recognition and pay increases, but he placed the conflict within a grand struggle of workers seeking to be recognized by their societies in the past for the wealth they generated and for their significance to the economic development of their societies.

His public speaking activity, though, was not limited to his hometown. He traveled to New York and Boston extensively between 1898 and 1901. He spoke on a variety of topics, especially the one he knew best: labor. Fox was a popular draw because he was an eyewitness to the events at the McCormick Reaper Works and Haymarket. He could speak about the anarchist movement in Chicago and the labor movement of the city, too. His experience working as a Knight, agitating for the eight-hour day, representing the Metal Trades Council, and as a member of the ARU gave him the ability to provide insight into the cause of labor along with an anarchist analysis of capitalism and the nation-state. During these public speaking tours in the Northeast, he developed strong relationships with such well-known anarchists as Harry Kelly as well as lesser-known figures in the movement such as the sheet metal worker and Dutch immigrant Alex Snellenberg. As he began to excel as a popular lecturer and as a writer, his devotion to the labor movement would be his primary focus for the rest of his career. Infusing the labor movement with anarchism was his distinctive contribution as a radical, a revolutionary, and a unionist. He would use his pen and voice as well as his organizing skills on the job to promote what he believed to be one of the best vehicles for revolution: a radicalized labor movement.[8]

Around the turn of the twentieth century, anarchists such as Fox were not the only radicals interested in mobilizing the American working class. Anarchists had to compete with socialists for converts. Most socialists embraced the ultimate end that anarchists sought: the abolition of the nation-state and capitalism and the creation a cooperative, egalitarian, and libertarian society. Socialists, however, argued that state socialism was a necessary stage in that historical process. Whether that argument came from the writings of Karl Marx and Frederick Engels or the writings and speeches of Debs, Fox rose to challenge the conviction that the control of the nation-state by socialists was necessary or historically inevitable. He pointed out that one only had to look at the socialist parties of Europe, especially Germany, to see that socialism posed no threat to the existing order. Two million socialists represented in the German Reichstag were no threat to the German kaiser. So much, he concluded, for parliamentary socialism. Socialism in the United States, he believed, had already been absorbed by the middle class and lost its revolutionary potential. Moreover, voting, whether for a socialist, a Democrat, or a Republican, was a passive means of giving away one's power to another. American workers needed to refrain from politics and use labor organizing—at the point of production—to permeate their work life with revolutionary possibilities, and anarchists working within the labor movement could be the ultimate radicalizing agent.[9]

Fox, though, was not unique in trying to connect anarchism to the labor movement, but he was one of the most consistent American anarchists to do so in the 1890s and 1900s. He was definitely influenced in this regard by Albert Parsons and Spies, but also by the fact that Chicago's anarchists in the 1870s and 1880s had been firmly established in city's working-class neighborhoods and factories as well as being members of labor unions. As a teenager, Fox listened to anarchist speakers who rallied for the eight-hour day and risked their lives in the pursuit of labor's emancipation. He would have read Lucy Parsons's compilation of her husband's writings and speeches—first published in 1889—in which it is clear that for Parsons anarchism was a working-class movement. The eight-hour day itself, he believed, was part of the class struggle, which Fox understood from personal experience. Moreover, European anarchists in the 1890s had a strong presence in labor organizations, particularly in Italy, Spain, and France. It is during that decade that anarcho-syndicalism begins to be widely articulated within the labor movement in Europe. The Italian Errico Malatesta would be one of the most important promoters of anarchists' active involvement in the labor movement. Malatesta was also an early advocate of the general strike as the most effective revolutionary tool that workers had at their disposal. He stipulated, however, that the general strike had to be directed toward social revolution, by anarchists in particular, for it to be successful. In fact, some scholars, namely Michael Schmidt and Lucien van der Walt, contend that "syndicalism, in essence, is an anarchist *strategy*, not a rival to anarchism." Much of Fox's writing and labor union activity would exemplify that assertion.

In a *Free Society* piece titled "Trade Unionism and Anarchism," Fox laid out his explanation for the role that anarchists played in labor organizing, emphasizing that it is only through the power of labor unions that workers can affect change in the workplace. To rely on politicians, the state, or the legal system would be a mistake for workers because the only power they have is at the point of production. Labor unions themselves—with workers organized by both trade and industry—would replace individual (or corporate) ownership of the means of production and the structures of the nation-state, which he contended were both enemies of the working class. This essentially syndicalist strategy will be at the foundation of his activism, writing, and economic and political thinking for the next two decades. Moreover, unlike many of his contemporary American anarchists, Fox was staying consistent with the heart of the modern anarchist movement as it emerged in the nineteenth century. One has only to look to

Bakunin's vision of the First International and to Parsons and Spies's influence on the Pittsburg Manifesto to see that the working class and their unions were the vanguard of the social revolution and held within their organizations the foundation of a new society.[10]

As a writer and lecturer, Fox was a rising star in the anarchist movement in Chicago and worked to make the city an important center for anarchism. He was instrumental in bringing to town Pyotr Kropotkin, the most internationally famous anarchist of the period. His *Conquest of Bread* had been translated into English and was widely read in anarchist circles and beyond. In addition, Kropotkin was a regular contributor to *Free Society* and many anarchists and others read his work in *Freedom*, the most widely circulated English-language anarchist-communist periodical in the world. Kropotkin was invited to speak at a number of universities in the Northeast in 1901, but Fox persuaded him to come to the Midwest. Kropotkin gave a lecture on "Anarchism: Its Philosophy and Ideal" at the Central Music Hall. Clarence Darrow, one of the nation's leading labor attorneys by the 1890s, acted as chair and opened the meeting. Fox remembered Darrow introducing Kropotkin with the words "In Russia they exile their great men; in Chicago we hang them," the latter point a reference to the Haymarket Martyrs. Fox was impressed by Kropotkin's scientific rational for anarchism. Kropotkin, as a naturalist and a geographer, argued that anarchism was a natural phenomenon and that collectivism, not individualism, was borne out in human history and in nature. Fox, in his personal interaction with Kropotkin that year, found him quite interested in the American labor movement. During the reception given after Kropotkin's lecture, the two talked for an hour. At the time, Kropotkin was urging anarchists throughout the world to emulate the anarchists of Spain, Italy, and France who were actively engaged in the labor movement. He was impressed that Fox, a well-known anarchist, was an elected union official—he was president of the Blacksmith Helper's Union in Chicago—and that he had been and continued to be an active trade unionist. Fox was far from the only anarchist in the Chicago labor movement. Quinn was affiliated with the Chicago Federation of Labor, Lizzie Holmes was with the Women's Federal Labor Union, and Anton Johannsen, at different periods, was a member of the United Brotherhood of Carpenters and Joiners (UBCJA) and the Amalgamated Wood Workers International Union of America (AWIU) just to name a few.[11]

Fox along with other comrades wanted to further develop the anarchist movement in Chicago, but without a locally produced paper they believed that the movement could not grow. He, along with Parsons and Clemens Pfuetzner (a cobbler by trade), persuaded Abe Isaak to bring *Free Society* to Chicago. They promised that the paper would have much greater financial support and a larger readership. Pfuetzner alone contributed $400 to assist with the expenses incurred by the move and another $50 so that Isaak and his wife Mary and their children—Pete, Mary, and Abe Jr.—would have plenty of fuel for the winter. The publication and printing of the paper was a family affair. The first issue of *Free Society* from Chicago appeared on 3 February 1901. The city's anarchists were able to provide a house on Carroll Avenue for the periodical to be produced and for Isaak and his family to live. Fox lived close by on the same street where he supervised the renting of "nicely furnished rooms, with gas, bath, and library; from one dollar per week upwards." By this time he was living with Esther Abramowitz, a Russian Jewish immigrant from Lithuania, a garment worker, and an anarchist. She arrived in the United States in the early 1890s and had two children that decade—David and Sylvia—during her marriage with fellow Chicago anarchist and dentist Martin Rasnick. Her sister Annie was married to Eric Morton; eventually the couple would relocate to San Francisco. Fox, to support himself and his family, continued to work as a blacksmith, for which he was paid $10.50 for a sixty-hour workweek. He assisted in the production of *Free Society* along with Rasnick, Enrico Travaglio, Julie Mechanic, Alfred Schneider, and Michael Roz. Travaglio, an Italian immigrant and sailor, learned the print trade after moving from San Francisco to Chicago and became a skilled compositor. He was the typesetter for the publication. Adding to the circle of Chicago anarchists was Hippolyte Havel, who had arrived back in 1899 after meeting Goldman that year in London. He traveled frequently, sometimes with Goldman, but after *Free Society* arrived in the city he worked as the "news and book agent" for the anarchist paper, even living in the same house as the Isaak family.[12]

The anarchist community that Fox and others strove to build up in the late 1890s seemed to be at its most vibrant by the beginning of the new century. The Social Science Club and the Anarchist Club had regular meetings with a host of speakers from Chicago, other parts of the country, as well as Europe and Latin America. Isaak began publishing in *Free Society* a directory of anarchists in the city with their trades and professions

CONSTITUTIONAL SAFEGUARDS.

From the pages of *Free Society*, 1902. Courtesy Newberry Library, Chicago, Illinois.

including their contact information. The anarchists were simply following the lead of socialist and union periodicals that featured the same type of directory so that comrades could patronize fellow comrades. Readers of *Free Society* could find a variety of trades and services provided in the eight-page anarchist weekly newspaper. Fox acted as secretary of the *Free Society* Sustaining Club. The group met every Wednesday at the newspaper offices on Carroll Avenue. Fox also oversaw the Anarchist Club, which offered a series of lectures to educate the public about anarchism. Unfortunately, along with active support of the paper in the city, some tension arose. Isaak thought that the sustaining club was trying to exert too much control over the paper, especially the editorial section. Some in the anarchist circle thought that Isaak was running the paper too much as a family affair and not making it a community endeavor. At one point Parsons and others in the group suggested that Isaak open his account books, so that all could be aware of how the money was being spent as the paper's subscription base was growing rapidly. He made all the finances available for anyone who cared to view them and showed where the money went in terms of paper, presswork, and postage. He was a bit disturbed, however, when it was made clear that his family—who set the type and did most of the work to get the paper published—had to live on $11.20 a week "and none of the grumblers suggested that such wages were inadequate for the amount of work performed."[13]

Despite these ripples in the waters of the Chicago anarchist community, the city was an important center of radical activity and seemed to be experiencing a renaissance of sorts. For the first time in almost ten years, the city had an English-language anarchist-communist newspaper with a national and international circulation. Anarchists such as Fox and visitors to the city such as Goldman had venues for their speaking engagements. Comparably vibrant anarchist communities were thriving in New York, Boston, Philadelphia, Cleveland, and San Francisco. Every day the movement was attracting new members, especially through the anarchist press and public lectures by anarchists. In August 1901 a young man, who called himself Fred Nieman and said he was an anarchist from Cleveland, introduced himself to Isaak at the offices on Carroll Avenue and spoke with him about anarchism and the movement in general. He needed a place to spend the night and Isaak suggested that Nieman inquire at Fox's home because he thought he had at least one room available. The stranger knocked on Fox's door that same evening. Fox wrote years later that "coming from the office of *Free Society*, nearby, I assumed he was a comrade from out of town. On learning he was from Cleveland, I asked if he knew certain well known anarchists there. His negative reply convinced me that I was wrong. He could not be an anarchist in Cleveland and not know these people." Although suspicious, Fox offered him a room for the night anyway. Fox thought of him as "a good looking chap of about twenty four, with a girlish face and sensitive blue eyes, he impressed me as a youth seeking in his own quiet way a solution to the riddle of poverty in the midst of plenty. He retired and I saw no more of him." Isaak, though, had serious concerns about Nieman based on the conversations he had had with him and because of a letter he received from Cleveland anarchist Emil Schilling. Schilling had met Nieman and thought his questions about secret anarchist societies and violence indicated that he might be an agent provocateur. Isaak, who had had similar conversations with him, decided to publish a warning about Nieman in *Free Society*.[14]

Nieman turned out to be none other than Leon Czolgosz, the assassin of President William McKinley. Secret Service agents apprehended Czolgosz immediately after he shot the president on 6 September in Buffalo, New York (McKinley would die eight days later of gangrene caused by his gunshot wound). He later confessed to the crime and declared himself an anarchist. Fox read about the shooting in the Chicago newspapers and recognized the picture of "Nieman." He immediately thought that all anarchists would be under suspicion. His thoughts were confirmed, for in the next issue of the city's newspapers editorials claimed that an "anarchist plot" was behind the shooting. Fox had already been planning to travel to New York for an extended stay before Czolgosz's act. Esther and the children had left ahead of him before the shooting, a practice they had done in the past "due to monetary considerations" when traveling as a family. After selling off his "house hold" belongings, he had taken a room with his friend and Esther's ex-husband Rasnick on Newberry Avenue. Fox did not know it at the time, but on the evening of the day of the shooting police went to the *Free Society* offices on a tip from a reporter who had interviewed Isaak that day. Isaak— who had nothing to hide—told the reporter that Czolgosz had visited him at the Carroll Avenue house and had spent a night at Fox's home. The reporter related that information to the police.

When the police arrived at Isaak's home, they arrested all the men present: Isaak, Isaak Jr., Havel, Travaglio, Pfeutzner, and Schneider. The officers and detectives also seized anything they thought incriminating, from issues of *Free Society* and other anarchist literature to personal letters and photographs. Later that evening, Mechanic came to the house, where she also resided. As Mary Isaak and her daughter related what had taken place only an hour earlier, police returned and arrested Mechanic and both mother and daughter. At the police station, Isaak went through a third degree of sorts. Alone he faced the chief of police, several lawyers, and reporters. Just before the interrogation, Jane Addams tried to get the anarchists released only to be respectfully shown the door. Isaak was asked repeatedly if he supported the killing of the president and murder in general. For Isaak, the assassination attempt was due to the fact that "where there is tyranny there is bound to be assassination." He did not support nor would he condemn Czolgosz's act. While the anarchists were being held and questioned at the city jail about the shooting, the police returned yet again to the house and found Fox's current address. The following afternoon when Fox returned home from work, he discovered that "two portly cops were waiting for" him. Rasnick and Roz (who was there paying a visit that day) had already been arrested. The police officers arrested Fox in connection with the assassination.[15]

The shooting of President McKinley by a self-proclaimed anarchist set off a wave of anti-anarchist and anti-radical hysteria that swept the county. The newspapers were filled with wild accusations about anarchists and their terrorist schemes. It did not matter that almost no anarchists supported Czolgosz and many condemned the shooting of the president. Nevertheless, there was a great deal of guilt by association. It also did not help that anarchists in Europe had assassinated or attempted to assassinate heads of state throughout the 1890s and into the new century. Some anarchist periodicals still published articles supporting "propaganda by the deed," even though most of these articles had very sophisticated interpretations of what such deeds meant. Nevertheless, Johann Most's *Freiheit* carried an article by Karl Heinzen—a German revolutionary and theoretician active fifty years earlier—on political violence that appeared just two days before the president was shot. Police arrested Most, who was tried and convicted of publishing work that disturbed the peace. He would serve the better part of a year in prison for carrying the article.

In the days following the shooting, federal agents, police forces in several major cities, and mobs of angry citizens began to move against well-known anarchists and anarchist communities. In New York, a mob attacked the offices of Yiddish-language anarchist newspaper *Freie Arbeiter Stimme*. Another anti-anarchist mob raided the anarchist community in Guffey Hollow, Pennsylvania, forcing twenty-five families to flee the area. In western Washington, a Loyal League of North America formed "to accomplish the utter annihilation of anarchists and anarchistic teachings." The anarchist Home Colony in Puget Sound narrowly avoided a raid. In the end, most of the anarchists arrested following the shooting of McKinley were residents of Chicago, though Harry Gordon and Carl Nord would be arrested in Pittsburg on 9 September. Goldman, who upon hearing of Isaak and the others' arrests, decided to travel to Chicago to offer her assistance. She was met by Max Baginski, a German immigrant anarchist and editor of *Chicagoer Arbeiter-Zeitung*. On his advice, she went into hiding when it was clear she was to be arrested as well. She stayed for a time at Charles Norris's home until her whereabouts were discovered. Police surrounded the house on 10

September and had a warrant to enter. At first, Goldman pretended to be a Swedish servant girl, but she eventually gave up herself up to law enforcement and joined the other anarchists in jail.[16]

A few days before Goldman's arrest, Fox entered the county jail. The police did not initially question him. He was simply placed in the same cell as Rasnick and Roz. He noticed that the cell they occupied was the very same one Parsons had found himself in fifteen years earlier. Fox, remembering that Parsons had "sang his favorite song, Annie Laurie, on the eve of his legal murder," decided to launch into a verse of the song. Without knowing it, his "voice reached the *Free Society* staff in another part of the jail, a signal that" he too had been incarcerated. The day before police arrested Goldman, all the Chicago anarchists in custody—nine men and three women—were arraigned and charged with conspiracy to kill the president. The judge denied the men bail and remanded them for ten days. The women—Mechanic and Isaak's wife and daughter—were given $3,000 bail, though later that day all charges were dismissed against them due to lack of evidence. While the president lived for a week after the shooting and actually looked as if he might recover, Fox and the other anarchists were able to mingle with other prisoners during the daily exercise period. However, once McKinley died on 14 September, the anarchists were kept separate from the rest of the prisoners. Fox had an opportunity to speak with reporters on the day of McKinley's death as did several other anarchists in custody. Fox was quoted as saying "I am not a believer in the principles of government of which McKinley was an official representative." He continued:

> I feel no loss politically; another will take his place. His death is a result
> of the unequal conditions, socially, politically, and economically, which
> surround him and all of us. The same conditions are a result of thousands
> of deaths every day, and it is because I desire to change these conditions that
> I am an Anarchist. The government converts the discoveries of sciences into
> implements for taking human life, and I am opposed and deplore the
> taking of human life. I am opposed to government. As for Mrs. McKinley
> I have the same sorrow which I have for my cellmate of yesterday who
> heard of the death of his child and wept bitter tears. I sympathize with
> suffering whether it be in the prison cell, the reeking tenement, or in the
> White House.[17]

After about a week, the anarchists were brought before the court again. While waiting for the proceedings to begin, Fox was taken away to be questioned by the chief of police, Francis O'Neill. His anarchist comrades and Fox himself did not think that was a good sign. They believed at the time that he was going to be taken to Buffalo to be tried and executed with Czolgosz. To Fox's surprise, O'Neill had no questions for him regarding a conspiracy to kill the president. The police chief asked, "What is the method by which the Anarchists hope to bring about a realization of their ideal?" Fox remembered thinking "Here was my opportunity. These club swinging bums are an ignorant lot who never read anything but the sport page. Now let them listen to a lecture on Anarchism." Fox explained that anarchists

> have no ready made plan for the birth of the new order of society, that is something for a later date. Their present concern is with the spreading of knowledge. The workers must know before they can do. We call for the elimination of the landlords and capitalists and the organization of co-operatives in which every man and every woman will have an equal share. No rich, no poor, no unemployed, no crime, no policemen, no jails. For who would steal when there is an abundance of everything. When the workers in sufficient numbers get these ideas under their domes they will get the urge to try them out; and it is not for us at this early date to know just how they will go about it. All will depend on the circumstances of the moment. Ours is a long range program. It may not be realized in our time. When it does come we have reason to believe the landlords and capitalists won't fall in line. We don't expect to convert many of them; and there will be need for strong policemen, like yourself, Chief O'Neill, to lockup the Morgans and the Rockefellers of the time; for they are sure to start a counter revolution, a revolution of force against a revolution of ideas. In such an affray you can easily guess on which side to find the Anarchists. Thus you see that, like yourself, Chief, I am a revolutionist. But I don't confine my revolutionary urge only to the Emerald Isle.

As Fox concluded his lecture, he noticed a smile on O'Neill's face, for the police chief, as many Irish in Chicago, favored a revolution in Ireland to throw off British rule. O'Neill thanked him and Fox was taken back to the rest of the defendants to everyone's relief. Fox thought that the fact that he, being the only American-born anarchist currently being held, puzzled the police, who may have thought that Fox was a "feeble-minded boob out of whom they might be able to extract valuable information." However, the police who escorted him voiced sympathy for his ideas and thought it a shame that he had been arrested, which surely would undermine a political career, which at least one police officer thought possible for the working-class Chicagoan. It is evident from his lecture that Fox believed all working men and women, including the working-class police of Chicago, could participate in the creation of a new society that would emancipate them all, with the driving force being ideas rather than violence.[18]

Fox and the other anarchists remained in jail for a couple more weeks. Chicago comrades tried to make their stay in jail as pleasant as possible. For example, food was brought in from a nearby restaurant. Fox's union offered him a vacation upon his release. He refused that but accepted financial assistance to join his family in New York. As the days passed, it was looking like the accused would be released, for Czolgosz implicated no one in the shooting save for citing the inspiration he had received from a Goldman lecture and some anarchist literature he had read. Meanwhile, some outrageous claims were made in the newspapers about the possibility of storming the jail to lynch the anarchists, guilty or not. The sheriff took the threats seriously and prepared for an assault on the building. Those threats, in the end, subsided rather quickly. After several weeks of trying to connect the shooting to the anarchists in custody, prosecutors and investigators dropped the charges. News floated through the jail that they were to be released. Fox remembered an outpouring of support from the non-anarchists in the jail as he and his comrades were set free.[19]

Soon after his release from the Cook County Jail, Fox left Chicago to rejoin his family in New York City. He found work as a millwright in a cabinet shop and eventually he, Esther, David, and Sylvia found a place to call home in Manhattan on Avenue D, near the East River and close to the German anarchist community. While settling into a life in New York, Fox thought that a measured anarchist reaction, in print, to the assassination of McKinley and the public, state, and federal government's attitude toward and treatment of Czolgosz and anarchists in general was in order. The hysteria that followed in the wake of the president's death was evident from the editorial pages of the country's major newspapers to the pulpits of its smallest churches as a call went out to purge the nation of anarchists. State and federal officials openly considered restricting immigration into the United States, especially that of radicals and anarchists. Anarchists themselves varied in their opinion of Czolgosz's act. Some openly condemned him, and others considered what he did the behavior of a madman or someone too unintelligent to see how harmful he was to the movement.

Goldman was one of the first anarchists to address the assassin's act and to place it within a larger context as well as to provide some sympathetic understanding. Writing in *Free Society*, which had suspended publication for several weeks due to most of the staff being incarcerated, Goldman wrote "The Tragedy in Buffalo." In her article, she argued that Czolgosz was a product of several decades of war waged on the working class of America as the industrial revolution transformed society and made "life, liberty and the pursuit of happiness" increasingly difficult for the American people. Even though politicians and newspaper editorialists wanted to characterize him a European, Czolgosz was an American. But more than being a simple product of the suffering of the American working class, Czolgosz could not accept the status quo and sought to be a historical agent of change. He himself said that he "did it for the American people." For Goldman, he was that rare individual who could not bear the suffering borne by the many, whether by workers in a mine or child laborers in a textile mill, while the few profited. He could no more accept that then accept the brutal imperialist suppression of Filipino independence. Goldman, though, went on to suggest that Czolgosz's shooting was "natural" in that violent acts were a natural outgrowth of a violent society. Only when the daily violence that the working class in the United States and around the world experienced at the hands of capitalists and governments would violence cease.[20]

Fox followed Goldman's lead by writing his own commentary on the assassination. His motivation, however, also involved a response to Theodore Roosevelt's statements regarding anarchists as he became the nation's president. Roosevelt was quoted as saying that "anarchist speeches and writings are essentially seditious and treasonable." This, coupled with extreme editorials such as in the Washington *National Tribune* which called for lynching "every avowed Anarchist," convinced him that he needed to challenge Roosevelt by clarifying for the public what anarchism was, contextualizing it, and explaining Czolgosz's action. Thus, as anti-anarchist legislation made its way through Congress, Fox's *Roosevelt, Czolgosz and Anarchy* appeared in early 1902 with the assistance of New York Anarchists in publishing and distribution. Fox used the pamphlet to confront the distortions

A PERIODICAL OF ANARCHIST THOUGHT, WORK, AND LITERATURE.

VOL. IX. NO. 28.   CHICAGO, SUNDAY, JULY 13, 1902.   WHOLE NO. 370.

Free Society masthead. Courtesy Newberry Library, Chicago, Illinois.

leveled at anarchists by politicians such as Roosevelt. For Fox, the would-be oppressors of anarchism were out to oppress free speech and a free press. That effort was futile because ideas cannot be legislated out of the country. In fact, from Fox's perspective, the tirades against anarchism only stimulated the public's interest in this alternative theory of society. In the pamphlet, Fox noted the oppressive acts of the federal government against workers who struggled against exploitive employers and the violent suppression of Filipinos in their struggle against American imperialism. Although Fox did not support Czolgosz shooting McKinley, he argued that McKinley reaped what he had sowed. Anarchism, according to Fox, had little to do with Czolgosz's act, for the man was "tortured to the limit of endurance by the sight of a suffering humanity." He was no "common assassin, but a lover of mankind." From Fox's perspective Czolgosz just as easily could have been influenced by the Declaration of Independence as by an anarchist speech. The influence that would have come from anarchism, however, would be the truth that "Labor creates all wealth, that to the producers belong the product, and that by the eternal law of Justice and Equity only the producer should enjoy it."

Fox went on to argue that all forms of government are inherently oppressive, and he cited numerous well-known historical figures who supported that claim by invoking the ideas and writings of Americans like Thomas Paine, Thomas Jefferson, William Lloyd Garrison, and Henry David Thoreau, European thinkers such as Leo Tolstoy, Edmund Burke, and Herbert Spencer, and of course anarchists such as Kropotkin and Pierre-Joseph Proudhon. His point was not that they all supported an anarchist theory of society but that, from his perspective, they championed liberty and freedom from oppression, especially the oppression that comes from state power. It is clear in the pamphlet that at its heart Fox's anarchism was a libertarian social philosophy that should not be alien to Americans or feared by them. According to Fox, "Under Freedom—Anarchy—an enlightened public opinion will take the place of laws and jails. The basis of society being love and comradeship instead of brute force . . ." For Fox, anarchism promised a kind of secular millennialism that would usher in "Peace, Love and Brotherhood" as the "inevitable consequences of Anarchy." Moreover, "the Anarchist is essentially a man of ideas, and he is forever searching for fertile soil in which to plant them. With tongue and pen, he battles with the hosts of ignorance and authority. Being an Evolutionist, he knows that only through ceaseless agitation will his ideas gradually take root and finally become the dominant thought in the world." In the end, to achieve an anarchist future, the people must emancipate themselves. It is their ideas "that enslave them," not a ruling elite. Killing a tyrant, a king, or a president, he contended, will not free the people. Therefore, the spread of ideas through the written word was essential to the oeuvre of anarchists. For some, it was their life's work.[21]

With anarchists placing so much importance on presenting their ideas to the public, especially in written form, shutting down their publications and hampering their use of the mail systems were effective weapons. Although the Home Colony anarchists were never under serious suspicion by federal authorities that they were part of a conspiracy to assassinate President McKinley, the group did produce a widely circulated anarchist newspaper, *Discontent: The Mother of Progress*. Under the Comstock Act of 1873, postal officials had great leeway in prohibiting what they defined as "lewd and obscene" material from the mails. On 24 September, Charles L. Govan, James W. Adams, and James E. Larkin found themselves under arrest for violating the Comstock Act. Adams wrote the offending article, which advocated free love. Larkin was editor of the paper at the time and Govan was the printer, though charges were eventually dropped against Govan. The case went to the federal court in Tacoma. The prosecution's case was seriously undermined, however, when Judge C. H. Hanford made it clear that he found the article radical but not obscene. The victory for the Home anarchists was short-lived, for a grand jury brought indictments against Mattie D. Penhallow, the postmistress for Home, and Lois Waisbrooker, editor and publisher of *Clothed with the Sun*, an anarchist-feminist newspaper. Waisbrooker had penned an article on free love, claiming "that there can be no sin nor crime in mutual sex relation." Penhallow was accused of

A photograph taken of Jay Fox in New York City in 1902. Courtesy University of Washington Libraries, Special Collections, UW 28604z.

mailing the "obscene and lewd" article contained in the newspaper. Although the charges against Penhallow were dropped and Waisbrooker had to pay a simple fine, Home lost its post office. The immediate effect was the suspension of *Discontent*. These actions of the federal government seem to support Fox's contention in his pamphlet that the suppression of free speech and ideas were at the heart of the anti-anarchist crusade.[22]

In a more direct manner, however, the federal government did move against anarchists, though the move was against immigrant anarchists in particular. According to historian Michael Heale, "Congress, for the first time in American history, finally concluded that it was legitimate to turn people away from the United States because of their political beliefs." In 1903, Congress passed an immigration act that President Roosevelt signed into law. The new statute prohibited anarchists from entering the country and denied immigrant anarchists already in the country the opportunity to become naturalized citizens. The irony is that Czolgosz was not an immigrant but a native-born American of Polish parents. A major reason members of Congress went after immigrants was that they could not agree on how to suppress domestic anarchists without overextending the powers of the federal government. Picking up the slack, though, were state legislatures. For example, New Jersey, New York, and Wisconsin created legislation that outlawed "criminal anarchy." The statutes were similar to the federal immigration act in that anyone—citizen or immigrant—was forbidden to advocate the forcible overthrow of the government or the assassination of government officials.[23]

In New York, the state legislature passed the Anarchy Act of 1902, which stipulated that a conviction of committing "criminal anarchy," in writing or in speech, would lead to a ten-year prison term or a fine of $5,000. Two of the act's provisions hampered anarchist activity in the state and in New York City in particular. One made it illegal to form a group that advocated overthrowing the existing political system. Another made it illegal for two or more individuals to meet to discuss "outlawed doctrines." Despite this draconian law, the anarchist movement in the city continued to grow. In the words of historian Tom Goyens, "The anarchist movement . . . refused to go underground," for "meetings and publications continued." Anarchists' defiance of the law did lead to arrests, however. For example, a small cadre of young male and female anarchists successfully distributed most of the twenty-five thousand copies of the first run of

Roosevelt, Czolgosz and Anarchy in New York, leading to repeated arrests. In another instance, at a memorial service for former Chicago governor John Altgeld, two anarchists gave away two hundred copies of Fox's pamphlet before being arrested. At a public meeting that Fox chaired honoring Most before he was to serve his prison term, two speakers on the platform were arrested for their speeches: William MacQueen, the Scottish editor of *Liberty*, a New York anarchist-communist newspaper, and Most himself. MacQueen was released on bail only to be arrested again a month later for "inciting a riot" for speeches he gave in conjunction with a Patterson, New Jersey, silk weavers' strike where a clash between strikers and police broke out on 18 June 1902. The Austrian anarchist Rudolf Grossman was also arrested and charged with the same "crime." Both anarchists received five-year terms at hard labor.

The most celebrated case of an anarchist prosecuted under these new laws was John Turner, a British labor leader and anarchist whose writing appeared in *The Rebel, Free Society, Discontent,* and other US anarchist publications. He traveled for the second time to the country in 1903 to lecture and study industrial working conditions. After a lecture he gave at the Murray Hill Lyceum in New York on "Trade Unionism and the General Strike," federal immigration officials arrested him for violating the Immigration Act of 1903. Following his arrest, the Free Speech League, which had formed the year before, rushed to his defense. Several prominent anarchists, along with a score of progressives, made up the league and the Turner Defense Committee that took on the British anarchist's case. Turner lost his challenge to the law, which had moved all the way to the US Supreme Court. He was deported in 1904. In the end, despite such governmental attacks on anarchists' free speech rights, many self-avowed anarchists in New York seemed to be able to circumvent the law. Using terms such as "radical," "liberty," "freedom," and "progressive" rather than "anarchism" or "anarchist," anarchists met openly in groups, engaged in public speaking, and continued to publish their newspapers and pamphlets. Sometimes they even flouted the law without repercussions.[24]

During this period, the ethnic makeup of the movement in New York was changing. As German immigration diminished in the 1900s, Italian, Jewish, and eastern European immigration increased. With this influx of new immigrants mixing with the native-born anarchist residents of the city, the movement became more international in character, even using the label "International Group" instead of "Anarchist Group" to both reflect members' multi-ethnic makeup and to avoid violating the Anarchy Act. In fact, Fox became secretary of the city's anarchist International Group, which had the express goal to spread the ideas of "freedom" to the American people. In New York, Fox found himself, over the next several years, in an even more vibrant anarchist community than the one that he had left in Chicago. Along with the pool of anarchists from different parts of Europe and the United States residing in the city were some of the most widely circulated anarchist publications in the country, including Benjamin Tucker's *Liberty*, Saul Yanovsky's *Freie Arbeiter Stimme*, Most's *Freiheit*, and MacQueen's *Liberty*. Numerous public speaking venues were available as well, from Cooper Union to the Radical Reading Room. Fox became a popular, featured speaker at the Radical Reading Room on Forsyth Street, which was in the heart of the radical East Side and near his home. His reputation within the anarchist circle of New York as an insightful commentator on the current state of the labor movement and strategies that the working class could employ to overthrow the existing economic system led to speaking engagements throughout the Northeast, particularly in Boston.[25]

3. Labor's Revolutionary Potential

IN CONCERT WITH HIS ACTIVE LIFE AS AN ANARCHIST, FOX CON-
tinued to make his living during these years as a millwright. The shop
he worked in, however, was nonunion, as were all of the cabinet shops in
and around New York City. That changed when the AWIU—which originated in Denver, Colorado, but moved its union headquarters to Chicago
in the mid-1890s—began to organize the cabinet shops in New York. The
Chicago organizer that had unionized Fox's shop was called back west,
leaving the position open. Fox's coworkers elected him to be business agent
of the local, for which he was paid four dollars a day. For Fox, this would
be the first time in his years of labor union activity that he would be a paid
union official. Moreover, he was quite proud that the rank and file of his
shop chose him, an open anarchist, for the position. Some had questioned
whether an anarchist could "consistently function as a union official," but
his commitment to the cause of labor won them over. From Fox's point of
view, a revolutionary should be ensconced in the labor movement as an
active participant, for labor unions were the foundational form of organization for workers as a class and the union experience itself was "the primary school for the education of the workers in their economic rights as
human beings." Fox's work as a business agent required him to be a walking delegate for several unionized cabinet shops. He had elected shop stewards

in three workplaces who assisted him in day-to-day operations, which included handling minor grievance procedures, providing information for his reports, and collecting union dues. Fox's duties kept him quite busy, and he received no overtime pay for his participation in meetings of the locals and committees, which always took place in the evenings, as well as the weekly Sunday meetings of the Central Labor Council in which he took part. He found working with shop owners not as difficult as he thought it would be. Most he thought were "willing to discuss the problem of Labor and Capital in a reasonable manner as it applied to their individual cases."[1]

Fox, as both secretary and business agent for Local 172, presided over meetings held every Thursday at the local's headquarters on Third Avenue, amid the German anarchist community. Germans, moreover, were heavily represented in woodworking trades in the city. The headquarters was not too far from where his family resided, so Fox could walk to his local. In 1903, he was elected president of the woodworker's council. Morton, his anarchist comrade and brother in-law from Chicago, also relocated to New York and had been elected as the council's secretary. Fox wrote for the trade union's publication as well, *The International Wood-Worker*, on his local's progress in the city and other topics. For several years, jurisdictional disputes broke out between the AWIU and the UBCJA. The carpenters and joiners were on strike in summer 1903 over a wage dispute, and during the strike action a contractual agreement was worked out between the AWIU and employers to supply men to the worksites. The UBCJA's contract had run out, though its representatives cried foul and called on city and state officials to arbitrate the dispute. The arbitrators ruled that as the earlier agreement had expired both union organizations were free to seek contractual agreements with the employers. The UBCJA went so far as to try to revoke the AFL charter of the AWIU, though that was dismissed. Since the first efforts by the AWIU to assert itself in the city, the carpenters and joiners expressed their opposition to the new trade union. Therefore, no love was lost between the two labor organizations. Nevertheless, Fox's union was in effect scabbing on striking fellow workers. This experience, multiplied by hundreds of such disputes among trade unions, will underscore for him the necessity of industrial unions to prevent such conflicts in the future and bring about greater labor solidarity.[2]

In addition to working as a union official, Fox actively participated in the city's anarchist movement, especially as a public speaker. He spoke at the Radical Club—the lectures of which were free and open to the public every Wednesday evening—on the topic of anarchist communism, a talk he had given in other venues and would continue to give over the years. At the Liberal Society, where he gave the same lecture, he took an evolutionary approach to the subject, probably influenced by Pyotr Kropotkin's series of articles published in the British magazine *The Nineteenth Century* that became his book *Mutual Aid: A Factor in Evolution*, or by the book itself, which was published in New York in 1902. Fox argued that anarchist communism was not "a beautiful dream" made possible by "a community of Angels," but "a natural and logical sequence of evolution." He provided an analysis of the evolution of human society in which cooperation and communalism were the basis of self-preservation. Moreover, in his idealized view of the earliest human societies, he thought of them as anarchist communist, for "they had no government. No classes or castes existed among them; they lived on a basis of equality—the natural condition of society without government and private property." However, the concept of private property corrupted this early stage of human development, and through private property came power and the exploitation of certain individuals over others; classes and slaves soon followed. Nevertheless, rebellion of the lower classes became a significant feature of human history whereby people sought to return to liberty and equality.

Fast-forward to his own time. The complexity of the capitalist economy made anarchism seem an impossibility due to the simplicity of its tenets. Fox argued that, to the contrary, out of the contemporary factory emerged trade unions and the demand for liberty and quality continued. In his lecture, he went on to discuss how anarchist communism would work in a future society. Here, the influence of Kropotkin again is apparent, namely his *Conquest of Bread*, originally published in French, which was serialized in *Freedom*, the British anarchist-communist journal, the previous decade. Kropotkin laid out in some detail how an anarchist-communist society could function. Fox's lecture followed some of the essential elements of Kropotkin's theory of society. In another lecture, Fox explained the differences between anarchism and social democracy. Social democrats, he argued, wanted state control of the means of production that would be managed by elected representatives. The wage system, though, would still exist and power would transfer from private or corporate ownership to state ownership. Authority would still be in the hands of a potential oppressor, while anarchist communism called for public ownership without the state. The means of production would be controlled by the workers themselves. Given Fox's experience at Haymarket, he was a featured speaker at commemorations of the execution of the Chicago anarchists. At Boston's Paine Memorial Hall, he gave such a lecture at a memorial meeting. In New York, he participated in meetings of the *Freie Arbeiter Stimme*, which were chaired by Saul Yanovsky, the publication's editor. Yiddish-speaking Jews were becoming a significant element of the city's anarchist movement as the German anarchists of an older generation were passing from the scene. Esther Abramowitz may have helped Fox bridge the language gap when discussions went back and forth between English and Yiddish.[3]

Writing was Fox's primary activity as an anarchist, and he honed his craft in *Free Society*, his primary venue. His topic of choice was the labor movement and issues relating to the working class. He was concerned with workers being their own agents of change and not allowing themselves to be bought off by the powers that be. For example, he was not terribly supportive of Labor Day as practiced in the country every September, for it was a time when the government allowed workers a day to celebrate the significance of their work. At least, given the numbers involved on that day, a demonstration of sorts was possible. Nevertheless, he did not support socialists' efforts to revive May Day and have American workers join other laborers around the world who celebrated it as the true Labor Day because it was on 1 May 1886 when workers across the country, particularly in Chicago, launched a strike for the eight-hour day. In Europe, where governments refused to recognize 1 May as Labor Day, he thought defying authority was good propaganda for the movement. In the United States, however, American conditions needed to be understood when trying to reach the working class. Imitating Europe would not garner much support among the American working class for socialism or anarchism. Fox clearly remembered 1 May 1886 from personal experience but thought trying to revive May Day would be like trying to revive a corpse. Better to put one's energy into the movement at hand and radicalize the existing Labor Day that Americans celebrated.

Moreover, bringing the anarchist message to American workers was Fox's primary calling as a writer. He, like most anarchists of his generation, saw in the working class the origin from which the revolution would emerge. Unlike his generation of anarchists, however, he was far more similar to

Albert Parsons of the previous generation when it came to the labor movement. He reasoned that "Anarchists should identify themselves more closely with the great practical movement of the toilers," for he acknowledged that many anarchists thought of trade unions as "reactionary institutions" with which they should not waste their time. For example, Fox's fellow anarchist Harry Kelly dropped out of the labor movement in 1904, partly due to his union's conservativism and majority rule decision-making. Fox, though, argued that unions were more progressive than they were given credit for being and that his fellow anarchists should continue their participation in labor unions. He was in line with John Turner, the British labor leader and anarchist, who believed that as voluntary associations seeking to change conditions at the point of production, unions had incipient anarchist potential, and with Errico Malatesta, who saw the revolutionary potential of the general strike, which was unlikely to happen unless labor unions played a decisive role. *Free Society* reprinted Malatesta's thoughts on the general strike, which appeared in *The Torch* several years earlier.[4]

In the pages of *Free Society*, Fox wrote a series of articles titled "The Strikers at Work" in which he commented on the history of the labor movement, contemporary unions, and strikes. A topic that took up a considerable amount of space in his column was the Pennsylvania anthracite coal strike of 1902. He began by explaining the causes of the strike, pointing out the process by which a miner mined hard coal, his costs involved (e.g., having to purchasing his own blasting powder and other tools of the trade), and how he was paid by the ton of coal mined. Fox also was sure to include the day laborers and other workers in the coal industry and their working conditions, pay, and support of the strike. With the two sides deadlocked, Fox analyzed the behavior of the court system, with the implication that the state had already sided with the mine owners as labor agitators were given stiff prison sentences for trying to spread the strike. For Fox, as well as for labor unions in general, court injunctions held particular ire. They were used to break strikes by interfering with the exercise of free speech and free assembly. He also cautioned the labor movement that to appeal to the Congress for support was not realistic as Congress was the servant of capital. It would make more sense to appeal to J. P. Morgan, who had helped resolve the coal strike of 1900. When the Greater New York Central Labor Unions passed a resolution calling on the president to convene a special commission to resolve the coal strike, Fox asked rhetorically what they expected.

Surely, they did not think that Congress was any less dishonest than state legislatures, which seemed rife with corruption. He chastised the labor body for having any faith in the state, but he acknowledged that workers were still under the spell that the government could do something in their interests. They needed to understand that

> workingmen—especially unionists—must learn these common facts of political life, and look elsewhere for aid in their trouble. Let that knowledge be within themselves, in the recesses of their own hearts and minds. They must READ AND THINK. They must encourage and develop the spirit of solidarity among themselves; cluster together in their trade unions and educational clubs, exchanging their best thoughts with one another, thereby raising themselves above the blinding powers of superstition which has kept them in the mire of poverty for ages past. Parties and leaders will conduct men from one slavery to another. Only their own clear thoughts will lead them to final emancipation and liberty.

Fox was not alone in his thinking. It was still quite common for labor leaders and labor journalists to council workers to rely on themselves and their organizations rather than hope for legislative cures. All Illinois workers had to do was to point to the unenforced eight-hour-workday statute passed in the state legislature in 1867 to see the futility of state intervention on the side of labor. In the end, President Roosevelt was able to resolve the strike through arbitration, though not without great resistance from coal mine owners and railroad barons arrayed against the 150,000 striking workers. Fox did not think that the coal mine workers succeeded in the strike. Their union was not recognized and they did not gain the eight-hour day. However, nine hours was better than ten and a wage increase was not to be dismissed.[5]

Another theme in his writing was to grapple with what would be the most effective means of getting the message of anarchism to the people. *Free Society* was where most of his work appeared in the early 1900s. Among the themes he explored as a writer was the quality of anarchist discourse. He thought it needed to operate at a high level of cool rationality but infused with a sense of brotherly and sisterly love. The intellect as well as the heart needed to be the targets for anarchists when they were appealing to readers. From Fox's perspective, "the coming man and woman must not hate, must not have enemies. The doctrine of hatred ought not to be preached." Furthermore, he argued that "Intelligence directs all the great movements of the world," and "Knowledge must be our guiding star to the land of Freedom." Also, anarchists needed to embody the qualities that would make anarchism possible, namely tolerance, comradeship, and the acceptance of differing opinions. More than leading by example, anarchists needed to refrain from denunciation, hate, and rage, for such rhetoric was what underlay all types of government. He cautioned anarchists to "talk less, and read and think more." Fox did not want to be seen as advocating the prohibition of individuals from writing and speaking for the cause. However, he urged anarchists, especially younger ones, "to a deeper study of the fundamental principles underling the philosophy of Anarchism, and to a better knowledge of the language in which they propose to work. Unless we give this important matter more attention the cause will suffer greatly, our individual advancement crippled and Anarchism be deprived of representatives of its exalted ideals."[6]

Free Society exemplified a print culture of inclusion. Letters to the editor, a variety of contributors, and open discussion of articles and letters submitted was ever present. Even though anarchist communism was the ideological underpinning of the journal, a variety of opinions appeared in its pages as to what anarchism actually was, how a social revolution would bring about anarchism, and how a future anarchist society would function. Unlike socialists and later communists with their party platforms and ideologues, anarchists were largely free of dogma or any type of central control. Anarchists, of course, had their influences and strong, sometimes authoritarian personalities, but the movement itself tended to be an evolving system of ideas and methodologies subject to frequent and open debate.

Although *Free Society* had a core group of readers and was a significant newspaper to spread anarchist communism, the publication was under serious financial strain. Abe Isaak put out several pleas to the readers that subscribers needed to be in good standing with their subscriptions and that more subscribers were needed. The Radical Club arranged a theater performance to raise funds for the periodical. Those interested in attending the play—*The Jewish Sappho*—could purchase tickets at a number of businesses in the city. Emma Goldman spoke between the acts on "The English

Propaganda," in other words on the importance of an English-language anarchist-communist journal. At about this time, supporters of the publication thought relocating it could improve its financial situation. Anarchists in New York, and Fox in particular, wanted to see the paper moved from Chicago to New York, where he was currently living as was Goldman and other high-profile anarchists. In some respects, New York appeared to have a more vibrant anarchist movement in the early 1900s, but it had no English-language anarchist-communist paper, for other such periodicals in the city had folded. Goldman was especially supportive of the move, but there were varying levels of support in other quarters, especially among the foreign-language anarchist press. For example, Yanovsky, editor of *Freie Arbeiter Stimme*, did not like the competition, at least according to Fox.

In the end, a group of East Coast anarchists promised Isaak fifteen dollars a week to publish the paper. This was more than he and his family had ever earned producing the paper in the past. He, along with members of his family, moved *Free Society* to New York in early 1904. Years later, Isaak recalled the move as a serious mistake, even more of a mistake than leaving San Francisco, where he and his family had been quite content. Isaak thought he had not inquired fully under what circumstances the paper was to be supported. The *Free Society* Group, which was created to assist in the paper's production, interfered with Isaak's management of the enterprise, which grated on him to no end. Still, the paper ended up failing due to a lack of subscribers. *Free Society* suspended publication at the end of 1904, and Isaak transferred the subscriber list over to *The Demonstrator*, an anarchist-communist newspaper published out of the anarchist village of Home Colony. At the last minute, Isaak was approached by a wealthy gentleman sympathetic to anarchist communism who was willing to finance the publication, though Isaak politely refused. He had lost interest in the movement and was probably disillusioned by the behavior of some of his comrades.[7]

Filling the void left by the publication was *Mother Earth*, the first issue of which came out in mid-March 1906. Goldman was the publisher, a major writing contributor, and a significant fundraiser for the magazine. Max Baginski was the publication's first editor. *Mother Earth* would become the most significant English-language anarchist-communist periodical in the United States for the rest of the 1900s and 1910s. The journal, though, would cater more to bohemian counterculture sensibilities than to the work life of common laborers or to union men and women. Nevertheless, the availability of that media platform was still months away, and without *Free Society* Fox, who could only write in English, needed another venue for his anarchist writing. He found that new outlet with *The Demonstrator*, one of a series of Home Colony anarchist newspapers. In late 1905, James F. Morton Jr., the community's newspaper editor, decided to step down from his position. Morton had published in *Free Society* and in other anarchist, radical, and progressive publications for years. For the last several years he edited *The Demonstrator*, writing a weekly column in which he commented on many topics of the day. Although he was committed to Home Colony as an experiment in anarchist living and in publishing an anarchist newspaper, he decided he needed to move to New York and devote himself to a more thorough type of writing than was possible as editor of the newspaper. In addition, he received little financial compensation from his work as editor, so he was compelled to find other means of livelihood, which took up a considerable amount of his time. In New York, he would be able to devote himself to the kind of writing that he longed to do.[8]

Morton, with the support of *The Demonstrator* Publishing Group, persuaded his friend and comrade Fox—who had moved back to Chicago by 1905—to take over as editor of the newspaper. Around the same time Chicago anarchists sent a circular letter addressed to every name on the subscriber list of *Free Society*. The readers were asked about whether they would support starting a new anarchist paper. The feedback was not encouraging. Nevertheless, the English-speaking anarchists of the city wanted to establish a paper to spread their ideas and to share some of the burden of education being shouldered by the foreign-language anarchist press. The way this was to be achieved created a rift among Chicago anarchists. Some insisted that a paper needed to be produced in an urban environment so as to be firmly connected to the labor movement. According to these advocates, such as Lucy Parsons, Chicago should be the center of anarchist agitation. The city's radical tradition and reputation as the most unionized city in America seemed to support the argument. The anarchists of the city had already organized several fundraising picnics which seemed promising. Others, though, namely Fox, suggested that "a paper published in the backwoods of Washington" could be effective. The cost of living was very low in the community and plenty of volunteer labor would be available. Even though Fox was committed to the labor movement, he also still supported socialist colonizing efforts in the Far West. Home Colony was proving its longevity over other socialist communities and he may have seen this as his chance to participate in the effort. Therefore, he may have been less than forthcoming about why he wanted the paper out west. In addition, he did remind his comrades that it was not that long ago that the best English-language anarchist newspaper with a national circulation, *The Firebrand*, was published out of Portland, Oregon. Fox argued that it would be possible to expand *The Demonstrator* into an eight-page anarchist-communist weekly, exactly what the movement needed to replace *Free Society*. Some money had already been donated for a newspaper venture by Chicago anarchists and others from around the country.

With the two factions divided and the funds in Fox's possession, he thought it best to ask the donors what they preferred. According to him, most wanted the money to go to *The Demonstrator*. Parsons was infuriated by this because she thought the process was compromised by Fox, who she believed already intended to relocate the propaganda effort and himself to Home Colony. In the end, Parsons started her own short-lived newspaper, *The Liberator*, in Chicago, while Fox began to write extensively for *The Demonstrator*. In some respects, he complemented the writings of Andrew "Al" Klemencic, who wrote extensively about labor issues for the paper. Klemencic, born in Trieste of Slovenian decent, represented the Colorado Journeymen Tailor's Union at the founding convention of the IWW; he had been active in the labor movement since his arrival in the United States in 1890 and, coming from Colorado, had been a frequent contributor to *Free Society*. When he passed away in 1906, Fox took on the role of labor reporter and commentator. It was at Klemencic's suggestion that Charles Govan, the editor of the paper after Morton departed Home, put the IWW union symbol above the editorial page. Fox had objected to that because he wanted the newspaper to be free to critique the IWW, the AFL, or any other labor organization and to not come off to readers as biased. Nevertheless, Fox, to the disappointment of Govan, did not take over as editor and his relocation was delayed by a couple of years. Historian Charles LeWarne suggests that Fox suffered an eye injury, most likely at his workplace, in May 1906 that postponed his departure for Washington. Therefore, it was up to Govan and others on the editorial board of the paper to determine editorial policy and continue the publication.[9]

Even though Fox had his sights set on relocating to Home Colony, he had a satisfying professional and personal life in Chicago. His friend, fellow anarchist, and labor organizer Johannsen found Fox employment as a machinist in a woodworking shop. Esther contributed to the family income by working as a domestic servant, cleaning the homes of the more well-to-do. Together they were able to support themselves and Esther's children Sylvia and David in a modest apartment in a working-class neighborhood at the north end of the city. In many respects they had a typical working-class life. They rose early in the morning, ate a sparse breakfast, and commuted to their jobs. At the end of the day, Esther had a meal ready for Jay and the children, often a simple plate of beans and rice, after which Jay smoked his pipe and enjoyed the company of his family. Later, as Esther tended to the evening dishes and put the children to bed, Jay turned to his extensive correspondence with other anarchists and radicals or began work on an article for the anarchist or labor press. Jay and Esther enjoyed an active social life among the city's small but committed community of anarchists. Among that community of anarchists, which included anarchist individualists as well as anarchist communists, labor militants, and radicals, was Johannsen, his wife Maggie, and Matthew Schmidt, who was a woodworker in addition to laboring in the building trades. Schmidt would later be involved in a series of bombings and would face charges in relation to the Los Angeles Times Building bombing in 1910 among others. On some evenings, the circle of anarchists and radicals stayed up late at a Chinese restaurant discussing "philosophy, and love, and psychology" along with issues of the day over plates of chop suey and pots of tea. In some respects, Esther struck a romantic figure in the community. Although on the surface, Jay and Esther's life together resembled a patriarchal relationship and home life, they both believed in free love. Jay was more of a supporter of the concept, while Esther was a practitioner. Jay did not hinder Esther's "longings" to be with other men, even if that meant she "left for weeks at a time." While she was away, Jay contented himself with his work and caring for the children.[10]

The call to actively participate in the anarchist movement was an ever-present feature of Fox's life. He was very much devoted to writing and public speaking both in Chicago and in the Northeast. In Chicago, he was a frequent speaker at the Social Science League and made several trips to Boston and New York to lecture on anarchism and the labor movement. In addition, he continued to seek out both the labor and anarchist press for his writing. With the *International Wood-Worker,* he found a receptive forum for his work, beyond some of his earlier writing which dealt primarily with union matters when he was a business agent and walking delegate in New York. The publication was the monthly periodical of the AWIU. After the periodical moved from Denver to Chicago in the mid-1890s, the editors offered a German-language section, for Germans and German Americans were well represented in the skilled woodworking trades and furniture making in the city. Fox was not the only openly anarchist labor writer to pen articles for the *International Wood-Worker.* Lizzie Holmes was a frequent contributor as well, writing on diverse topics. Her columns were the featured articles of numerous issues. T. Putman Quinn, one of the anarchists to bring *Free Society* to Chicago, also had articles published in the periodical. In addition, the pioneering labor journalist Eva Valesh was a frequent contributor as well.

It is striking the radical and potentially revolutionary positions that were presented in the publication over the years. Fox, for example, in response to miners' strike in Colorado in 1903–4, wrote an article admonishing the Western Federation of Miners (WFM) for attempting to secure arbitration or, worse, compulsory arbitration, for he warned that the employer will only agree to it if the union is strong and it can lead to nothing more than a compromise. And for looking to the state legislature, that was not worth much either, according to Fox. Colorado passed an eight-hour-workday law in 1899 only to have it ignored by mine owners and ultimately declared unconstitutional by the state supreme court. Eight-hour legislation was attempted again but failed to remedy the situation, as mine owners were powerful enough to refuse to implement such a law. In the final analysis, Fox maintained that only with a general strike, when workers and their unions struck as one, could the eight-hour day be implemented. Such an action would succeed or fail based on the ability of the workers to demonstrate solidarity. In another article in the journal, Fox sought to explain to readers how trade unionism was a challenge to the capitalist system. Employer associations, he noted, pulled their resources together to crush trade unions because they interfered with the autocratic hold employers wanted to maintain over their workers. He continued, "Despite all the power of money, which buys the tongues of the shrewdest lawyers, the pens of cunning editors, and the services of legislators and governors, soldiers and police—in spite of all, the giant of organized labor is growing larger every day, and no power on earth is now able to check its growth. Hail to the new emancipator of man, the ever-progressive trade union!"[11]

The trade union movement was indeed growing during the early years of the new century. Labor militancy was on the rise as well given the recalcitrant behavior of employers, especially those in large industries. Therefore, Fox's aggressive language and anti-government rhetoric was welcomed in some labor circles as unions could rarely count on local governments to support their interests, though exceptions did exist. The collapse of the Knights and the inability of the AFL to effectively organize the vast majority of American workers led many in the labor movement to search for other means to improve working conditions and challenge the industrial capitalist system. Out of this frustration grew the industrial union movement, which had its origins with the Knights, though in the 1890s, in the Far West, the WFM was the primary proponent of this organizing strategy. In order to broaden its reach, the federation was instrumental in creating the Western Labor Union, which became the American Labor Union in 1902. But this effort to further galvanize the American working class met strong opposition from the AFL.

In early January 1905, however, a new effort emerged from a conference of industrial unionists to bring together the largest number of workers and labor advocates as possible, regardless of political affiliation. In May of that year, *The Demonstrator* carried "A Manifesto" that was also published in revolutionary periodicals, socialist journals, and labor newspapers throughout the country. It was a call for workers to come together for a convention in Chicago in June to form a labor organization that would unite all workers, be they skilled or unskilled and regardless of ethnicity, race, gender, or national origin. The manifesto suggested that the organization would be international and devoted to the concept of class struggle. It was intended to be both a practical labor union as well as a revolutionary organization. Delegates to the convention could represent specific unions or simply represent themselves. Fox was aware of the coming convention but had serious reservations. He was supportive of the amalgamation of existing trade unions, thinking that that would enhance the power of labor so that trades would not be scabbing on each other in strikes or lockouts. He had experience working to amalgamate the metal trades in the 1890s in Chicago, and the concept dated back to 1870s. In his view, amalgamation was an organic industrial unionism that should be an evolutionary development, derived from the experience of laborers themselves. It needed to come from their own initiative in order to be fully embraced. He had concerns about creating a new labor federation and new labor unions that were parallel to those that already existed, which could perpetuate and amplify the current problem of jurisdictional disputes that disrupted labor solidarity and created confusion for workers. Nevertheless, Fox attended the convention in the hope that his reservations and concerns would be unfounded and that his pessimism would give way to optimism. He along with Debs, Parsons and Mary Harris "Mother" Jones acted as delegates, though they represented only themselves.[12]

Fox was one of a number of anarchists and labor leaders to attend the convention that were hostile to government and dubious of its ability to assist the working class in its conflict with capital. Salvatore Salerno is one of the few historians who have extensively examined the role of anarchists at the founding convention of the IWW. He notes that the Haymarket Martyrs and the "Chicago Idea" permeated the convention atmosphere. Fox, who acted as a delegate and a labor journalist for the convention, corroborated both of Salerno's points in his first article in *The Demonstrator*. In a detailed report on the founding of the IWW in Chicago, Fox provided a concise narrative of events and an analysis of key speeches. He began his report by noting the importance of Chicago as the birthplace of the IWW, for it was "significant that many of the 200 delegates to the industrial workers' convention gathered about the tomb of our martyred comrades and drank deep into their hearts the full meaning of the labor struggle." He was in strong agreement with William Trautmann, former editor of the *Brauer-Zeitung*, the newspaper of the Brewery Workers' Union, who took to task the failure of Samuel Gompers and the AFL to meet the needs of the American worker. Fox provided an ample quote from the speech by Daniel DeLeon, head of the SLP and Socialist Trade and Labor Alliance. Fox was most impressed by DeLeon's seeming willingness to acknowledge that "the political expression of labor is but the shadow of the economic organization" and that the ballot box was insufficient without the power of a "thoro [*sic*] industrial organization of the productive workers." For Fox, "DeLeon and his political associates [were] coming closer to the Anarchist position all the time." Thomas J. Haggerty, a priest and editor of the *Voice of Labor*, gave a speech following DeLeon in which he took DeLeon's comments one step further by celebrating the inclusive nature of the IWW. He argued that "this convention ought to be broad enough to allow any kind of a revolutionary workingman to come into the proposed economic organization." Haggerty was instrumental as secretary of the constitutional committee in writing the preamble of the IWW's declaration of principles. Fox went on to assert that the "strongest revolutionaries" at the convention "came from the far west." He continued that "the delegates from the Western Federation of Miners had no word of praise for politics" and that William Haywood, secretary of the WFM, made clear in his speech that the labor union was the instrument of both practical gains for the working class and the foundation for its eventual emancipation. Here was the "Chicago Idea" expressed twenty years or so later, with the same anarchist implications as when it was inaugurated by Parsons and Spies in 1883. However, in the new century, a firmer commitment to organized labor is evident among a core group of anarchists and socialists in that labor unions could attain immediate improvements in the lives of working people and simultaneously be the foundation of a new, cooperative, and egalitarian society.[13]

In *The Demonstrator*, Fox had a forum to examine the labor movement and explain the significance of trade unions and industrial unionism to the publication's anarchist and progressive readers. In a September 1905 article, Fox argued that the labor movement was something that the employer class feared above all other challenges to its economic power. Union membership was growing by "leaps and bounds" during the early years of the twentieth century, he contended. In fact, union membership had doubled between 1897 and 1901 to about one million members and had doubled again to almost two million by 1904. As of 1905, though, membership did not increase, and it remained static or fell slightly over the next several years. Nonetheless, the great gains by labor since Fox plunged into the movement as a self-declared anarchist in 1897 would have buoyed his hopes for the continued unionization of the American working class. Within these unions, Fox championed the sentiment of equality, which if not a pervasive sentiment within all trade and industrial unions was an aspiration for many union brothers and sisters. Corporate leaders, Fox suggested, dreaded "the possible outcome of a condition of equality among men. They fear[ed] the loss of the privileges they now enjoy of exploiting the workers, first as wage earners, second as buyers." Fox believed as the anarchists of an earlier generation did that the "progressive trade union" was "the new emancipator of man." Nevertheless, he had a word of caution for the working class, for wage-earning men and women needed to continue to actively join and create labor unions, and most important they needed to work together as trades or as industries. Solidarity was the key to success. A means to attain this, he argued, was for trades to amalgamate such as the garment workers of New York were currently doing. For Fox, amalgamation was the natural, evolutionary, and worker-driven action to create industrial unionism.[14]

In a subsequent article, Fox viewed the IWW as a potentially positive and unifying force in the labor movement and thought that the "new Industrial Union" could be helpful in creating a climate of solidarity among the working class. He was troubled, however, by the prospect of the IWW creating rival unions to current craft and trade unions, thereby dividing workers rather than unifying them. He was also concerned that progressives and radicals, especially anarchists, were departing the established trade unions and going over to the IWW, deserting "their less progressive comrades in the old unions, leaving them to shift for themselves." Fox would rather see progressives and radicals stay in the established trade unions of the AFL and continue to work at radicalizing the federation into an emancipatory labor organization. To create a separate federation as the IWW was doing could work to reduce labor solidarity as competing labor unions vied for members. Fox believed that "without taking a man from the old craft unions, or organizing a single scab, there are yet enuf [sic] nonunion men and women in the country to make a union larger than the Federation of labor [AFL]." Fox thought that that was the plan the IWW set for itself at the Chicago convention—that is, organizing the unorganized workers. He hoped that the current conflict between the IWW and AFL would subside if the Wobblies (i.e., members of the IWW) exercised "a more temperate and conciliatory attitude . . . toward the old organization."

Fox's perspective is interesting on several levels. First, he seems to have underestimated the deep resentment that many anarchists, radicals, and socialists had for the AFL, for members of the new federation did intend to replace the AFL. His misreading of the intentions of those hostile to the AFL is understandable. The January 1905 conference of industrial unionists, the manifesto that the delegates issued, and the June 1905 convention itself did not specifically call for a new labor federation to replace the AFL. Nevertheless, that is precisely what members of the IWW began to do during the new federation's first year of existence. Fox shared much of their criticism of the AFL, but he never felt comfortable with dual unionism. Second, his concern that radicals would leave the AFL, thereby ensuring that the federation would remain conservative, predated by several years the critique of the IWW by revolutionary syndicalists such as William Z. Foster. He asked rhetorically "if it would not have been better for the new unionists to have stayed within the ranks of the old union and pursued their propaganda there for the industrialization [industrial unionism] of the labor movement rather than to have deserted to a new union with the direful results that are sure to follow." And third, those "direful results" was the strife of union factions competing for control of trades and industries that took place soon after the conclusion of the June convention. With the IWW and AFL on the verge of war with each other, Fox reasoned the only real benefit would go to the employer class.[15]

Fox made clear in much of his writing that the common foe—capitalism and the employing class—needed to be always in the sights of organized labor. He consistently voiced great distress whenever internecine conflict broke out within the ranks of labor. In "The Labor Struggle," published in *To-Morrow: A Rational Monthly Magazine*, he presented to the readers of this Chicago-based anarchist publication an overview of labor history from the ancient world to the present, touching on key episodes of worker rebellions and the constant struggle that workers faced throughout history. Approaching history from a labor theory of value, Fox argued that workers—be they skilled, unskilled, slaves, or peasants—have had to rise up to fight the employing class, which only compensated labor with the bare means of existence. The current wage system was simply the latest example of an effort by employers to cheat workers out of the full fruits of their labor. The trade union, he argued, was the most effective organizational weapon that workers had at their disposal. He reasoned that "intelligent working men know that the politics of the country is controlled by the men who control the stocks and bonds and possess the title deeds of its wealth. It is quite natural then that they should eschew politics and direct their efforts to the conquest of bread." The nonpolitical and direct economic action conclusion that the educated worker would naturally come to needed to be further enhanced with the understanding that there can be no "reconciliation between capital and labor." Moreover, "nothing short of a complete change of the system of production and distribution will satisfy the new aspirations of the workers."[16]

Faith in organized labor and in the working class was central to Fox's vision of the anarchist transformation of society. That faith was shared by many in the anarchist movement. The general strike for the eight-hour day in May 1886, with its epicenter in Chicago and significant anarchist participation and leadership, resonated among anarchists, socialists, and trade unionists worldwide. For anarchists, however, the labor movement posed significant problems as a vehicle for revolution. In the United States, which had emerged in the new century as the largest industrial economy in the world, conservatives dominated the leadership of most unions as well as that of the AFL. Therefore, the focus of most trade unions in the country was on wages, hours, and working conditions for their members and not on revolution or even the expansion of labor organizing to unskilled workers. The IWW hoped to fill in that gap, but it was still in its infancy. In Germany and Great Britain, most of the trade union movement was wedded to the partisan politics of the Social Democrats and the Labour Party respectively. Seizing control of the state through Parliament or the Reichstag in conjunction with a heavily organized labor workforce seemed to hold sway over the socialist path toward the transformation of society. France, Italy, and Spain nurtured more radical, anti-statist labor movements, which led to the development of revolutionary syndicalism. By the mid-1900s, the Confédération Générale du Travail (CGT) in France was of particular importance because of the role anarchists were able to play in its operation. Within this context, some of the more prominent members of the international anarchist community—meeting in Belgium and the Netherlands in 1906—called for an international anarchist conference. Such events had taken place in the past, but little had emerged that was significant to furthering the advancement of the anarchist cause, unifying the movement, articulating a common anarchist message, or reaching the toiling masses. The one scheduled to meet in Amsterdam in late August 1907, which Fox supported and Goldman and Baginski attended, would reveal a major tension in the anarchist movement between "mass anarchism" and "workerist" anarchism.[17]

Despite the concerted efforts of both republican and monarchial governments to "exterminate" the anarchists in their countries over the past three decades, almost one hundred anarchists managed to meet in Amsterdam from 26 to 31 August to discuss a range of issues that confronted the movement. Unlike previous anarchist conferences that were disrupted by law enforcement officials, the Dutch government largely left the attendants alone to conduct their affairs without interference. Moreover, the Dutch press reported on the conference proceedings without distorting the message or demonizing the participants. In this relatively free and peaceful atmosphere, anarchists from throughout Europe and the Americas, for the first time in perhaps a generation, could delve into the problems unique to an international libertarian movement. After devoting the early sessions to reports by the representatives from specific countries on the state of the movement in various parts of the world, the conference sessions focused on key issues that ranged from anarchism and organization, to syndicalism and anarchism, to individual action and collective action, to the creation of an Anarchist International Bureau, to the general strike and social revolution.

By far the most important topic, which at times spilled into other sessions, was syndicalism and its relationship to anarchism, or more broadly collective action versus individual action. Speaking for the necessity of organization and for anarchists to become essential to the labor movements of their respective countries was Pierre Monatte and Amédée Dunois, both prolific writers and members of the CGT. They embraced what would be later be called revolutionary syndicalism, and in 1907 they were convinced that the labor movement had an intrinsic anarchist component that anarchists must enhance by their active participation. They realized that trade unionism and even industrial unionism could be mired in mere reformism. Therefore, with anarchist participation, the trade union and the industrial union could become the structure of a new society. Also, organized workers would be the vanguard of the general strike that would bring capitalism and the state to its knees. Unions would be the mechanism that society could use to reestablish itself, resuming the production and distribution of goods and services in an egalitarian and cooperative manner.

Rising to challenge what some believed was too narrow a vision of the anarchist movement and too close of an association with labor unions was Malatesta. He presented an argument that he first qualified by noting he had been an early advocate of anarchists joining labor unions and working closely with the laboring classes. He maintained that he still believed that was essential and important work for anarchists to do, so that they would not be confined to ivory towers of purism. Nevertheless, he argued that unions were "only potentially revolutionary." Also, to only focus on wage laborers left out huge sections of society that needed to be included in the social revolution. And third, he believed that anarcho-syndicalists were mistaken if they thought the revolution could be achieved peacefully with the general strike and that armed insurrection was unnecessary. Although in the end the conference participants passed resolutions supportive of both sides in this debate, the Amsterdam Congress was significant for endorsing anarcho-syndicalism. In the short run, many anarchists committed, or recommitted, themselves to working more closely with labor unions. Emerging from the conference was the weekly, multilingual *Bulletin of the International Syndicalist Movement*, which circulated worldwide until mid-1914. In the long run, however, the debate would continue, and, with time, a clear drift would take place between anarchists (and their anarcho-syndicalists allies) and revolutionary syndicalists (and those syndicalists who felt no need to qualify the term).[18]

Although Fox did not attend the Amsterdam Conference, he did enter the debate by maintaining a position he had held for some time. In "Trade Unionism and Anarchism: A Letter to a Brother Unionist," which appeared in *Mother Earth* in November 1907 and was republished as a pamphlet by the Social Science Press in Chicago the following year, Fox staked out a position more closely aligned with Monatte and Dunois than with Malatesta. In a conversational style that would be a standard feature of his writing, Fox presented his perspective in response to a "letter" he received from a union brother asking about anarchism's relationship to the labor movement. Fox first explained that when a worker begins to ask critical questions about the compensation for his labor, the length of his workday, and the conditions of his employment, he reveals a discontent that was a sure sign of his intelligence. The worker, according to Fox, either organizes or joins a union to address these issues in order to force the employer to give into his demands, or he becomes an anarchist and envisions a society "without employers, or governors of any description." He went on to state, "Thus you see the same condition of mind and intelligence produce the unionist and the Anarchist, who are often one and the same person. In striving to better his lot in the present, he is a unionist; in mapping out a condition of freedom and equality for the future, he is an Anarchist." Although the unionist and anarchist share the same starting point, the unionist is preoccupied with attaining "a fair day's pay for a fair day's work," though not having a clear definition of either. From the anarchist's perspective "a fair day's pay" is only fair if workers receive the full fruits of their labor and nothing less. This proposition, he thought, was something "that any workman or woman can easily understand." Therefore, once they understood the proposition as members of organized labor, their "union will have deeper and more definite significance."[19]

Before he explained the greater significance of trade unionism, Fox felt compelled to articulate the anarchist perspective more thoroughly. One common critique of anarchists was that they were utopians. He did acknowledge that anarchists had "faith in the goodness of man," but anarchists also were cognizant of human weaknesses, chief among them being selfishness. Anarchists thought that through "power-free relationships" they could overcome that type of behavior in a society in which selfishness could not lead to exploitation or the use of power over others to benefit oneself at the expense of others. Whether in trade unions or government itself, it was clear to the anarchist that all power corrupts. Union members needed to keep a watchful eye on labor officials and government, for the latter by its very nature of supporting the employing class offered no benefit to the working class. In fact, the government assisted the capitalists in taking from workers a significant portion of the full fruits of their labor. The trade union could be the vehicle of ending the exploitation when union men and women come to the conclusion that to free themselves "from exploitation they must take back the land and tools, by refusing to pay rent to the landlords, and by refusing to allow the capitalist to buy and sell the product of their toil and control their labor." How then would workers do this, he paraphrased the question of the brother unionist. Not through government, he answered. That was the solution of the employer, who wanted the worker to use the ballot box. The well-meaning socialist had the same response. How, Fox asked rhetorically, could the enemy of labor, the state, magically become its friend through the ballot? It was a fantasy. To support his position, he noted in recent elections in several states that eight-hour-day legislation was never implemented or was ruled unconstitutional. Workers, though, did have a means to force change in their conditions: the strike.

As labor organizing continued the world over with more workers laboring within the context of labor unions and as more unions engaged in strikes to better their members' well-being, the strike could be extended "and it only require[d] time and experience to develop the desire for a General Strike." For Fox, the general strike was a distinctly anarchist tactic because "it is a non-invasive method. It forces no man; it avoids him; it lets him alone." However, it was the method by which workers could take control of the means of production and distribution and thereby usher into being a new society. Underlying the arguments in his article is the premise that unionists need anarchists to gain the ultimate victory of emancipation from both employers and the state. Implicit also is that anarchists need unionists to reach the masses of the working class. Fox's reasoning had the same practical application of anarchism to the world of the worker as Monatte and Dunois's position expressed in Amsterdam. It also shared the problems that Malatesta identified in terms of vagueness, the narrow focus on workers without attention to the rest of society, and the faith in a non-violent revolution.[20]

Despite the reservations of Malatesta, many anarchists voiced much support for the movement to engage the working class in a more concerted manner. None in the United States was more committed to this effort than Fox, and his pamphlet sold well, especially overseas. A key to awakening the revolutionary possibilities of trade unions and industrial unions was getting the anarchist message to workers. From the pages of *Mother Earth*, a call was issued by some of the most prominent anarchists—such as Alexander Berkman, Kelly, Voltairine de Cleyre, Hippolyte Havel, and George Bauer—to establish "a practical weekly, a fighting champion of revolutionary labor." A newspaper to be circulated among workers they thought would complement the "theoretical, literary and educational" focus of *Mother Earth*, which perhaps did not speak to the direct needs of the laboring classes. Lost in this call was the work of Home Colonists in publishing *The Demonstrator*, an anarchist-communist publication that featured extensive news relevant to workers and labor organizers. Fox, starting in 1905, had become a frequent contributor along with Klemencic, who, like Fox, was an anarchist and veteran unionist, and had written for the publication almost from its inception. Perhaps anarchists from the industrial Midwest and the East Coast had a prejudice that prevented them from promoting *The Demonstrator*. Or perhaps they considered the paper too closely associated with the anarchist colony. Regardless, nothing came of this call.

The desire for an anarchist weekly devoted to working-class issues did not subside, as Fox explained in an appeal to readers of *Mother Earth* in fall 1908. Here he invoked the spirit of the Amsterdam Congress, for "it [had] agreed upon the policy of going into the unions and encouraging these organizations to move toward Direct Action." He asked his anarchist comrades to support a newspaper designed to "carry the message of Anarchism to the workers; a paper that will, as it were, step into the factory, walk into the union, or stop on the street corner and discuss, in a familiar way, the questions that are vital to the here and now." He advised his fellow anarchists to accept the fact that the working person is interested in issues of the moment: wages, job security, and working conditions. And finally, he implored anarchists that "if you want to interest the worker in the future, you must become interested in the present. The practice of standing high up and, preacher-like, megaphoning the people is played out. The men who influence the world to-day are they who step down from their pedestal of learning and mix with the crowd." He may have wanted to emulate in the United States the *Voice of Labour*, edited by the British anarchist John Turner, of the Shop Assistants' Union, which featured articles by anarchists and left-wing socialists that advocated for direct action by workers and encouraged radicals to participate in the labor movement. Fox, who was back living in New York at the time, began a lecture tour starting in Boston and extending to the Pacific Coast. Fox was featured at several public speaking engagements in which he lectured on "Industrial Unionism and Trade Unionism," drawing on his pamphlet and on other topics such as "Why I Will Not Vote." He hoped to have a fund collected in New York when he returned, so that he could launch an anarchist labor weekly newspaper. He would have his opportunity with the demise of *The Demonstrator*.[21]

As with many anarchist periodicals, Home Colony's newspaper struggled financially. Its subscription list was never very large and many of its subscribers were chronically delinquent in paying. Compounding the publication's problems were disagreements in the community over the role of the paper. Should it be devoted to the colony and its residents, to the wide array of anarchist ideas and perspectives, or should it try to expand its reach and attempt relevance on issues both national and international? Over the course of its publication editors and contributors tried to accommodate many of the aspirations contributors and subscribers had for the periodical. However, satisfying everyone was not possible. To provide a clearer focus and direction for the paper, and with the hope of increasing circulation and subscriptions, *The Demonstrator* Group, a number of likeminded Home residents, took control of the periodical in August 1907. The group decided to proclaim the paper an anarchist-communist journal, even though contributors had spanned the spectrum of anarchist theory from individualist to communist and it had usually leaned anarchist communist for most of its existence anyway. Nevertheless, anarchist communists were the most vocal and organized of the anarchists of Home and they set about to revitalize the newspaper. Even though the paper projected an anarchist-communist orientation, it did continue to provide space for other libertarian points of view. Moreover, in an effort to free the paper from unwanted interference by some of Home's colonists, especially those who were not anarchist communists, the group broke free of the Mutual Home Association (MHA), the colony's governing body. Although, this coup was an effort to save the newspaper, it was to no avail, for *The Demonstrator* suspended publication in 1908. Even if Fox had relocated to Home before the paper's demise, he probably could not have saved it. Perhaps it was for the best—at least for him—because he would be free to create a new publication that would be under his direct control, though he would have a core of like-minded anarchists in the community to offer their support.[22]

4. The Agitator at Home

THE BCC MOVEMENT THAT FOX HAD CHAMPIONED IN THE 1890S had by the late 1900s been largely discarded by most supporters in favor of other methods, both reformist and revolutionary. Even though the BCC's Burley Colony still existed in western Washington and was firmly in the ranks of the SPA, it had stagnated by 1906. Moreover, Equality, the first colony established by the BCC, ceased to exist by 1907. In contrast, the anarchist Home Colony—founded in 1896 by three families of the failing socialist Glennis Colony—was a vibrant community in the 1900s. Anarchists of various stripes resided in Home and even non-anarchists were welcomed into the community. Unlike Burley and Equality, Home had no well-outlined theory of society or socialized businesses. The bylaws of the colony were kept purposely simple. Residents were free to work together or work separately to support themselves and their families. Over the years, the community's newspapers continually promoted personal liberty and voluntary association as the colony's anarchist hallmarks. Fox had wanted to move to Home, but he was not in a financially sound position to move himself and his family to the Far West. Finally, in December 1908, Fox left New York for the Pacific Northwest, having arranged beforehand a number of speaking engagements along the way. In his own words, I "talked my way across the continent to the evergreen state of Washington." He arrived first in Seattle and met up with his anarchist comrade, Alex Snellenberg, a sheet metal worker with a shop in the city. Fox was quite taken by the mild

A portion of Home Colony, circa 1910. Courtesy Washington State Historical Society, Tacoma.

winter weather of the coastal region. After a short stay in Seattle, he took a steamer to Tacoma and there transferred to Home's main transportation source: the *Tyconda*. Upon docking at Home on Joe's Bay, the colonists of Home gave him a warm welcome. He stayed at the residence of George H. Allen, one of the founding members of the colony. After a short stay, he returned to Seattle to earn enough money to bring Esther, David, and Silvia out west.[1]

Back in Seattle, Washington politicians and business leaders had devised the Alaska-Yukon-Pacific Exposition to celebrate the special connection of the city and state with Alaska, Canada, and the Pacific, especially Japan. More importantly, the political and business establishment wanted to advertise to the nation and the world the maturity that Seattle and the state of Washington had reached in the hopes of attracting "home-seekers" and capital investment. The exposition, which was scheduled to open 1 June 1909, had support from the state legislature to build several permanent buildings on the grounds of what would become the University of Washington, situated just north of downtown Seattle. Through another friend in the city, Jenny Lavroff, Fox found work as a janitor in the exposition's Arts Building, which would become the university's chemistry building. While employed in Seattle, Fox visited the IWW union hall and reading room at

212 Washington Street near the original "skid row" in the heart of the "wage-slave" market, due to the number employment offices found there, particularly relating to mill and logging camp work. The IWW had been trying to organize workers in the timber industry for several years without any long-term success. The Wobblies he met were despondent over not having a full-time organizer and asked if Fox would be interested in the position. Although he was sympathetic and was especially pleased to see the IWW trying to organize loggers, he declined. He told them he came out to the region to become the editor of an anarchist newspaper at Home Colony. However, he promised to give the Wobblies favorable publicity. Eventually, Fox had earned sufficient funds to bring Esther and the children to Washington. Together they lived in Seattle until the conclusion of the exposition and were able to relocate to Home in fall 1909. Fox bought two acres of land at Home and built a house, fulfilling the basic requirements for joining the MHA and becoming a full member—along with his family—of Home Colony.[2]

Although lacking a newspaper, the community that Fox and his family joined was in full bloom. As of 1910, Home had a population of 213, living in sixty-eight homes. Of the total number of residents, seventy-five were children. In fact, the increasing number of children in the community required building a new school that year. Home colonists hailed from many parts of the country and from Europe, and they were proud of their multi-ethnic community, which comprised gentiles and Jews, immigrants and native-born Americans. The village had three cooperative stores, a meeting hall, a warehouse, and a wharf. As most members lived in homes with two acres apiece, it was difficult to earn a living by farming. Some cooperative industries did exist, though largely consisting of modest cordwood or lumber mill operations. The community had a minimum hourly wage for labor, but most residents had to leave Home periodically to work in Seattle or Tacoma, or travel farther distances to California. Fox was no exception, for he had to leave occasionally to find employment, such as to San Francisco in summer 1910, to earn capital to help fund a new colony newspaper. He stayed with Morton, Annie, and their daughter Anita, who had relocated to the city from Chicago and lived in a mixed working-class neighborhood of immigrants and native-born Americans. In addition, Fox wrote for Morton's anarchist publication *Freedom*. Home hosted lecturers and activists such as Emma Goldman and the IWW's Bill Haywood and

Esther, Sylvia, and David at Home Colony. Courtesy Washington State Historical Society, Tacoma.

welcomed promoters of everything from vegetarianism to Asian spirituality to speak at Liberty Hall. From Fox's perspective, the success of Home rested in the community's claim to be "merely a preparatory school that taught the essentials of freedom and cooperation, without delving too deeply into applied socialist economics in the unfavorable atmosphere of capitalism that surrounded it."[3]

The anarchists of Home had weathered many storms, which included threats from residents of Tacoma to overrun the colony in the wake of McKinley's assassination, the loss of the village's post office in 1902 due to federal harassment of the community's newspaper *Discontent*, and the collapse of *The Demonstrator*. Nonetheless, Home's anarchist spirit continued to burn bright among most colonists. The colony's resources were in better shape than they had ever been, and a significant number of residents were eager to make another effort at promoting the anarchist cause through a newspaper. Fox had at his disposal a simple, but effective, printing press that the anarchist, free love, and labor advocate Ezra Haywood had used in the 1870s. In addition, a number of residents were willing to donate their labor to the publication. Of special assistance was George Jones, a resident printer by trade. He could instruct Fox in setting type and other aspects of newspaper publishing. Moreover, Rebecca August, a Russian immigrant, anarchist, and friend from Chicago, also relocated to Home. August acted as *The Agitator*'s proofreader and lived with Fox, Esther, Sylvia, and David. Along with Jones and August, David helped Fox in publishing the paper, primarily by learning how to set type, a skill that would translate into employment in the trade years later in New York.[4]

Fox's commitment to and enthusiasm for this new publishing effort helped to reinvigorate the community's anarchism and better connect Home to the larger national and international movement. As editor of *The Agitator*, Fox could provide an anarchist labor perspective that he and others in the movement thought was lacking and would be a perfect complement to the more literary and diverse subject matter in Goldman's *Mother Earth*. As if to underscore Fox's commitment to both the labor movement and to anarchism, the first issue of *The Agitator* featured a front-page article— penned by Fox—commemorating the 1 May 1886, general strike for the eight-hour day and the events that led to the Chicago anarchists' subsequent martyrdom in November 1887. Fox's eyewitness accounts of these momentous events in the history of labor and of anarchism in Chicago helped connect contemporary anarchists to the martyrs of their past. Included in this first issue were letters and speeches of the Haymarket anarchists, which emphasized their devotion to the working class and to one another as comrades in the great class struggle, together condemned by the state for daring to challenge the economic hegemony of the capitalist system. Subsequent November issues of *The Agitator* contained commemorations, featuring Fox connecting the Chicago anarchists to direct action and industrial unionism. Fellow anarchist, writer, and public lecturer Jack Wood wrote of the anarchists' last moments before their execution and his interpretation of what they stood for and why the authorities needed to silence them. Lucy Parsons penned her own commentaries on the historical significance of Haymarket, the "farce" of their trial, the execution, and the funeral, drawn from her eyewitness accounts and her historical interpretation.[5]

In the pages of *The Agitator*, Fox was maintaining a tradition in the anarchist, radical, and labor press of remembering the Chicago anarchists and connecting them to the heritage of anarchism or to the labor movement, and especially the struggle for the eight-hour day and the right to free speech. Moreover, remembrances were not limited to the press, for labor and radical groups in Chicago and in cities throughout the United States held similar ceremonies. And, of course, the inspiration behind May Day, the international Labor Day, drew from the 1886 events in Chicago. The anarchists of Home Colony had annual memorial meetings and commentary in the pages of its newspapers. And when Fox joined the community, he became an avid participant. He ventured north to Seattle to participate in commemorations as well. In November 1911, the IWW headquarters of the city, led by Wobblies F. R. Schleis and Floyd Hyde, organized a memorial meeting that included speakers and music by the Russian Workers' Society. With five hundred people in attendance, Fox was the principal speaker and narrated the events of Haymarket and the historical significance of the Chicago anarchists.[6]

The Agitator, Fox promised, would continue the fight for a libertarian, cooperative, and egalitarian society for which the anarchists of Chicago gave their lives. He did not promise any blueprints for a social revolution or for the future society. He believed that the people themselves, when they were sufficiently educated and organized, would bring about the revolution and determine the nature of the new society. The role of *The Agitator*, like the role of the anarchist in general, was to educate the working class on their historic potential, radicalize their institutions (particularly labor unions), and to enlighten laborers by presenting the ideas of scientists, humanists, and social scientists denied to them in what meager education that they had received as children or what was available in the mainstream media. Fox and the contributors to the newspaper presented an array of literature in a digestible form for "the toilers." His hope was for the periodical to find its way into the neighborhoods and factories of the working class. Subscribers were encouraged to leave issues on streetcars and workbenches, at union meeting halls, and to hand *The Agitator* to workers, who may not have the time to listen to a speech but could find time to read. He encouraged "agitator groups" to form around the country in support of the publication through writings and donations. These affinity groups could provide reports from their regions on the problems and successes of the movement. The most successful unit in this network of support was the Agitator Group of Seattle.[7]

Support for the newspaper was an ongoing concern for Fox and for other anarchists who were equally committed to its role as an English-language working-class revolutionary publication. In the interest of full disclosure, Fox published periodic financial reports for the paper that indicated his salary and that of his assistants and the material costs involved with publishing the paper. Included in these reports were the receipts of subscribers. Most subscribers were individuals, some rather prominent such as Jack London, and organizations subscribed as well, primarily IWW locals on the West Coast and in British Columbia. Another means of sustaining the newspaper were fundraising events. The Agitator Group of Seattle was the most successful at generating revenue. Even before the newspaper's first issue appeared, the group sponsored an excursion to Home Colony, by steamship, in summer 1910. Due to the success of that visit to Home by interested Seattleites, the group organized another excursion to Home Colony in June 1911. Tickets were available for purchase at several downtown Seattle locations. The steamer *Fairhaven* left at 8:00 a.m. for the day trip to the colony with food available aboard ship. When guests arrived at Home, they were treated to baseball, boating, dancing, and "other amusements" along with dinner. The group also sponsored events in the city itself to gain donations for the paper. The first of these fundraisers was the "all-Nations Peasant Ball." Attendees paid a fifty-cent entry fee at Redding's Academy and were encouraged to dress in the attire of a worker from any country.

On the evening of the ball, participants created an International Peasant Colony at the venue with specific rules that were intended to be broken, incurring ridiculous punishments. At the event, participants were satirizing an array of institutions of state and church, creating mock trials for "outlaws" along with orchestrating farcical wedding ceremonies. Representing *The Agitator* at the ball was David, wearing overalls, logger boots, a printer's cap, and a sash with the paper's name across it. Periodic day trips to the colony in addition to social events, including balls, dances, and celebrations, in Seattle, San Francisco, and New York proved to be important sources of revenue for the newspaper. Moreover, Home anarchists were following in an anarchist tradition by creating their own libertarian space and an anarchist subculture as they tried to garner support for *The Agitator*.[8]

Despite fundraising events, Fox felt compelled to stress to readers on a regular basis the need for more subscribers, especially in the Midwest and East. He lamented the fact that those who supported the idea of a revolutionary newspaper a year or two earlier had failed to provide the necessary financial support once *The Agitator* was launched. In addition, he continually emphasized the necessity of such a paper to propagate, in English, anarchism, direct action, and a radicalization of the labor movement. His longtime friend and fellow anarchist Martin Rasnick, starting in Philadelphia, began organizing support for the paper in the Northeast early in 1911. Fox made his own trips to West Coast cities to lecture on a variety of topics and to encourage people to subscribe to *The Agitator* at the conclusion of his lectures. Hampering support for *The Agitator*, however, was the plethora of radical publications at the time. *Mother Earth*, with Alexander Berkman now as editor, became a direct competitor for readership, for he was equally committed as Fox to providing a focus on labor issues. *Mother Earth*—in the end—could absorb the eastern radical readership that Fox sought. *The Agitator* also competed with London's *Freedom*, which had a long-standing international English-language anarchist readership. And on the labor front, the IWW had a western newspaper and an eastern newspaper, the *Industrial Worker* and *Solidarity* respectively. Fox, however, never discouraged support for radical and revolutionary newspapers and always ran a section in *The Agitator* with advertisements for *Mother Earth*, the *Industrial Worker*, *Freedom*, and many other radical and revolutionary newspapers and periodicals in English and in other languages. Still, he continued drumming up support for his paper and routinely noted in what cities, in the United States, Canada, Australia, New Zealand, and Great Britain, agents for *The Agitator* could be found.[9]

Although *The Agitator* would be primarily an anarchist and labor newspaper, Fox treated a variety of topics that he thought would be of interest as well as be of educational value to his readers. For example, an important cause that swept through anarchist circles, in the late 1900s and early 1910s, was the Modern School movement, which *The Agitator* championed. In fact, the masthead of the newspaper proclaimed it to be "A Bi-Monthly Advocate for the Modern School, Industrial Unionism and Individual Freedom." Francisco Ferrer, one of the movement's most significant proponents, was martyred by the Spanish government in 1909. His death helped accelerate the spread of libertarian education beyond Europe to the United States. The alternative educational system proposed by Ferrer and his supporters dovetailed well with the anarchist insistence on individual, ethical self-direction. For anarchists, education from childhood through adulthood that stimulated free thought, creativity, and egalitarianism was vital to the creation of a new society. The contemporary educational system and the institutions of society—as presently constructed from the anarchist perspective—maintained the hegemony of the state, the church, and capitalism. A libertarian educational alternative, however, could revolutionize society through an intellectually liberated working class. Just as the radicalized union could be a mode of "social transformation," so too could the Modern School.[10]

The historical role of the anarchist was to assist the working class in its own emancipation. To do that, anarchists needed to be able to reach the people by exercising their free speech, aided by a free press. Fox championed that freedom in the pages of *The Agitator*, especially regarding Wobbly free speech fights, which were usually the result of trying to industrially organize migratory laborers, especially those in agriculture and logging. An important IWW organizing strategy was to go to where workers congregated in downtown western cities (e.g., where they sought work through employment agencies or from employers themselves, who would frequent downtown locations in search of temporary workers). Beginning in 1909, the IWW engaged in numerous free speech fights—mostly in western states—when city officials tried to suppress Wobblies from holding street meetings. IWW members would disregard city statutes against holding open-air meetings. Speakers would stand on a platform, in many cases a soapbox, to explain to workers the necessity of joining the union. One by one such speakers would be arrested, eventually filling up city jails and clogging up court proceedings with their trials to the point where city officials, primarily due to the expense involved, would be forced to rescind the ordinances. Fox reported to his readers on the fights in Fresno, California, Vancouver and Victoria, British Columbia, Kansas City, Missouri, Aberdeen, Washington, and San Diego, California. Moreover, he published firsthand accounts from participants, eyewitnesses, and IWW free speech organizers, who in some cases made appeals to readers to join in the ongoing struggles with city officials. Of particular interest to Fox was the fight in San Diego, in part due to the excessive violence perpetrated by vigilantes and police, which included tarring and feathering Ben Reitman, Goldman's companion and lecture tour manager, the brutal expulsion of free speech fighters from the city, and the killing of Joseph Mikolasek, anarchist, Wobbly, and contributing editor of the Bohemian anarchist weekly *Volné Listy*. Fox published moving accounts of the atrocities committed in these conflicts with thorough coverage of San Diego. He argued that the direct action tactics of the IWW could—in dramatic fashion—reveal how fragile free speech and a free press were in the United States.[11]

The residents of Home Colony prided themselves on their personal freedom and the accepting attitudes of their fellow colonists, especially when individual behaviors were unconventional. The open admission of incoming colonists by the MHA worked well for years as newcomers were of a similar world view as older residents. As the colony grew, however, some new residents arrived who did not share the same live-and-let-live perspective. They may have been more drawn to the low cost of living, remoteness, or cooperative enterprises than the principles of the colony itself. A practice the new residents objected to was nude bathing in Joe's Bay. For years, colonists, male and female, young and old, bathed in the cool waters of the bay, most with some sort of undergarment but others wearing nothing at all. The latter bathing was usually done in secluded areas or some distance from the shore by those slipping into the water from a boat. During the record-breaking heat wave in summer 1911, some colonists took refuge from the heat by bathing nude in the bay. Residents who objected summoned the local deputy sheriff to have the bathers arrested for indecent exposure. Most of those arrested were women. The reaction to this betrayal of the colony's principles was swift. Those who initiated the arrests were boycotted by their fellow colonists and a serious degree of factionalism broke out among the residents. Fox came to the defense of the nude bathers—whose cases were moving through the court system—in an editorial titled "The Nude and the Prudes." In his article, he advocated for the right of residents to bath with or without clothing and argued that there was nothing vulgar about the human body. Rather, any vulgarity was in the mind of the "offended." He went on to explain to readers the history of the colony and its culture of personal liberty. The "prudes" were violating that basic premise of the community. In his article, he urged a boycott of the "prudes" to either force them to change their ways or to leave the community. As if to underscore Fox's argument regarding the celebration of personal liberty in the community, a marked increase of nude bathing occurred, resulting in more arrests.[12]

Fox knew from reading a Tacoma newspaper that authorities were preparing to arrest him for his editorial in *The Agitator*. The police action came in August, almost two months after his article appeared, on the charge of encouraging disrespect for the law, a statute enacted in the wake of the anti-anarchist hysteria following the McKinley assassination. That law would serve prosecutors of radicals in the state well for years until Washington passed its criminal syndicalism legislation in 1919. Out of fear that he might leave the area, a deputy sheriff arrested him in the dead of night. He went peaceably and ended up spending a brief period in jail until he could secure his release on bond. Once released, Fox returned to Home and resumed his editorship of the newspaper. He wrote of his arrest and connected it to issue of free speech and freedom of the press. He made clear to his readers that the authorities' goal was to shut down *The Agitator* and subvert one of the most important instruments the working class had at its disposal: a free press. He noted that "today the free press is the most vital element in the education and organization of the working class. It is our medium of thot [sic] exchange, and we cannot grow without it." Encouraged by his supporters—the Agitator Group of Seattle, Home residents, writers and subscribers of the paper, IWW locals, and the radical and labor press, especially the *Industrial Worker*—he argued that the paper would carry on even if he had to serve a prison sentence. Fox also found support among local and national free speech advocates. *Mother Earth* reprinted his article and encouraged readers to contribute to Fox's legal defense. In Pierce County, in which both Home and Tacoma are located, radicals established a free speech league, with Home colonist Nathan Levine serving as secretary. The body sought financial support for Fox's legal defense and secured significant support from the New York Free Speech League.[13]

Fox's trial began 10 January 1912, with many Home residents attending the proceedings and some called on as witnesses either for the prosecution (the "prudes) or for the defense (the "nudes"). From the very beginning, the prosecution, a pair of young politically ambitious lawyers, Grover C. Nolte and August O. Burmeister, sought to prove that Fox's editorial inspired residents to break the law. They also made anarchism a central element of the case. The defense attorney, James J. Anderson, objected, on the ground of irrelevance, to Nolte's question to jury members regarding whether they believed in anarchy. That objection, along with most of his others, was overruled. A large portion of the trial was taken up by the prosecution trying to link further law breaking, specifically an increase in nude bathing, to Fox's article. The defense suggested that warm weather more than words motivated residents to bathe in Joe's Bay and that the offended of the colony were looking to be shocked. Fox did not appear as a witness during his trial, but he did address the jury in the defense's closing remarks. He argued that free speech and freedom of the press were the foundations of a free society and that agitation is how a society improves itself: "Show me a country where there is the most tyranny and I will show you the country where there is no free speech." Moreover, he and Anderson noted that criticism of laws and statutes occurred regularly in the press and editors of those newspapers are not brought before the courts for their editorials. The prosecution not only tied Fox's article to law breaking but to the anarchism of the colony itself. In Nolte's closing statements, he argued that Home colonists had no right to "do as they damn please" for they resided within a state that provides freedom but within the context of law and order. Before the jury left to deliberate the case, Judge William O. Chapman instructed them that the statute did not require that the accused advocate the disobedience of any specific law "but to law in general or law as the basis of government."[14]

The jury deliberated for two days and returned a verdict of guilty, though they asked for leniency. Anderson immediately requested a new trial but was denied. At a sentencing hearing the following month, Fox received a sentence of two months in jail. However, he was able to secure bond for his release as Anderson—though he was continuing to defend the nude bathers as their cases came before the court—sought to appeal Fox's conviction. Fox received support from across the country from anarchists, labor radicals, and progressives. Moreover, he was in touch with the New York Free Speech League, led by Theodore Schroeder, Lincoln Steffens, Bolton Hall, and other prominent progressives, and was willing to accept their interest in supporting his appeal. The league issued a pamphlet titled *The Free Speech Case of Jay Fox* in September 1912, in which the authors argued the unconstitutionality of the Washington state statute that Fox violated. The pamphlet also included Fox's article in full so that readers could judge the contents for themselves. In the following months, Anderson submitted a lengthy appeal to the state supreme court in which he argued that the law under which Fox was convicted was unconstitutional on both state and federal grounds and completely arbitrary in nature. In addition, Anderson argued that Fox's article never urged the breaking of the specific law in question or any other law. In November, the state supreme court unanimously refused to overturn the county court's ruling, citing Johann Most's 1902 conviction in New York for inciting disrespect for the law with his publication *Freiheit*.[15]

Meanwhile, Fox continued his work on *The Agitator* and decided to publish a series that was requested by the *Tacoma Daily Ledger*. However, according to Fox the editor refused to publish the piece, which "barks too loud at the system," because it did not "quite suit" what Fox called a "subservient capitalist sheet." In the series, which Fox titled "The Agitator in History," he explained the significance of the agitator as a necessary historic actor who could stimulate dramatic historical change. Fox drew on both religious and political history to highlight individuals that readers could readily identify with as great disturbers of the peace. His use of such figures was not necessarily original. Radicals had interpreted Moses and Jesus as revolutionaries before. Fox, however, wanted to demonstrate the role that a signal individual could have in radicalizing the people and thereby influencing the course of history, primarily by overthrowing or challenging the existing ruling elite. He drew on American political history as well, reframing Thomas Jefferson and George Washington in a more radical light and reminding readers that "in one generation we hang the agitator and in the next crown his memory with glory." He argued that this point was especially true for men such as Elijah Lovejoy and William Lloyd Garrison, whose efforts helped to shift public opinion against African American slavery in the United States.

Times of great struggle, however, were not over according to Fox. The agitator was needed more than ever as the ranks of the poor and exploited working class grew and the concentration of power and wealth of the plutocracy increased. As in the past the agitator must lead the people to the next stage of freedom. To suppress the agitator will only lead to rebellion and the ruling elite will pay a steep price, as the French peasants demonstrated in 1789. According to Fox, "Revolution is nothing more than pent up evolution broken loose. Dam up the river of progress and you will have a tremendous flood on your hands. Let the agitators alone, and they will keep the river clear of obstructions.

Although Fox was somewhat self-effacing, he did place his own efforts within the context of the agitator in history. Here he articulated the basic message that anarchist communists had for the next stage of societal evolution. The present economic system was not responding to the needs of most people. Therefore, a cooperative system needed to be tried. With political systems, he lauded the contribution to political evolution by such figures as Thomas Jefferson. However, anarchists could go a step further from representative government to self-government. He placed himself with Henry David Thoreau, who improved on the thought of Jefferson: "That government is best which governs not at all, and that is the kind of government we will have when men are ready for it." Fox's own actions as editor of *The Agitator* fell into this sweep of history, particularly in his recent conviction over his article "The Nude and the Prudes." Although he strenuously denied that he advocated breaking any law, he argued that his conviction rested on his exercise of the right to free speech. Moreover, his struggle to advance free speech had a material connection to those of the past, for his newspaper was printed with the very same press Heywood used decades earlier when he published one of the first American anarchist newspapers, *The Word*.[16]

In his newspaper, Fox paid close attention to the activities of agitators, rebels, and revolutionaries, both domestically and abroad, in the realms of free speech, labor organizing, and outright rebellion. Although Europe and Latin America dominated foreign news, Fox did publish material concerning Asia. In Japan, the anarchist movement was in its infancy, but an early advocate of radical Western political theory and political economy was Kōtoku Shūsui, who translated and published the works of Kropotkin, Bakunin, Marx, and Tolstoy among others. He, along with his wife and over twenty associates, were accused of plotting against the imperial family in 1910. They were tried in a hasty manner without much time for an adequate defense. The court found twenty-four guilty and sentenced them to death, including Kōtoku, by hanging. Fox published appeals from the anarchist community, especially New York and Chicago where large demonstrations took place. Fellow anarchists and free speech advocates condemned the accusation, the court proceedings, and the death sentence. Fox published a letter he had sent to the Japanese ambassador in Washington, DC, in which he commended the Japanese for standing up to Russian aggression in the 1905 war between the two countries and applauded the Japanese for incorporating Western science, technology, and progressive social change in recent years. However, he expressed his disappointment that Japan would take such a "barbarous" turn with Kōtoku and the anarchists and socialists who received the death penalty. Their "crime," in his opinion, was that they simply disseminated ideas unpopular among the ruling elite. Fox also published the correspondence he had had with Kōtoku in 1908 in which he complemented Fox on his pamphlets *Roosevelt, Czolgosz and Anarchy* and *Trade Unionism and Anarchism: A Letter to a Brother Unionist*. Kōtoku agreed with Fox that anarchism was a nonviolent movement and that anarchists had an important role in radicalizing the labor movement. Eventually, twelve anarchists and socialists including Kōtoku were put to death. In *The Agitator*, Fox condemned the executions, though he asserted those killed did not die in vain. He wrote, "Hemp will hang an agitator but it will not throttle an idea. By hanging eleven men and a woman on the gallows, Japan has hung their ideas in the stars."[17]

One of the most important foreign news stories to appear in the pages of *The Agitator* was the Mexican Revolution. Almost every issue of the paper contained reports on the progress of the revolution, appeals to American workers to support Mexican workers and peasants, or the writings by the revolutionary Ricardo Flores Magón. For anarchists, the revolution across the border was the ultimate example of direct action on the part of the rural and urban proletariat. From the beginning of the revolution, anarchists, including Magón, stressed that the insurrection had to have economic emancipation as a goal in order for it to effect social as well as political change. Fox regularly published Magón's writings in translation from his publication *Regeneración* and essays written for the radical and labor press in the United States. *The Agitator* also carried pieces by the English anarchist William C.

Owen, who at the time was living in Los Angeles and edited the English-language page of Magón's newspaper. Magón, along with his brother Enrique and a number of other associates, had been living in exile in the United States since 1903. They were able to direct revolutionary activities in northern Mexico and played a role in the Cananea strike in 1906. However, the following year Magón and most of his associates in exile were arrested and jailed. After their release from prison in Los Angeles in 1910, they were able to resume publishing their newspaper, which was the principal organ for the Partido Liberal Mexicano (PLM). Between 1910 and 1912, the PLM was transitioning from a liberal-left, anti–Porfirio Díaz coalition to an explicitly anarchist organization, particularly as socialist and liberal elements of the PLM in Mexico began to side with Francisco Madero's broad-based revolutionary coalition. Magón and the PLM junta in Los Angeles remained true to their anarchist principles and still had support in northwest Mexico, where they were able to tap into a long-standing agrarian anarchist tradition. In Baja California, the PLM launched an uprising in early 1911 that also included an invading army of Wobblies and assorted adventurers.[18]

Magón and Owen had a particular interest in seeking out support from Fox, for *The Agitator* could be useful in disseminating news about the revolution and a forum for the PLM's revolutionary agenda. Fox and *The Agitator*, Magón and Owen reasoned, were better connected to radical elements and militant labor on the West Coast than the anarchist press in other parts of the country. Especially significant was the need to rouse support from the American working class by publishing, in English, direct appeals for support and to distribute literature in a systematic manner across the country. The great fear of Mexican and American anarchists was that the United States would intervene to protect American industrial and commercial interests in Mexico and bring the revolution to a halt. Therefore, with American troops massing at the border with Mexico, it was imperative that American workers refuse to support an invasion. To mobilize American labor support for the PLM and the revolution, Fox published a letter that Magón had sent to Samuel Gompers, president of the AFL. In the letter, Magón called on Gompers to publicly endorse the Mexican revolution and the PLM, encourage American labor support, and pledge that the AFL would resist an American invasion. Although Gompers gave his tacit support to both the revolution and the PLM, he like many in the American labor movement along with most socialists and progressives, including Debs, welcomed Madero's military victory in spring 1911 and supported the interim government. From the anarchist perspective Madero was a mere reformer who would make only modest changes to the economic system and would never threaten the great landowners of Mexico nor the foreign control of the country's natural resources and industries. He would not help Mexicans achieved what Magón and the PLM called for, namely "land and liberty."[19]

Fox issued pleas for financial support of the junta's legal defense after they had been arrested by federal agents in Los Angeles. *The Agitator* carried articles by Magón, Owen, and others, which further articulated the goals of the social revolution and put the events in Mexico into a larger historical context with reference to a worldwide revolutionary movement determined to overthrow the capitalist system. Fox and Owen, in particular, tried to tie events in Mexico to the struggles of American workers and the repression they faced by state and federal governments. Despite these efforts, the revolution in Mexico was leaving Magón and the PLM behind. Forces loyal to Madero had to contend with Emiliano Zapata and his supporters in southern Mexico, along with other rebel groups, who, though not self-identifying as anarchists, embraced much of the PLM agenda and even adopted the rallying cry of "land and liberty." Meanwhile, in Los Angeles, Magón, his brother Enrique, and other members of the junta stood trial in summer 1912. Within a matter of weeks, the defendants were found guilty of violating the federal neutrality law because of their connection to the rebellion in Baja California along with other activities in Mexico. They were sentenced to almost two years in prison at the federal penitentiary on McNeil Island, Washington. In early August, Fox visited the prisoners and wrote with admiration of their sacrifice for the cause they shared with workers everywhere. He chastised American workers for not doing more to assist the revolution and castigated American socialists for advising Mexican peasants and workers to become democratic socialists and turn to the ballot rather than to direct action.[20]

Fox—along with his fellow anarchists, but also socialists, Wobblies, and some progressives—had great respect for Japanese, Mexican, and Filipino revolutionaries, who were attempting to throw off the yoke of oppression, be it imperialists, capitalists, or a ruling elite. He could feel a connection to these rebels and agitators, for his own ancestors and relatives faced similar oppression from the British back in Ireland. Neither racism nor ethnocentrism obscured his appreciation for those who spread libertarian and egalitarian ideas or who engaged in direct action to bring about a more just society. In fact, he thought of them as part of a worldwide revolutionary movement and, moreover, that they could lead and inspire that movement with their actions. In addition, Fox frequently wrote with admiration for his Jewish comrades and for Jewish immigrant workers, many of whom were on the front lines in fight for liberty, equality, and labor organizing. Rousing American workers to their historical role was at the heart of the overall mission of *The Agitator*. Fox's hope was that providing readers with news and analysis about revolutionaries and rebels would motivate American workers to engage in direct action. He also wanted to educate his largely native-born, white working-class readership to the fact that workers and intellectuals in Asia and Latin America and immigrant workers to the United States were not so different from themselves.

His newspaper was filled with international news and commentary and domestic stories deemed relevant and educational to workers and to the labor movement in general. In addition, he carried articles from other newspapers, both radical and mainstream, along with essays written by a variety of anarchists and labor advocates. A regular feature of the newspaper was Fox's "The Passing Show" column. The feature was similar to the "Observation and Comments" column in *Mother Earth,* in that both dealt with a variety of issues from an anarchist perspective, though Fox focused more on labor than any other subject. He paid particular attention to the labor movement on the West Coast and in British Columbia. The open shop drive by employers in Los Angeles received special attention, especially as Harrison Gray Otis, the editor and owner of the *Los Angeles Times*, advocated for the elimination of unions entirely and for outright blacklisting of union leaders. When the Times Building was blown up in October 1910, apparently in retaliation for Otis's antiunion rants in his newspaper, a number of labor organizers were suspected by local police. Law enforcement officials arrested John and James McNamara of the International Association of Bridge and Structural Iron Workers' Union (BSIW) for the bombing, though other suspects continued to be pursued. Rumors spread that two possible accomplices, Matthew Schmidt, Fox's friend and comrade from Chicago, and David Caplan, had made their way to Home to hide out. Caplan had, in fact, lived at Home with his wife several years previously. Fox may have become acquainted with Caplan in 1909 or earlier and it is possible

Fox and Caplan discussed dynamite and its uses in conflicts between capital and labor.

The William J. Burns Detective Agency, which the city of Los Angeles hired, pursued the suspects. Burns himself was one of the agents who went to the colony. Fox was among those under surveillance. Burns was assisted by an informant in the community. "Mr. Blank," whose identity remains unknown but may have been a recent arrival, claimed that Fox was mixed up in some "dangerous" activity that involved a trip to San Francisco in 1910 before the Times Building bombing. In the end, Burns and his detectives found nothing, though some evidence exists that Fox knew of Caplan's whereabouts and may have assisted him in evading law enforcement, for it seems likely that Caplan had stayed briefly at Home and then hid out on nearby Bainbridge Island.[21]

Fox's involvement in assisting Caplan elude authorities is inconclusive, but he was very forthcoming about his position on violence as a strategy to advance the interests of labor and the working class generally. It is highly unlikely that Fox was aware of the bombing campaign that James McNamara directed, from 1906 to 1911, against employers who used nonunion labor for their building projects. Fox, like many labor advocates, believed in the innocence of the McNamara brothers and urged labor organizations to assist in their defense and applauded those organizations and individuals that did. For Fox, this was a classic battle between labor and capital, with the state framing a case against labor organizers. He connected their plight with that the Haymarket Martyrs and Haywood and the other officials of the WFM in the assassination of former Idaho governor Frank Steunenberg. When the McNamara brothers confessed to the crime, Fox, like other prominent anarchists such as Goldman, Berkman, and de Cleyre, did not abandon them. He placed their actions within the context of a "great social war." He did this in a manner similar to what he had done with President McKinley assassin Leon Czolgosz. He did not necessarily support the actions of the men because of the deaths resulting from the bomb blast, but he understood their direct action as part of a larger struggle to defeat industrial capitalism, a system of exploitation that brought about the deaths of thousands of working people every year in mining accidents, railroad mishaps, and workplace fires, many of which could be prevented if the drive for profit over human life did not dominate the economic system.

Fox was one of many writers of the era who commented on the dangerous industrial workplaces that workers were forced to endure. Moreover, he, along with de Cleyre in *The Agitator*, admonished socialists, progressives, and trade unionists who rushed to condemn the McNamara brothers. Although he did not outright endorse their form of direct action, he did commend them for fighting back and not relying on the SPA as a panacea for labor's struggles, for workers themselves had to bring about their own emancipation.[22]

The only way to achieve that emancipation was through a variety of forms of direct action that he and other anarchists endorsed. The method he continually advocated—which distinguished him from most American anarchists and which had the most long-term, pragmatic possibilities— was industrial unionism. In the pages of *The Agitator*, Fox carried numerous stories on strikes in different parts of the United States and abroad. He pointed out time and again that strikes by individual trade unions within industries tended to fail because other tradesmen and -women in those same industries continued to work. Even though they may have had sympathy for their striking fellow workers and may even have contributed to their strike funds, the nonstriking trades were—in reality—scabbing on their fellow workers. Only by trades combining into industrial unions could they have the power to bring an industry to a halt and have their demands met. Fox cited the efforts by the metal trades in San Francisco where, by combining their efforts, they established the eight-hour day. Moreover, when workers assembled into large, confederated industrial unions they would have the power to overthrow the exploitive capitalist system and replace it with a cooperative economic system that could meet their needs. With employers combining into ever larger corporations, he argued that the "A.F. of L. will have to change its form or it will be beaten out of existence." And he lauded the IWW as "the advance guard in the march of the toilers towards industrial unionism." In addition, he cited the example of British and French workers who had turned away from political action and focused on direct action in the workplace through the industrial union movement. He cited the anarchist John Turner, but especially trade union leader Tom Mann, as guiding lights for industrial unionism in Great Britain. Fox published Mann's open letter of resignation from the Social-Democratic Party in which he argued that political action was ineffective and that

"Direct Industrial Organization was the best strategy whereby the workers can ultimately overthrow the capitalist systems and become the actual controllers of their own industrial and social destiny."[23]

Even though prominent unions in the AFL such as the Brewery Workers Union (BWU) and the United Mine Workers (UMW) were organized industrially, craft or trade unionism still dominated the American labor movement. Gompers had some support for industrial unionism even in the early days of the AFL's formation. Nevertheless, the federation primarily comprised a large constituency of trade unions. The leadership of those unions and the rank and file tended to be committed to the needs of their respective crafts. For example, when the WFM sought to rejoin the AFL after leaving the IWW, its admission was delayed by the leadership of the International Association of Machinists (IAM), who feared that machinists at work in mines would be compelled to join the WFM. Fox was highly critical of such fiefdom politics within the AFL. Nevertheless, he continued to hold out hope that industrial unionism would win out eventually. He argued that the AFL should follow the lead of the IWW and "the syndicalists in France," and the "Departmentism" within the federation should be allowed to evolve "into real, progressive, Industrial Unionism." Moreover, the radical potential of industrial unionism had been a feature of the labor movement for some time, for those unions had either an explicit socialist platform or a clear socialist leaning, which was clearly manifest in the BWU, UMW, ARU, and the WFM.

Nevertheless, industrial unions were not emerging from the labor movement at the pace Fox had hoped, outside of the IWW, which only formed industrial unions. In addition, Wobblies were not increasing their numbers as of 1911 either. Therefore, Fox reiterated his call for anarchists to follow the lead of their comrades in Europe and to work within the labor movement. European anarchists, Fox claimed, followed the recommendations of the Amsterdam Congress in 1907. They became better organized in their respective countries and made a concerted effort to join the labor movement and tried to radicalize trade and industrial unions. Fox took some comfort in the December 1910 Philadelphia meeting of the Federated Anarchist Groups, which demonstrated that anarchists were making some effort to organize in the United States like their European counterparts. Unfortunately, no consensus emerged among the participants concerning the labor movement. Fox lamented the fact that some anarchist communists were against organization of any kind, for fear that it would undermine their libertarian principles.[24]

In *The Agitator*, Fox explained to his readers that labor unions were an ancient and organic organization that emerged from the experience of working people as far back as ancient Egypt and Rome. These were institutions of labor solidarity that had a communistic character from the very beginning. Industrial unions were a contemporary manifestation of an old concept in which all members were equal and the union represented the interests of all in common. Anarchists needed to understand that labor unions were not a structure imposed from above but built from the bottom up and could be under the control of the workers themselves. Unions, then, had the capacity to be libertarian organizations. Moreover, he tried to interpret a variety of expressions of solidarity and successes through direct action as a result of industrial unionism, giving further evidence that political action was unnecessary to advance the cause of labor. He attributed IWW free speech fights to the solidarity that comes through industrial unionism and considered the ability of the Shop Federation on the Rio Grande Railroad to win the eight-hour day by applying the "industrial principle." Furthermore, he admired the East Coast transportation workers' strike in summer 1912 when workers joined together regardless of trade. Therefore, he was quite dismayed when Wobblies, who were at the forefront of the industrial union movement, had critics within their ranks such as Frank Bohn. Bohn wrote an article in the *International Socialist Review* that attacked the direct actionist, anti-political element in the IWW and argued that without political action the IWW would die out as a labor organization. Fox thought that "the I.W.W. was founded on the failure of craft unionism on the one hand and labor politics on the other." Fox helped to keep this debate going in the left press by publishing an article by B. E. Nilsson that was rejected by the *International Socialist Review*, which was written in response to Bohn's article (titled "Is the I.W.W. to Grow?"). Nilsson took Bohn to task for referring to the anti-political element in the IWW as "Fanatics" who promoted an ineffective "Spittoon Philosophy." Nilsson explained the flawed reasoning that political action through any party, socialist or otherwise, could change the conditions of workers in the US, for those who controlled the means of production controlled the state. He pointed out that in countries like Germany where the socialist party had a substantial presence in government and controlled the largest labor unions, few tangible benefits for the working class were achieved through such political action. In France, where direct economic action dominated the labor movement, Nilsson argued that much more had been done for workers through their own direct action in the workplace.[25]

Moreover, Fox republished an article by Charles E. Russell from the *International Socialist Review*. Here he could point to Russell's concern that even when a labor government was established, such as in Australia, it became nonrevolutionary. Fox noted a similar problem with political action by analyzing the case of the British Labor Party that formed in an effort to bring the voice of the working class to Parliament. However, no meaningful legislation had been passed to benefit workers. In addition, Ramsay McDonald, chair of the Labor Party, openly criticized the concept of the general strike, syndicalism, and the IWW as a "mere escapade of the nursery mind." The British labor leader did not seem to understand where the English working class was headed. Fox believed that he would be left behind as British workers moved toward industrial unionism and direct action at the point of production. Fox noted two industrial strikes, one by sailors and other by railroad workers, which demonstrated success through labor solidarity and ending craft divisions. Nevertheless, he lamented the fact that the striking railroad workers were willing to accept the promises of a "Royal Commission" to investigate the workers' demands. Fox conceded that workers had a long road ahead to learn from their mistakes. And on this question of whether the IWW would grow or not, Fox published a report from I. N. Stanter of the tremendous growth of the IWW in San Francisco among Italian and French workers, particularly in the North Beach area of the city.[26]

Of the many strikes Fox covered in *The Agitator*, the Lawrence textile strike held special interest for him as well as for the Seattle Agitator Group. Fox had spoken to a group of textile workers in Lawrence, Massachusetts, in 1908 as they struggled with poor working conditions, low pay, and long hours. He greeted the strike in January 1912 with great enthusiasm as it evolved into one of the most significant IWW-led actions in the Northeast. The strike began spontaneously when a small group of textile workers walked out due to a wage decrease. Employers had to reduce the workweek to fifty-four hours as mandated by the Massachusetts legislature. Rather than keeping the existing wage rate as they had done in the past when hours needed to be cut back, employers decided to slash wage rates. The spontaneous walkout generated a citywide strike in the textile industry and the IWW quickly took leadership of the action. The small Italian IWW local in Lawrence invited Wobbly Joseph Ettor to help organize the striking workers. His leadership along with that of Haywood and Arturo Giovannitti proved decisive in infusing a strike over a wage dispute into a call for the abolition of the wage system. Moreover, it demonstrated the power of industrial unionism and worker solidarity among an ethnically diverse workforce. The behavior of employers, city officials, and the AFL helped to demonstrate to the public the plight of the workers and their families in the industry. The striking workers had many supporters throughout the country due to extensive newspaper coverage. The Agitator Group in Seattle in concert with IWW locals raised funds for the striking workers and later for the legal defense of Ettor and Giovannitti. But the group did not stop there. In addition, the group was able to build on its initial efforts at organizing Seattle tailors into an industrial union. Jack Solomon and Beckie Beck, fellow anarchists from Chicago who came to Washington along with Fox, used the Agitator Group headquarters as an organizational center to found IWW Local 194 of the Clothing Workers' Union. The local boasted of winning several strikes for their members in the greater Seattle area. The ultimate success of the Lawrence strike and the industrial union in Seattle seemed to bode well for the IWW and the concept of industrial unionism.[27]

Although Fox's labor coverage was overwhelmingly devoted to male workers, he did write about women workers in the pages of *The Agitator*. In some respects, his thoughts on women in society had evolved over the years. In several speeches and essays from five or more years earlier, he argued that women were inferior to men in part due to nature but also due to societal expectations, which he believed most women embraced. His sexism, however, was mitigated by women entering the wage-labor workforce in larger numbers every passing year. Therefore, he began to argue rather consistently that women needed to be in the front ranks of the labor movement. He understood that they had unique concerns in the workplace, for they were often paid less for the same work performed by men and faced open discrimination and arbitrary treatment from employers. They also worked in mass production industries and could be part of the overall trend toward industrial unionism. In early 1910 he was in Philadelphia, drumming up support for *The Agitator*. There, he witnessed the trolley workers' strike that evolved into a general strike that engulfed the city and much of its working class. Clashes between striking workers, scabs, police, and security guards were common. One image that stuck in his mind was that of a striking female worker with a child in her arms having been beaten by the employer's guards. He wrote of the blood streaming down her face from the blows from the guard and concluded that "neither age, sex, nor condition serves to defend the head from the club" of the servants of capitalism.

Fox asserted that women workers consistently experienced the same brutality of the capitalist system as men did. He used the Newark, New Jersey, Anchor Lamp factory fire in November 1910 and in the Triangle Shirtwaist Fire in March 1911 in New York City as only the most recent examples, as it was primarily women and girls who perished in the fires or jumped from factory windows to escape the flames only to die from their fall. For Fox, women and child workers paid the same price as male miners and railroad workers in their employment in an economic system that placed profit above safety in the workplace. Although he believed that many young women preferred marriage and family life to factory work, he argued they were capable of direct action in the workplace just as their male counterparts. He cited as an example a pearl button factory strike in Muscatine, Iowa, in which the female workforce walked out rather than accept the low wages offered by the employer. In addition, whenever there was a report of a new union of women workers, strikes by women workers, or literature published devoted to women's labor, he celebrated the efforts of women to join in the labor movement. On the latter, he wrote a favorable review of the Woman's Trade Union League magazine, *Life and Labor*, which appeared in 1911.[28]

Even though Fox, in general, underappreciated women's intellectual capacities in comparison to men's, he had great admiration for the intelligence, activism, and writing ability of the women he considered friends, comrades, and allies. He carried essays by several female writers, who wrote on a variety of topics, but the three most prominent women anarchist writers whose essays were published in *The Agitator* were Parsons, Goldman, and de Cleyre. He had personal and professional relationships with all three women for years. Although they had sparred on occasion, most recently over the location of *The Agitator*, he was closest to Parsons. She wrote several pieces concerning the Haymarket anarchists, the trial, and their final days. She was also responsible for providing Fox with their writings, speeches, and courtroom testimony that he featured in his newspaper. Fox updated readers on her travels to a variety of cities in the Midwest and Northeast, where she lectured on the anarchist and labor movements and brought the speeches and writings of the Haymarket anarchists to unions and working-class groups. He thought her work was one of the most effective means by which the workers of the country could be radicalized. She wrote in the pages of *The Agitator* of the warm receptions she received in union halls and at worker gatherings where she would sell anarchist literature, which was one of her main sources of income. Her book *Life of Albert R. Parsons* was always available in "The Workers' University" column of *The Agitator* along with a number of other works by fellow anarchists and radicals as well as writings by social scientists, historians, novelists, and poets. Readers could purchase the publications through Fox.[29]

Even though Goldman had her own publication, Fox carried several pieces written by her on a variety of topics. He found her explanation of why she was an anarchist and why anarchism was a higher form of socialism to be both inspirational and educational. After she published *Anarchism and Other Essays*, Fox published a glowing review of her book by Owen. Thereafter, Fox carried her book in "The Workers' University." He published her thoughts on the Mexican Revolution and pleas for other radical causes and for specific anarchist comrades in need. And as with Parsons, he carried information on her lecture appearances.[30] The major work by de Cleyre he published was her impassioned plea for the public as well as for socialists, progressives, and unionists to understand that the actions of the McNamara brothers within the context of a class struggle and that the loss of life in the bombing was not intentional. When she died in June 1912, Fox wrote a moving tribute to her. He commended her for her humanism, anarchism, and revolutionary spirit. According to Fox, her ability to refuse to help the prosecution of her attempted assassin, which took place ten years earlier, distinguished her as a higher form of human being. He was able to reconcile her ability to forgive her mentally ill would-be assassin and still support the Mexican Revolution. For Fox, there was no contradiction, for it was her deeply felt humanitarianism that made her an anarchist and a revolutionary. Later in the year, he used *The Agitator* to promote an effort by Chicago anarchists, among them her close friend Anne Livshis, to publish her works, both her essays and poetry, in pamphlet as well as book form in order to continue her influence on the revolutionary anarchist movement.[31]

Fox seemed to have found in Home a community that supported his efforts to bring an English-language anarchist publication to the movement. In the village, he developed several long-lasting friendships among the colonists such as with Lewis Haiman (who had a barber shop in Tacoma) along with Allen and many others. Moreover, he also found in Home a personally satisfying environment to help Esther raise her children. Both Sylvia and David helped with the publication, especially with transporting letters and packages to and from the post office and soliciting subscriptions from visitors to the colony. Esther bore a third child, Rebecca, who was probably born in late 1911 or early 1912. Even with the responsibilities of parenthood, Fox and Esther stayed connected to a number of comrades in Seattle, Tacoma, and San Francisco though frequent travel. They did not always make these trips together since Esther, in particular, visited anarchist friends in Seattle frequently. It was there that she may have met William Z. Foster. At this period in Foster's life, he was spending a great deal of time in the city. Foster was involved with the West Coast–based Wage Workers Party (WWP), a left-wing alternative to the SPA and the authoritarian Socialist Labor Party. He journeyed across the state to cover the Spokane free speech fight for the WWP's newspaper and ended up becoming a Wobbly in the process after spending two months in jail. Foster, like many radicals in Seattle, made the trip to Home. He visited the settlement for the first time in winter 1912 and made several others over the course of that year. According to Lucy Robins Lang, a resident of Home, Foster, though younger and more sociable, had a similar appearance to Fox: "They were about the same height, both slim and lithe, and both imperturbable." She also noted in her memoir that "between them moved the dark and voluptuous Esther Fox, a figure of Oriental romance." Fox had never hindered Esther's romantic relationships with men over the years, though it may have proved unsettling to find Esther romantically involved with Fox's new friend Foster, which happened sometime during 1912; by the end of the year she relocated with Foster to Chicago with all three of her children.[32]

As difficult as this was for Fox, he threw himself into the work of his newspaper and took an active part in community life of Home, which seemed as vibrant as ever. The new schoolhouse that had been built for the growing number of children in the community also served as a venue for public lectures by radicals and reformers who visited the village. Moreover, there were well-attended Esperanto classes meeting weekly that were taught by Allen. With a number of new anarchist publications appearing in the artificial international language it was essential that Home anarchists to stay current with this new effort to bridge the language barriers posed by a global movement. The anarchist nature of the colony could still be seen in such gatherings as an "All Nations Peasant Ball," another of which was held in 1912. *The Agitator* continually informed readers as to which steamers to take to reach Home. Accommodations were available for visitors at a local hotel, run by Bessie Brout and her son. The community had a robust gardening sector, mainly cultivated by the women in the village. Rasnick, who had briefly settled in Seattle to practice dentistry, brought his practice and second wife to Home. As a result of changes in the MHA bylaws in 1909, residents had the right to retain title to their land. This new policy stimulated property sales and new arrivals to the community. Many newcomers arrived from the West Coast, but others came from the Midwest or Northeast and some even from Europe. The community was becoming more demographically diverse.[33]

In some respects, the community was more vibrant, but it had become more conflicted. Economically it struggled. The two dry goods stores, Joe's Bay Trading Company and the Home Grocery Company, competed in a village that only needed one such establishment. The Trading Company found itself at odds with the MHA due to its inability to pay rent for its space on the community-owned wharf. Many members of the community, both male and female, had to travel for employment. Some of the more fortunate could find work in the region and return to Home on the weekends. Others had to travel out of state and stay away for months at a time. Due to dwellings being vacant and an influx of new residents, petty theft occurred in the community. This is what had prompted residents of the village to request a deputy sheriff in 1909. The irony of that could not have been lost on the true believers in the community. Moreover, it was that deputy sheriff, Jim Tillman, who arrested the nude bathers. The incident of "The Nude and the Prudes" helped to demonstrate in stark relief the divisions among residents. Nevertheless, the radical element continued to dominate the social and cultural world of Home while the "Prudes" remained a minority. In March 1912, the secretary of the MHA felt compelled to remind residents of the community's basic mores in "Home, What It Stands For," an article published in *The Agitator*. The previous fall, fifty-three residents of

Home formed "A propaganda group of the I.W.W." They pledged to produce "pamphlets and leaflets" and promised that "the cause of the one big union will be vigorously pursued." Even though the village possessed a unique quality as a radical community, the anarchist idealism of the early days was clearly on the decline.[34]

5. The Syndicalist in Chicago

IN LATE 1910, FOX ASKED HIS COMRADE RUDOLF GROSSMAN TO write an essay on the current labor movement in Europe. Back in 1902, Grossman had skipped bail rather than serve prison time for his conviction of "inciting to riot" during the Paterson, New Jersey, silk weavers' strike. He fled the country and eventually settled back in his home country of Austria, where he was publishing his own newspaper, *Wohlstand für Alle*, in Vienna. He wrote under the pen name Pierre Ramus for periodicals in the United States, including *The Agitator*. Fox wanted his readers to get a firsthand account of recent labor history and current developments in the European labor movement. Fox published Grossman's essay in early 1911. In the article, Grossman explained that the labor movement had a revolutionary capability in the 1870s, but that workers in many countries had been seduced by universal suffrage, thus moving away from economic action to political action. Political parties, which had taken hold of many labor unions, had little to show the working class of Europe after nearly thirty years of political action. In the last ten years, workers had begun to move away from politics, Grossman argued, and returned to the radicalism called for by the old the International Workingmen's Association. In France that could be seen in the syndicalist movement, which had a strong anarchist influence. French syndicalism used several revolutionary tactics that could be emulated: avoid the small factory strike and organize for a "local territorial general strike," engage in work slowdowns and sabotage to get demands met by employers, promote an anti-militarist agenda, and create workers' cooperatives. Grossman contended that this trend was not limited to France but could be seen in many Latin countries as well as in "authority-ridden Germany and Austria."[1]

Although he appreciated Grossman's essay on the labor movement in Europe, Fox wanted something more in-depth for *The Agitator*. Foster, who had spent over a year in Europe studying labor unions, especially in France and Germany, returned to the United States convinced that the IWW needed to be radically transformed. Fox announced to his readers, in an April 1912 issue of *The Agitator*, that Foster would author a series of essays, titled "Revolutionary Tactics," that would "include a critical examination of the tactics pursued by the Socialists, Anarchists, Syndicalists and the IWW, and a comparative analysis of their general effect upon organized labor." Fox urged his readers, many of whom were members and sympathizers of the IWW, to keep an open mind when reading the series. Fox hoped that Foster would bring some needed discussion to the revolutionary direction of the labor movement.[2]

Foster had sent dispatches back to the United States while in Europe that were published by *Solidarity* and the *Industrial Worker*. When he returned, he resumed his effort to bring news of the labor movement in Europe and the success of the "boring from within" strategy adopted by French and British trade unionists to radicalize existing trade unions rather than creating an alternative revolutionary labor federation. He first tried to bring his message to the IWW annual convention in September 1911, but found little support, except from members of the western group of "decentralizers." Therefore, he turned to the Wobbly press. He did not find a necessarily welcoming audience, for Wobbly distrust of trade unionism and the AFL was a frequent feature in IWW newspapers. Most Wobblies believed that craft unionism would not evolve into industrial unions. Nevertheless, Foster joined a running discussion in the IWW press of the basic question of why, after years of organizing, free speech fights, and publication efforts, the IWW was not growing. Foster argued that the primary reason for the IWW's stagnation was that it was beholden to a belief—enshrined at its creation—that trade unions could not be radicalized and made revolutionary. He used the transformation of the French CGT as the best example in Europe of how conservative trade unions could be radicalized through the boring within tactic. Labor unions in Spain and Italy were following the lead of the French, but so too were British trade unions, especially in the wake of the successful railroad and transportation strikes. Tom Mann, formerly an advocate of the IWW in Great Britain, adopted the French model and established, with other like-minded trade unionists like Guy Bowman, the Industrial Syndicalist Education League and the *Industrial Syndicalist*, a monthly publication.

Foster believed that "building from without" simply was not working. His prescription was for the IWW to become a "propaganda league" and bring the "principles of revolutionary industrial unionism" into the trade unions rather than creating a separated labor federation. In response to Foster, editors of the two Wobbly newspapers opened their columns for responses. The debate went on for several weeks with contributors either agreeing with Foster or arguing against his proposal and observations. One of the most insightful arguments against Foster was written by J. S. Biscay in the *Industrial Worker*. Biscay argued that the reason the IWW did not grow was due to lack of organizing on the job. Building from without had been shown to work if IWW members did so at the point of production rather than exerting so much energy bringing their message to workers on the street or at Wobbly locals. Moreover, to adopt Foster's suggestions would cause the IWW to disband. Even if members then tried to bore within the current craft unions, they would probably have little to show for their efforts, because radicals would be overwhelmed in the craft unions by conservative members who were wedded to their trades. In addition, migratory workers in agriculture and logging, who were being organized in the West, were not even eligible for union membership in the trades. Therefore, how could they bore? By December, *Solidarity* announced that all had been said on the topic and closed the discussion. The *Industrial Worker* made no such announcement, but Biscay's piece was the last to appear on the topic.[3]

Silenced in the Wobbly press, Foster decided to take his message to the membership in a cross-country tour and to accept Fox's offer to present his ideas in full in *The Agitator*. Fox first met Foster when he came to Home during his hobo tour—that is, hitching rides on freight trains—in winter 1912. Fox remembered, "I was impressed by as few other labor agitators I had met. I was struck by his great earnestness of purpose and quiet determination to carry out the plan. He was devoid of the riotous egotism I had found so common in propagandists." Fox's newspaper was widely available to Wobblies, especially in the West, and was advertised regularly in the *Industrial Worker* and *Solidarity*. Foster began his series by explaining to readers that the IWW was founded with two primary goals: to promote the concept of industrial unionism and to create a new labor movement of revolutionary industrial unions. Foster contended that the IWW had been so successful with the first goal that industrial unionism was being embraced widely and promoted by labor and socialist newspapers throughout the country. Building a successful dual labor organization, however, had been a failure. This was the case not only in the United States but also in Europe, where IWW unions were anemic in comparison to other labor unions, especially those imbued with syndicalism. At the heart of the problem for the IWW was the Wobbly conviction that its federation alone was capable of being a legitimate labor organization and that all others were labor fakers and nonrevolutionary. Moreover, the indiscriminate way Wobblies tried to form unions regardless of whether existing unions were "good, bad, or indifferent" created confusion for workers, bred conflict, and unleashed scabbing by non-IWW unions. To Foster, the IWW was behaving arrogantly by discounting the possibility of evolution among unionized workers in the AFL and considering itself the only legitimate labor organization to unionize the working class. In addition, the IWW was "violating the principle of the militant minority" by withdrawing from non-IWW labor unions and therefore leaving conservatives in control and unchallenged. And finally, the IWW had no agreed-on strategy of how to deal with AFL or independent unions "that refuse to go out of existence."[4]

In *The Agitator*, Foster reiterated his prescription that the ailing IWW become an entirely different labor organization. He wanted the IWW to accept that "dual unionism" was a failure and to give up on creating industrial unions. Wobblies needed to organize into an educational body and do what they had been most successful at doing, that is promote industrial unionism. They should follow the syndicalists in Europe, especially the "British Syndicalist propaganda league," which as "a national dues paying organization" was "not trying to build up a new labor movement, but to revolutionize the old one." Reaching workers with a national newspaper that could focus on the labor movement rather than on one specific element would be essential for syndicalism in the United States, and so too would be newspapers devoted to specific industries to expose the corrupt elements of the trade union leadership and policies and move the rank and file to embrace industrial unionism and revolution. Moreover, he envisioned a national cadre of direct actionists who would assist the militant minority in unions throughout the country agitating for industrial unionism and who would participate "in every important labor war, asked or unasked, by the conservative unions." In addition, Foster envisioned a decentralized strategy of organization, letting the direct actionists on the ground decide for themselves the best policies for a given situation rather than relying on an executive body with centralized control. Foster, rather weakly, argued that the special role the IWW currently played organizing unskilled workers could be continued within an IWW reorganized as an educational league. What form that organization would take Foster left to the direct actionists in the field to decide; once the unskilled formed into unions they could stay independent or join the envisioned revolutionary and industrial AFL. After concluding his "Revolutionary Tactics" series, Foster authored another series that Fox published, "Syndicalism in France," which presented readers with a brief history, an overview of the movement, and an analysis of the CGT's structure.[5]

Fox heralded Foster's series on syndicalism and his criticisms of the IWW as an example of a rejuvenation of the spirit of the labor movement. He also found that Foster's views supported his own misgivings about the IWW, though he had been quite sympathetic to Wobblies and their organizing efforts, especially with unorganized workers too often ignored by the AFL. Fox argued that syndicalism was a process by which once again labor could be at the vanguard of a revolutionary movement. He reminded his readers that the IWW was an experiment and that experiments should be revised, and that the IWW was just a tactic rather than an end onto itself. Furthermore, he reported on the growing number of syndicalist leagues forming and provided space for the locals to promote themselves in *The Agitator*, which included Foster's Syndicalist League of North America (SLNA), established in Chicago in late 1912 with anarchists, militant workers, and former IWW members Samuel Hammersmark, J. A. Jones, Joseph Manley, along with a few others. In addition, he promoted a new syndicalist newspaper in Kansas City, Missouri, *The Toiler*. Foster's essays and Fox's promotion of syndicalism stimulated a response from readers. Some simply wanted a better explanation of syndicalism in relation to the IWW, which Fox was happy to provide. Others challenged Foster's assertions. In *The Agitator*, Fox published a letter received by his friend, labor organizer, contributor to the newspaper, and former Wobbly Jack Wood from none other than Tom Mann. The British labor leader wrote, "I am much interested in *The Agitator*. It does well and I see it is now Syndicalist. That is all to the good." Fox bid Wood much success in his "syndicalist lecture tour to promote the Syndicalist League of North American and *The Agitator*" in fall 1912.[6]

For Fox, syndicalism was a more pragmatic version of anarchists radicalizing the labor movement, whether syndicalists or industrial unionists realized it or not. Fox was not alone in that view, as *Freedom* in London and other anarchist publications made clear. However, Fox did not go as far as Foster in seeing the necessity for the IWW to turn into an educational organization unless that was what the membership overwhelmingly decided to do. He defended himself and his paper as not unleashing "attacks" against the IWW as some claimed, but that he was being critical, based on the evidence he found before him. Furthermore, he asked why should Wobblies concern themselves with syndicalists entering the AFL and independent unions? If Wobblies have abandoned them, what was the harm in radicals trying to transform them? Fox did not find much use for the outpouring of literature on syndicalism, except for the book by the historian and economist Louis Levin, which he had favorably reviewed as a scholarly and historical piece of writing. Foster and Earl Ford's pamphlet *Syndicalism* was seen by Fox as a practical guide for the movement and how it could be implemented across the country's industrial landscape. He advised readers to "send in a dime, get the pamphlet and read it" themselves. He added, "You have waited long enuf for a political Messiah to free you. Do it yourself." Underscoring the call for self-emancipation, Fox included an excerpt from *Syndicalism* in the 15 October issue of *The Agitator* under the title "Superiority of Direct Action." Here Foster outlined the failure of political action by socialist parties, especially in Germany, which had the largest socialist party in Europe, to attain any meaningful changes in the lives of workers. He contrasted that to the work of labor unions that had secured reductions in work hours, increases in wages, and improvements in working conditions. Both Foster and Fox placed the labor union as central to the emancipation of the working class. That form of direct action enabled workers to ultimately liberate themselves from their capitalist masters.[7]

By fall 1912, Fox was ready to become more deeply involved with the syndicalist movement. For him this was a revolutionary development that would give anarchism a practical application. Even though *The Agitator* was in the red, it was doing reasonably well in terms of subscriptions, fundraising, and circulation. Nevertheless, Fox made a dramatic decision: he moved himself and his newspaper to Chicago, where he hoped the city would again be the center of militant, working-class radicalism in the United States. Foster helped convinced him that the newly formed SLNA, centered in Chicago, needed a newspaper and that *The Agitator* with Fox as its editor was a perfect fit.[8] In a letter to his longtime anarchist friend Jo Labadie, Fox wrote, "Say, Jo, what do you think, I'm going back to Chicago. This berg is become too small for the A [*The Agitator*]. It's outgrown the state. We want to take the center of the Industrial stage. The Syndicalists want me to go there and make the paper the central organ of the movement. And this movement is going to grow, Jo. It's better than our pure and simple anarchy at this stage. I'll make 'em anarchists and they won't know it. It's a sugar coat as it were."[9] Fox's letter reveals his desire to be at the center of the revolutionary movement and labor activism, and to keep anarchism alive among the working class and within syndicalism. On this last point, he obviously did not think all syndicalists were anarchists and he felt he could play an important role to keep this "militant minority" sufficiently anarchist, in effect "boring within" those who were "boring within."

The Agitator reappeared as *The Syndicalist*, published out of Chicago, in January 1913, though Fox had to stay behind at Home due to "his entanglements with the law in the State of Washington." Regardless of his legal situation, the editorial and business elements of *The Syndicalist* remained under his control at Home, while Foster would oversee the actual publication. Foster, now in Chicago with Esther and her children, was assisted by Lucy Parsons, who had argued in the past that Chicago should be the location of a revolutionary labor newspaper. She, along with several prominent anarchists, began to see syndicalism's revolutionary potential and changed the title of her most popular speech from "Anarchism: Its Aims and Objects" to "Syndicalism: Its Aims and Objects." Unlike Fox and Foster, however, she remained a supporter of the IWW, even as she became more involved with the SLNA. In her boardinghouse on 1000 South Paulina Street in an immigrant Slavic neighborhood, she provided office space for *The Syndicalist*. In addition, Foster probably resided there, though the evidence is inconclusive as to whether Esther and her children lived in Parsons's boardinghouse or in another Chicago neighborhood.[10]

In the first issue of *The Syndicalist*, the publishers—Fox and Foster—explained to subscribers why the periodical had a new title and why the home base had changed. *The Syndicalist*, according to their statement, was simply the third volume of *The Agitator*, continuing a change in the publication that began eight months earlier when it gave space and support to the new syndicalist movement. Moreover, the move to Chicago, they claimed, was in response to readers across the country who had urged that *The Agitator* relocate to an industrial center to better serve the working class. Once "the editorial, business and publication ends united in Chicago," they declared that they were "planning to increase the size of *The Agitator* and make it a weekly." Of course, the paper would need support from its readers more than ever if it were to grow. They pleaded with their readers to renew their subscriptions: "Whether you believe wholly in Syndicalism or not, you surely cannot be out of touch with this new phase of the labor movement that is growing rapidly in every part of the country. Indeed, it will be our constant endeavor to keep our readers well posted on every phase of the labor movement and make *The Agitator* a real review of the labor world." Furthermore, with syndicalist leagues springing up in cities in the Midwest and West, *The Syndicalist* with its home in Chicago would be at the epicenter of the new radicalism and had the opportunity to be the country's most important English-language advocate for syndicalism.[11]

In many respects, *The Syndicalist* was not all that different from *The Agitator*, especially in its early issues. Fox's "The Passing Show" column continued to appear along with articles on the Mexican Revolution, news of strikes at home and abroad, commentary on the misguided use of the ballot box by workers, updates on Fox's legal woes, and other subjects familiar to readers of *The Agitator*. However, as one would expect, the paper had a much sharper focus on syndicalism, regionally, nationally, and internationally. Fox made clear in the first issue that the league was not a new party or labor union that workers were being encouraged to join. They could remain in the union of their choice. And it was in the workplace that workers could achieve their emancipation. They needed to engage in direct action, radicalize their unions, and work toward amalgamating their craft unions into industrial unions. Fox noted, "If you will follow up, closely, the causes of past failures you will not only improve your conditions under capitalism, but you can even destroy the wage system and institute co-operative pro-duction and consumption." To provide readers with the ability to be more engaged in the syndicalist education effort, *The Syndicalist* would be a clear-ing house for general coverage of the syndicalist movement and other labor relevant news. Even though industries and localities were expected to eventually have their own newspapers, until that happened *The Syndicalist* could be a vehicle for disseminating information specific to their interests. With a small fee from syndicalist locals, the publishers would provide space in the newspaper. Individual locals would be funding their own section of the newspaper, which they would have control over, though under the supervision of the editor. Each local with a department in the paper would receive a bundle of *The Syndicalist* that they could sell or give away. Fox and Foster hoped that this would be how their newspaper could expand into an eight-page weekly. Moreover, with fees paid by individual syndical-ist locals, the editor—Fox—would not have to expend time and energy solic-iting subscriptions and prodding delinquent subscribers to pay up in a timely manner. Although this scheme had merit, it was shaky from the beginning for only the Syndicalist League of Kansas City and League 1 of Nelson, British Columbia, consistently had space in *The Syndicalist*. Oddly, syndicalists in Kansas City suspended publication of *The Toiler* to support *The Syndical-ist*. *The Toiler*'s editor, Max Dezettel, announced in early 1913 that subscrib-ers would here on out receive *The Syndicalist*. Given Fox and Foster's vision of localities having their own syndicalist newspapers, it did not bode well for syndicalism in the Midwest to lose a newspaper. Nevertheless, perhaps Dezettel and local syndicalists thought it best to have a column in *The Syndicalist* until syndicalism had more fully developed in Kansas City.[12]

Remaining in the Pacific Northwest at the end of 1912 and not plan-ning to leave until early 1913, Fox sought to advocate for syndicalism in public talks along with performing his duties for *The Syndicalist*. He also took the time to organize speaking engagements on his inevitable train trip to Chicago. Before leaving the Pacific Northwest, the syndicalist Trade Union League in Vancouver, British Columbia, invited him to give a talk on the merits of syndicalism at the city's Labor Temple. According to Fox, "In order to dispel any suspicion that [the Vancouver league] might be a dual organization in disguise, the league has made it a rule to accept no member unless he carries a card in the union of his trade or calling and continued membership depends on the card being kept paid up." The league represented a cross section of supporters in the city. Fox traveled by steamer to Vancouver with a stop in Victoria, the capital of the province. He could not help but be impressed by the natural beauty of Vancouver Island and the other small islands of the Puget Sound. Once in Vancouver, Fox was welcomed by members of the league, some of whom were Wobblies, and taken to the IWW hall to meet even more Wobblies. The following day, Sunday, he gave his public talk to a large audience in the hall. Wobblies, trade unionists, socialists, and others listened attentively to Fox's explanation of the syndicalist movement and what it offered workers. He noted that the audience asked insightful questions at the end of his talk and that many seemed to have "the right impression of syndicalism."[13]

Fox returned to Home after his sojourn to Vancouver and was finally ready to depart for Chicago in February 1913. He had two stops to make along the way, Butte, Montana, and Minneapolis, Minnesota. His goal was to continue to spread the gospel of syndicalism as a body of ideas that workers could implement in their existing unions. Fox was convinced that Butte was a good place to advocate for a radicalization of organized labor. The city was, for the most part, a union shop, most workers had the eight-hour day, and few earned less than $3.50 a day. For years Wobblies and their sympathizers had tried to set up a rival miners' union ever since the WFM had left the IWW. Radicals still had a place in the WFM in the city, but they were countered by the larger and more conservative Butte Miners' Union. Given the tumultuous events of the previous year in Butte and the role Wobblies had played, Fox thought it was a good opportunity to lecture his audience on the dangers of dual unionism. He argued that for workers to leave their present union and join an IWW miners' union would only create more factionalism, sowing discord in the ranks of union members. In his talk, he still had positive points to make about the IWW, but he stressed that Wobblies should concern themselves with organizing the millions of unskilled workers in the West and throughout the country who had no union. Those that already had a union should stay put and radicalize it, turning it into a revolutionary organization. Dual unionism, he cautioned, would only weaken the labor movement of Butte and provide the capitalists with an opportunity to divide and conquer organized workers.

At his next stop, Fox encountered a very different city. Minneapolis was a metropolitan area that had only a small number of workers organized in a few skilled trades. The IWW had made little headway there over the years, though it had a foothold, at least seasonally, in the state's wheat fields. Still, Fox took a positive tone in his public talk at Federation Hall. He argued that workers of the city would unionize if they had proper assistance to do so, principally in the form of organizers and funding. One of the major questions he sought to answer for his audience was "What form of labor unions will you have under Syndicalism?" His response was "that Syndicalism is not a system, but an idea; that it is not a creation, but an evolution; that it didn't germinate in the brain of some philosopher, but that it is the offspring of the toilers' own experience in mill, factory, and on the farm." Even though syndicalism favored the industrial form of organization, Fox contended that its success depended more on the point of view of the workers than the union card they may or may not hold. Moreover, it was the workers' lack of knowledge that held them back more so than a lack of organization. As if to underscore this point, Fox noted that "these hungry Northwesterners gobbled up all my literature, and I landed in Chicago without a book." Within the circles of labor radicals, Fox and Foster had become so associated with syndicalism that one labor advocate wrote a short poem about the two of them:[14]

"The proper way," said Jay the Fox,
"To start the revolution
Is just to bore a hole or two
In existing institutions."
"Agreed," cried Mr. Foster.
"I have my gimlet ready,
My arm is long, my hand is strong,
My nerves are cool and steady."[15]

Even though it was still winter, Fox had a warm homecoming in Chicago after being away from the city for four years. Some of his old friends and fellow anarchists still lived there and he was quick to reestablish those connections. Probably the most important of these friendships was with Parsons. Despite their occasional conflicts, she offered him a room at her boardinghouse. Also, through his connections in the machinists' trade, he was able to return to familiar labor at a machinist's shop. Along with Foster, his evenings and Sundays were consumed by work on the paper and correspondence with anarchists, unionists, and others sympathetic to the syndicalist cause. In fact, correspondence was the primary way for the fledgling SLNA to get off the ground. Fox was quite pleased to be in Chicago to see the 1 March issue of *The Syndicalist* go to print. Another activity that gave him great satisfaction was giving public talks in the city. His venue in March was at the Masonic Temple and his topic was "Syndicalism." He was not alone in presenting a public lecture on the subject. Emma Goldman arrived that same month to speak on syndicalism at the Oakland Music Hall. She expounded on a host of subjects over the course of several days in the city, mostly at the music hall but also at the Lexington Hotel.[16]

In the years before the outbreak of the Great War, syndicalism had become a popular topic of discussion not only in labor circles but also with the public, particularly among newspaper editors. Academics had an interest in the subject as well, as several journal articles, dissertations, and full-length monographs were produced by scholars from a variety of disciplines. However, the primary interest in syndicalism was among labor advocates, socialists, and most particularly anarchists. Goldman, along with Hippolyte Havel and Harry Kelly, established a Syndicalist Education League in New York City in 1912 after a meeting in which "sixty friends and sympathizers" approved forming such an organization. Kelly explained in *Mother Earth* that the league's primary mission was "to spread the doctrines of Syndicalism and to organize the unorganized." In fact, Goldman had been using the term "syndicalism" in her public speeches and writings since 1908 after she returned from the Amsterdam Congress. Although she initially sided with Errico Malatesta at the conference in holding that a general strike could not be a substitute for a social revolution, by 1912 she had come out strongly in favor of how significant a truly revolutionary proletariat would be in overthrowing capitalism and the nation-state and ushering in a libertarian and egalitarian society. Syndicalism, she argued, could be the organizing principles on which could be established a new society "based on solidarity and economic well-being for all." Moreover, she came to see syndicalism as something that was not distinct from anarchism, especially with so many European anarchists in the syndicalist movement. She argued that "Syndicalism is, in essence, the economic expression of Anarchism."[17]

Anarchists on the West Coast were as equally attune to syndicalism as their comrades in the Midwest and Northeast. With the departure of *The Agitator* to Chicago and its reemergence as *The Syndicalist*, anarchists Frances Moore, former resident of Home Colony, her husband Travaglio, former compositor of *Free Society* and editor of Italian anarchist publications in San Francisco, and Hammersmark published *Why?* in Tacoma, Washington, beginning in January 1913. For the next two years, *Why?* became the principal English-language anarchist periodical on the West Coast. In similarity to the first year of *The Agitator, Why?* championed an anarchist critique of society, support for the libertarian educational movement, and radicalizing the labor movement. Along with the staff of the paper, a variety of contributors penned columns, many of whom had published in previous anarchist periodicals. In fact, Travaglio corresponded with the prolific Detroit anarchist Labadie and enticed him to submit poetry and essays to the publication. Labor issues were a common theme in the pages of *Why?* Moore, writing in the first issue, explained to readers that "boring from within [syndicalist leagues]" or "boring from without [IWW]" was not as important as getting "busy boring, from within, from without, upward, downward, east, west, north, south, [boring] everywhere." However, even though her tone was ecumenical when it came to labor radicalism and revolutionary activity, *Why?* exhibited a clear support for the necessity of the "militant minority" to radicalize existing unions. Radicals, the editorials argued, should not leave their unions or worse remain aloof from labor organizations, but should "teach them . . . how to fight with dexterity and for a definite aim."[18]

Even though advocates of syndicalism aspired to a nationwide movement, it only took hold among a loosely affiliated membership of unionists and propagandists in several industrial midwestern cities—most notably Chicago, Kansas City, St. Louis, Minneapolis, and Omaha—and several Far West urban areas both large and small—primarily San Diego, Los Angeles, San Francisco, Tacoma, and Seattle in the United States and Nelson and Vancouver in British Columbia. Syndicalists established perhaps a dozen or so league branches with a total membership never rising above two thousand. Typical syndicalists were skilled, native-born, white workers who were either former Wobblies, former socialists—soured on party politics— or anarchists. In either case, they believed the AFL could be radicalized, and many of the syndicalists sought to join AFL-affiliated unions and promote amalgamation of craft unions into industrial unions. The syndicalist movement, though, failed to penetrate the industrial Northeast beyond the advocacy of a small group of anarchists and radicals affiliated with Goldman, Kelly, Havel, and their Syndicalist Education League. In addition, there seemed to be no effort to establish the movement in the South. The SLNA had several newspapers to promote its program: *The Toiler* in Kansas City (which would resume publication in late 1913), *The Unionist*, a St. Louis weekly, San Diego's *The International*, and *The Unionist* in Omaha. *The Syndicalist*, in Chicago, was the league's primary organ.[19]

In the pages of *The Syndicalist*, readers could learn of the progress of league branches, educational activities, union infiltration, amalgamation efforts, and organizing drives. Kansas City had one of the most active branches, in which syndicalists claimed great influence with several unions including those of cooks, barbers, and office workers. The league branch had a headquarters and reading room open to all wageworkers seven days a week. Syndicalists, through an education and organizing committee, instituted a union membership drive for the International Journeymen's Barber Union Local 192 in May 1913. They successfully brought more barbers into the union, and the local was successful in ending the practice of barber shops operating on Sundays. Foster, writing years later, argued that league activists were able to gain influence within the city's Central Labor Council. A young Earl Browder, who would eventually become the general secretary of the Communist Party, was an accountant by profession and a delegate to the council. Although he did not think of himself as a syndicalist, he worked closely with syndicalists and believed as they did that working within existing unions would be more effective than the dual unionism of the IWW. Browder would contribute articles to *The Toiler* in fall 1913 and would later coedit the newspaper with Dezettel. Also, syndicalists, as well as Browder, assisted office workers in joining the local of the Stenographers, Typewriters, Bookkeepers, and Assistants Union. Browder eventually would become president of the union and Dezettel would also become a member. Browder and the city's syndicalist league helped to launch Kansas City's Labor Forward Movement, which emerged out of Minneapolis and St. Paul and modeled itself on the Men and Religion Movement that was sweeping across the country at the time. Embraced by the AFL, the Labor Forward Movement was an effort to revitalize union organizing and contributed to a surge in AFL membership in 1913. League members, Dezettel, and William T. Sheehan would become special organizers for the AFL in the city. In 1914, they participated in several organizing drives and promoted the amalgamation of trades into industrial unions. Dezettel would eventually become president of the Central Labor Council with Browder as a prominent member.[20]

Another hotbed of syndicalist activity was St. Louis and the cluster of surrounding small towns. The St. Louis Syndicalist League advocated the creation of a Federation of Strike Committees that could assist striking workers who in many instances waged isolated campaigns. The federation fostered coordination, communication, and solidarity among striking workers across the country. J. A. La Bille, editor of *The Unionist*, was a prominent leader of the league branch. A former Wobbly, La Bille led a "militant minority" of workers to fight for industrial unionism in the Amalgamated Association of Iron, Steel, and Tin Workers Union in 1912. The following year syndicalists assisted restaurant workers in the city, specifically waiters, to establish Waiters' Union Local 20 of the international body. The waiters received support from the Cooks and Bartenders Union as well in an especially hard-fought battle the local waged against Melshemmer's Café and McTague's Café, the owners of which tried to staff only nonunion labor, some of whom were African American strikebreakers. Syndicalists claimed an influence with moving picture operators—a growing trade—who were encouraged to join the AFL. The moving picture operators successfully organized most of the theaters in the city over the course of 1913. Another action touted by the city's syndicalists was a strike by Bell Telephone operators. The young women had support from electrical workers and the St. Louis Central Trades Council. Inexplicably, the union's national officers called off the strike, which was an important lesson for syndicalists that national leadership was slow to recognize the militancy and resolve of rank-and-file union members. Nevertheless, the switchboard operators were some of the first union workers recognized by the Bell Telephone Company.[21]

To the west and across the border in British Columbia, Wobblies along with anarchists embraced Foster's call for IWW locals to convert from union locals into centers of industrial union activism and to work within the AFL. In 1912, syndicalists split with the IWW local in Vancouver and created a separate local of the SLNA. The most prominent syndicalist outpost in BC, though, was in the small community of Nelson. There Wobblies voted to withdraw Local 525 from the IWW and create a syndicalist league branch of the SLNA, relinquish dual unionism, and bore from within AFL locals. The AFL's lead organizer in the city, George H. Hardy, preferred this move because the IWW had made strong inroads into organizing the city's civic workers, unskilled laborers, and teamsters. Moreover, most AFL electrical workers and carpenters carried Wobbly union cards. He may have hoped to co-opt the rival IWW local with conservative trade unionists in the newly formed Federation of Labor Unions (FLU), an AFL affiliate. However, A. L. Elliot, William Craig, and Jack Johnstone—now former Nelson Wobblies—believed that this was the right move to insure labor solidarity against contractors who only planned to hire FLU members. Therefore, instead of having a factional fight, former Wobblies chose to go "over to the F.L.U. individually and gain control of it." The *Industrial Worker* was rather critical of Johnstone, in particular, because of his syndicalist activity. In addition, Nelson syndicalists, in protest over *Solidarity* and the *Industrial Worker* closing discussion of Foster's ideas, decided that their local would no longer subscribe to IWW newspapers, but would subscribe and support *The Agitator* and later in 1913 *The Syndicalist*.[22]

Fox had a keen interest in the labor movement of the Pacific Northwest and tracked the progress of syndicalist agitation. In Washington, he took heart in the move by delegates at the Washington State Federation of Labor convention in 1913 to pass a resolution that "declared flatly for the industrial form of organization." The convention delegates also resolved that unions should refrain from entering contracts with employers because of the potential of scabbing on fellow workers who may be on strike while workers in another union maybe bound by contract to remain on the job. According to Fox, they were following the example of delegates at the Third Annual Convention of the British Columbia Federation of Labor held in Victoria at the beginning of the year, who opposed the attempt to endorse a labor party in the province, which would be a political arm of the labor unions and therefore an embrace of political action. Syndicalists at the convention pushed for industrial unionism and direct action. In addition, most of the delegates supported a resolution in favor of industrial unionism and an additional resolution to call a general strike in case of war. Amplifying the point on the vital importance of industrial organization was Hammersmark. Fox published his open letter to L. A. McCammot, the secretary of the Electrical Workers Union local, in which he argued that the electrical workers' strike against the Stone-Webster Company was doomed because only 20 percent of the workforce was organized. The other 80 percent would simply remain on the job and therefore scab. "Get together—syndicate," he demanded, after which he asked, "Why not form a Stone-Webster shop federation? Every man employed by this firm being eligible to membership."

The sentiment was clear in that strikes would be more successful if the entire workforce were organized as an industry.[23]

A special interest of Fox's was Pacific Northwest logging and lumber workers. He noted that after seven years of organizing efforts, the IWW had little to show for its work in the industry. The only stable and lasting union among these workers were the highly skilled members of the International Shingle Weavers' Union that numbered over a thousand. Despite entreaties made by the IWW, the weavers refused to join the alternative labor federation and resolved to continue to maintain their affiliation with the AFL. Nevertheless, tens of thousands of workers in the industry had no labor organization. At the Shingle Weavers' Union annual convention in January 1912, in Sedro Woolley, Washington, delegates voted to seek jurisdiction over all workers in the timber industry and asked for AFL approval. A loss of a major strike by the weavers in 1906, according to historian Philip Dreyfus, radicalized and motivated them to be more open to industrial unionism. Another strike in 1912 would further push the weavers from the narrowness of trade unionism. At recent AFL conventions, delegates expressed their concerns about the growing power of employers' associations. And a few industrial unions were issued charters by the federation. In the case of the timber workers in the Pacific Northwest, the AFL leadership was uneasy about the IWW's organizing efforts in the region. The federation's industrial union, the International Brotherhood of Woodsmen and Sawmill Workers, formed in 1905 to organize loggers and mill workers, lost its charter in 1911. Therefore, with support from AFL vice president John Mitchell, former president of the UMW, the Shingle Weavers Union received that approval in the fall.

In January 1913, the Shingle Weavers Union met at their next convention in Portland, Oregon, revised their constitution, changed the union's name to the International Union of Shingle Weavers, Sawmill Workers, and Woodsmen (the following year the union's name would change again, to the International Union of Timber Workers, henceforth IUT), and changed the name of their newspaper from *The Shingle Weaver* to *The Timber Worker*. Now operating as an industrial union, organizers began in earnest to bring mill and logging workers into their ranks. Fox took no side in this effort by the IUT and the IWW to organize the workers industrially. He believed that "the Syndicalists contend that the difference in the organizations will be in name only, so far as the woodsman is concerned." Fox printed a communiqué from a member of the IUT who endorsed the SLNA program and after two years of organizing and educational work believed an industrial union of lumber and logging workers would succeed. His local in Everett, Washington, subscribed to *The Syndicalist* and considered it "our paper."[24]

Fox and Foster put a great deal of energy into their newspaper over the course of 1913, believing that educating workers about their historical mission required information and analysis that could guide them. For Fox, in particular, "the aim of Syndicalism is to systematically prepare the toilers for that general strike." He used labor struggles of the day as instructive lessons to help prepare the toilers intellectually. In early 1913, the massive New York garment workers' strike was in full swing. It served as a clear example of how the most exploited class of workers—many of whom were Jewish immigrants but also Italian, central, and eastern European immigrants as well—chose labor solidarity by crossing lines of ethnicity and gender as perhaps a third of the strikers were women. According to Fox, "strikes in themselves, apart from their material benefits, are the greatest educational instruments we have got." He used as an example the British miners' effort to secure the five-day week as a benefit to more than simply the British miners, for "the shorter workday helps the man without a job. It helps everybody. It gives those who work time to read, while enabling the unemployed to get a crust without charity." Moreover, strikes teach "the power of concerted action, and reveal to us the great strength we possess. They draw us together in the close bonds of solidarity."

Breaking that bond of worker solidarity and undermining worker power was arbitration. Fox adamantly preached against workers who accepted arbitration rather than striking. In April 1913, the Chicago streetcar workers had their dispute settled through arbitration and ended up with an "award" not much different from what the company offered at the outset of the dispute and now the workers were bound to the agreement for the next three years. Another division to worker solidarity and empowerment was an attachment to political agendas. Fox used the example of a conflict within the IAM between a socialist leadership and a primarily nonsocialist rank and file that split the union in New York and came close to splitting the union in Chicago. Fox argued that socialists, though they may be sincere in their goals for the working class, only wanted to use the trade union for their political agenda. Fox believed that workers should never relinquish local control over their union and that the trade union should exist for its own sake. And as for the largest IWW led strike of the year that took place in Paterson, New Jersey, Fox lauded the fact that the workers held out for five months but criticized the IWW for not fully understanding the capabilities of the workers when it came to revolutionary tactics: "They were up against the real thing in Paterson—a mass of workers untrained in the art of striking, without funds to sustain a long strike, without organization behind them; a mass that was not in any way capable to withstand a long siege without great suffering." The workers would have been better off, Fox asserted, by playing one employer off another through separate negotiated settlements, something the IWW refused to support.[25]

The dangerous nature of many workplaces could be instructive to workers as well, whether that be due to a mine explosion, train wreck, shirt factory fire, or when workers were "crippled" daily on railroads and in factories. The cheapness of the lives of workers, from the perspective of the capitalists, reduced all workers—be they white, African American, Latino, or Asian, male, or female—to the same level. Workers were foolish, Fox contended, to seek outside help in making their workplaces safe. Only when workers took possession of industry would workplaces be made safe. And if they cannot be made safe, for example with the mining of coal, then "the mines will be closed entirely and we will turn elsewhere for our motive power. For then a worker's life will not be the cheapest thing on earth, but the dearest." Nevertheless, the struggle to take possession of the means of production could be a bloody one, as the West Virginia coal strike indicated. By May 1913 dozens of miners had been killed over union recognition and efforts to improve wages and working conditions, and their civil rights abrogated with the declaration of martial law. Moreover, the violent strike's resolution was also a lesson. At a convention called to consider an end to the action, UMW officials urged the miners to give up their strike or lose their strike benefits. Most workers decided to end the strike even without attaining many tangible concessions from the mine owners. Nevertheless, according to Fox, a militant minority at the convention vowed to continue the struggle. For Fox, the lessons were clear. He wanted his readers to understand that violence and oppression were inherent in the system they were trying to overthrow, that industrial union solidarity was difficult to achieve, and that workers had to be weary of even their own union leaders when it came to the ultimate goals of labor action.[26]

Even though Fox hoped that the newspaper would enlighten workers through coverage of strikes and other labor-oriented topics, it was critical that workers educate themselves by attending meetings, lectures, discussion groups, and reading rooms or subscribing to publications and buying literature. Fox did not consider other radical newspapers as rivals to his own and encouraged readers to subscribe to *The Social War*, edited by the English radical Edward Mylius in New York, *Kozos Tarsadalom*, a Hungarian syndicalist newspaper published in San Francisco, and *Frayhayt*, a Yiddish-language anarchist paper friendly to syndicalism. *The Syndicalist*, similar to *The Agitator*, printed information as to where workers could go to learn about issues relevant to them. Public talks were advertised, especially for Chicago. In addition, a West Coast speaking tour by the Wobbly Laura Payne Emerson on the topic of syndicalism was announced. Emerson was a member of San Diego's IWW Local 13, veteran of the 1912 San Diego Free Speech Fight, a writer for the *Industrial Worker*, and contributor to the IWW's famed *Little Red Songbook*. Her scheduled city stops were listed for readers, who were "urged to join in making these meetings a success" for "the well-known California rebel." The Syndicalist Publishing Association—again like a column in *The Agitator*—offered a list of books and pamphlets for sale to readers. The span of literature available was quite broad, with works of anthropology by Lewis H. Morgan, philosophy by Friedrich Nietzsche, geography by Élisée Reclus, educational theory by Francisco Ferrer, and Marxist theory by Paul Lafargue and Friedrich Engels. The limited published work by Fox and Foster was available, but one of the most prevalent genres on the list was anarchist literature, such as pamphlets and books by Lucy and Albert Parsons, Mikhail Bakunin, Alexander Berkman, William Owen, Leo Tolstoy, Emma Goldman, Émile Pouget, E. C. Walker, Voltairine de Cleyre, Pierre-Joseph Proudhon, and especially an assortment of writings by Pyotr Kropotkin.[27]

Fox and Foster opened their newspaper to a variety of writers who had their own columns. One such featured writer was Dr. Eva Trew, an adamant opponent of forced sterilization and the eugenics movement, both of which she argued were assaults on the working class, which was similar to an argument made by Fox in *The Agitator* when the state supreme court of Washington proclaimed sterilization constitutional for specific convicted criminals. She had previously written in *The Agitator* on issues pertinent to women. In *The Syndicalist* she had a column called "Twenty Questions on Direct Action," in which she presented a series of questions concerning a major principle of syndicalism that she thought might be asked by a worker, whose interest had been piqued by this new theory of labor organization and agitation. In some respects, she amplified arguments offered by Fox and Foster, but she also explained the practical realities that the working class faced in pursuing political action. While Foster argued in his pamphlet *Syndicalism* reasons for the failure of political action, especially in an international context regarding socialist parties, Trew pointed out in her column the rampant disfranchisement in the United States of migratory workers, immigrants, African American men, and millions of women. The only reasonable avenue for workers was to liberate themselves by direct action, in other words economic action, in the workplace. But she also wanted workers to free themselves of the intellectual confines of Christianity, patriotism, militarism, and faith in the intelligence and philanthropy of the capitalist class. She took a decidedly anarchist position on Christianity, arguing that Jesus and his followers were working-class revolutionaries and that governments and the Church, from the very beginning, had co-opted their message and turned it into a system of oppression. Likewise, patriotism was a means to divide the working classes of the world to do the bidding of politicians and capitalists. She reasoned that the workers themselves could manage society in their interests if they followed the syndicalist path toward an "industrial commonwealth." Moreover, Trew argued in favor of sabotage as an important component of direct action that would help bring about an overthrow of the current system. She echoed some of Pouget's sentiments from his *Sabotage*, widely circulated once it was translated into English.[28]

Another featured contributor was J. A. "Jack" Jones, an early member of the IWW and an organizer for both the IWW and the WFM. In 1907, he took his organizing skills to Minnesota's Mesabi Iron Range where he met and subsequently married Elizabeth Gurley Flynn, the famed "rebel girl." Their Wobbly activities took them to Missoula, Montana, where they participated in the Missoula Free Speech Fight in 1909. Jones stayed in the Far West while Flynn's Wobbly activities took her from coast to coast. Jones had remained a member of the WFM even after it pulled out of the IWW. He continued to believe that the federation could return to its former militancy through the boring from within strategy. Demonstrating his commitment to that approach, in 1912 he joined the SLNA. Nevertheless, he made the decision to leave the Far West and in the following year relocated to Chicago and found work as a painter, joined the painters' union, and wrote regularly for *The Syndicalist*. In his column, "Society Notes," Jones focused on sabotage and dark humor, both associated with workplace grievances, slowing down production, or simple malicious mischief. His writings were not necessarily unique in the radical labor press. Workers who subscribed to the IWW's western newspaper, the *Industrial Worker*, could find similar examples of dark humor related to the world of work, though they may not have found many explicit examples of sabotage as in *The Syndicalist*. Although sabotage was probably one of the most controversial aspects of the syndicalist movement, it was widely accepted by many syndicalists, Wobblies, and anarchists as well as by disgruntled workers throughout the ages.[29]

Internationally, the most important focus of *The Syndicalist* was syndicalism as a worldwide phenomenon. Special attention was paid to the possibility of an international syndicalist conference. The Industrial Syndicalist Education League (ISEL) in Britain held two conferences—in London and Manchester—in late 1912 calling for an international gathering. Even though trade unions were a major component of the Second International, delegates at the British conferences believed that the socialist organization, which required "a pledge of parliamentarism," prohibited syndicalist participation. Moreover, the International Secretariat of National Trade Union Centers—commonly referred to as the International Secretariat, which was supposed to be an international trade union organization—was controlled largely by socialists and therefore not interested in issues common to syndicalists. Also, except for the CGT, the International Secretariat had policies that excluded syndicalist organizations. Therefore, syndicalists felt they were forced to create a separate international labor organization, one they believed needed to be built on revolutionary industrial unionism and direct action. Guy Bowman, editor of *The Syndicalist and Amalgamation News* (formerly *The Industrial Syndicalist*) and general secretary of the British ISEL, called for an "International Syndicalist Congress [to] bring together the militant workers of all countries." Foster argued that such a conference was necessary to establish connections among the variety of syndicalist movements in Europe, the Americas, and other parts of the world. Moreover, he agreed with Kropotkin, who believed anarchism and syndicalism had great commonalities and that syndicalists needed to come to some common understanding of what type of new society they were striving for. Foster noted "the communistic theory of the C.G.T., the industrial state of the I.W.W.; the Pouget-Patuad theory of double federation of producing labor unions on one side and the federation of distributing co-operatives on the other; the theory that the miners will own the mines, the railroaders own the railroads, etc.; the shop organization theory, etc." as some of the most prominent post-revolution societal organizational models. Fox concurred that a better understanding of what a syndicalist future would mean was crucial for the movement. In addition, syndicalism, as an international revolutionary movement, was underscored in the pages of *The Syndicalist* with republications from *The Syndicalist and Amalgamation News* and London's *Freedom* that traced a direct connection between syndicalism and the expulsion of anarchists from the First Socialist International.[30]

The most important international figure in the syndicalist movement for both Fox and Foster was Tom Mann. After spending nearly nine years in New Zealand, Australia, and South Africa promoting and organizing for trade unionism and socialism, Mann began to sour on parliamentary politics and lost his faith that the labor movement could achieve its goals through political action. After his return to Great Britain in 1910, he, along with Bowman, traveled to France to study "the principles and policy of the CGT." Mann had only visited France a few months before Foster, but he was equally impressed by the French boring within strategy. When he returned to Britain, he and Bowman began publishing the *Industrial Syndicalist* and at the Industrial Syndicalist Conference in Manchester the conferees formed the ISEL, the subsequent model for Foster's SLNA. Fox had defended Mann and Bowman after their arrests and convictions in 1912 associated with "The Don't Shoot Leaflet" that urged British soldiers not to use violence against striking workers. Moreover, he had published accounts of Mann's organizing efforts in Great Britain and reprinted some of his speeches and writings in both *The Agitator* and *The Syndicalist*. Therefore, it was with great excitement that Fox and Foster could welcome Mann to the United States on his speaking tour in 1913. Mann's tour was sponsored in part by the Socialist Party, the IWW, and the AFL and took him to seventy cities. His book, part memoir and part revolutionary tract, *From Single Tax to Syndicalism*, appeared earlier in the year, in which he preached the gospel of workers' control of industry. The labor and radical press, along with mainstream newspapers, had covered his labor union activities for years. Especially noteworthy was his leadership of the 1911 Liverpool transportation workers' strike. As chair of the strike committee, Mann led tens of thousands of striking workers and was instrumental in successful negotiations with employers. Consequently, Mann's tour received extensive media coverage from large newspapers such as the *New York Times*, but also small newspapers such as the Italian anarchist *Cronaca Sovversiva*, the *Labor Journal* of Everett, Washington, the *Bridgeport Evening Farmer*, and the *Seattle Star*.[31]

In his speeches, Mann championed syndicalism as the best path to worker emancipation and received warm receptions. In the Seattle area, Parsons, who was in the Pacific Northwest on her own lecture tour, organized several speaking engagements for Mann, as did the Wobbly Sam Scarlett in Salt Lake City. Back in the Midwest, syndicalists organized Mann's lectures in Kansas City and St. Louis. His criticism of Gompers and the AFL was well received by Wobblies at their annual convention. He did, however, openly criticize political action and dual unionism and advocated the boring from within strategy, especially regarding the AFL. This led to some cooling of support by the IWW and the Socialist Party. Nevertheless, numerous other labor unions and associations sponsored his speaking engagements, including Foster and the SLNA. In Chicago, Mann spoke on 11 September at the North Side Turner Hall, sponsored by the city's labor league, and the following night at the same location sponsored by the painters' union. A major theme of his talk was labor solidarity. He argued that the capitalist class—in all countries—controlled the institutions of religion, education, and government for its own interests. Therefore, the working class needed to turn inward for its emancipation. In England he believed that labor solidarity had brought the working class "not so much nearer to heaven, but a little further from hell."

Even though syndicalism attracted a good deal of attention in 1913 and its adherents were enthusiastic, *The Syndicalist* was not doing well. The paper's headquarters moved to West Division Street and its schedule was reduced from twice monthly to once a month starting with the June issue. Fox explained to readers that the change in publication frequency was due to the slow summer months, but only one issue appeared in September and no others followed. The effort to have local syndicalist leagues pay to have columns in the newspaper did not expand beyond the three or four that consistently paid for space from the beginning, and individual subscriptions were not increasing either. Fox believed that "the slow growth of the movement was due to the fact that sufficent [sic] preparatory work had not been done before starting the new line of propaganda that required more than the usual explanation." A national constitution for the SLNA, which Foster proposed at the beginning of the year, remained unwritten at the close of the year. From 27 September to 2 October, the First International Syndicalist Congress took place at Holborn Hall in London, but the SLNA failed to send a delegate. Ironically, the IWW had a delegate present at the congress along with representatives from Europe and Latin America. As one might expect, the delegates had a variety of opinions on the direction the congress should take and the issues most important to the movement. Attendees discussed antimilitarism, the general strike, political affiliations, industrial unionism, direct action, and international connections. In the end the delegates were able to articulate a declaration of syndicalist principles for the international movement that included support for "autonomous industrial Unions," class struggle to overthrow capitalism and the nation-state, international labor solidarity, and the use of labor unions as the means to produce goods and services in the interests of the entire community. These sentiments were in harmony with much of what Fox, Foster, and others advocated in the pages of *The Syndicalist*. *The Toiler* out of St. Louis gave the congress high marks for encouraging decentralization, direct action, antimilitarism, and the general strike, though the editor hoped that at the next installment the congress would issue a clear statement opposing the practice for the divisions that dual unionism creates in the labor movement, a perspective that Fox, Foster, and most American syndicalists would heartily endorse.[32]

With the demise of *The Syndicalist*, Dezettel and several other syndicalists in Kansas City revived their newspaper in October 1913. As editor, he wanted *The Toiler: A Monthly Review of International Syndicalism* to be "the liveliest revolutionary magazine in America" and "to carry on a hearty agitation for syndicalism, or revolutionary unionism." *The Toiler* had some of the characteristics of Fox's paper in that Dezettel and his associate editors, Otto E. Cook and Earl Browder, tried to provide connections between various syndicalists leagues in the Midwest and Far West as well as international news of the syndicalist movement. A host of writers—including Foster, Browder, and Fox—penned articles for the newspaper that nurtured those connections. "The Rebels' Forum" column allowed syndicalists to discuss a variety of issues pertinent to the movement, particularly in terms of tactics such as sabotage, strikes, industrial unionism, amalgamation, and decentralization. In addition, the editors republished writings by Jack London, Anton Johannesen, Pedro Esteve, Louis Levine, Tom Mann, William Owen, and others, which gave readers a variety of perspectives on topics of the day. Nevertheless, the orientation of *The Toiler* tended to focus on the labor movement in Kansas City. The other syndicalist newspapers in St. Louis and Omaha tended to focus on local issues as well, while Laura Payne Emerson's *The International* in San Diego primarily contained republished writings out of the radical labor press pertinent to syndicalism plus several of her own articles. Given the focus of the remaining syndicalist newspapers, the SLNA did not have a primary organ in which to spread the message of syndicalism or to recruit new members and new local leagues.[33]

6. Boring Within

A CCORDING TO FOX, "AFTER A YEAR IN CHICAGO PROMOTING THE new adventure in Syndicalism we decided to lay off for a while." Although Fox and Foster's efforts to build a syndicalist movement with Chicago as its headquarters seemed to stall, their commitment to syndicalism did not waiver. Moreover, they were going to embark on one of the primary features of syndicalist activity in that they were poised to bore within an AFL-affiliated union. In the meantime, Foster continued to work as a train car inspector in Chicago and maintained an extensive correspondence, particularly among syndicalists. In addition, he assisted in organizing speaking engagements for Mann through the remainder of the year. Fox attended the seventh convention of the IWW, held in Chicago in September. Even though he was a member of the SLNA and a close associate of Foster, he was welcomed as a fellow worker and industrial union activist. He spoke to some of the delegates about the merits of the boring within strategy and expressed his concerns about the IWW's centralization. The Wobblies he spoke to heard him out, but no one seemed willing to drop out of the IWW and join the SLNA. Later, he returned to Seattle, where the AFL was holding its annual convention, which took place in November. He was motivated to attend with the goal of promoting industrial unionism and the amalgamation of craft unions. At the convention, he met J. G. Brown, a socialist and president of the recently created IUT. At the convention, the AFL provided the union with financial support to hire more organizers.

At Fox's urging, Brown selected Foster to be one of those organizers along with Andy Raynor. Raynor, originally from Wisconsin, had worked in the mills for over thirty years and was a committed advocate for industrial unionism. He was a shingle weaver by trade and member of Local 5 in Machias, Washington. Brown was aware of Fox's editorship of *The Agitator* and *The Syndicalist* and may well have read Fox's "The Passing Show" column in March in which he welcomed the AFL's interest in organizing the timber workers of the Pacific Northwest. The union's newspaper had already republished articles by both Foster and Fox that had first been published in *The Syndicalist*. Brown suggested to Fox that he write for the *Timber Worker* and assist the current editor, William H. Reid, who was also the union's secretary-treasurer. Fox began writing regularly for the newspaper in December 1913.[1]

When the shingle weavers decided to extend their jurisdiction to the entire industry in 1912, prices and production were up for lumber and shingles, making employment plentiful. A great deal of enthusiasm was evident among the membership of the IUT in 1913 during its organizing drives in lumber mills and logging campsites in the Pacific Northwest and beyond. The union created locals for specific trades within the industry and mixed locals when necessary. This method of organizing locals provided them with a good deal of autonomy, and mixed locals of shingle weavers, mill workers, and loggers promoted industrial union solidarity. The headquarters of the union was in the Maynard Building in Seattle's Pioneer Square neighborhood, and nearby the union operated a hiring hall and reading room in the Stetson Building. The location is significant in that downtown Seattle was an important destination for unemployed workers in western Washington who sought work or for seasonal and migratory workers who needed a place to spend the winter between jobs. Having a hiring hall, the IUT could compete with the city's employment agencies, which required workers to pay for a job. The union also competed with the IWW for members, and by 1913 the IUT had become openly hostile to the IWW. While the IWW had 640 members in good standing in its National Union of Forest and Lumber Workers, the IUT had 3,500 members in fall 1913. In addition, IUT's number of locals expanded from thirty-three in March to sixty-five in December. Most were in Washington, though the union established locals in Oregon, northern California, British Columbia, Wisconsin, Michigan, New Hampshire, and West Virginia.[2]

The IUT's organizers in the mills and logging camps and financial assistance from the AFL were crucial for the union to grow in membership. Equally important was the *Timber Worker*, a four-page weekly. Reid invited union members to write columns focused on issues relating to the "shingle mills, sawmills, and logging camps." In addition, he declared that the "paper will stand for industrial unionism," and members of the union took up his call for contributions. Every week organizers wrote columns about their activities. Press committees from various locals had their reports and notices published. The newspaper was a fountain of information about issues pertinent to the union membership, whether that be coverage of the state legislature, workplace organizing efforts, strikes, or working conditions. Labor news featured stories both domestic and foreign with the latter usually labor activity in Europe. Reid gave favorable coverage to Progressive Era reforms, especially direct legislation by voters and a minimum wage for women wageworkers. Writing in support of a minimum wage for women was Alice M. Lord, the business agent for the Waitresses' Alliance in Seattle. Lord was successful in leading the effort to achieve the eight-hour day for women wageworkers in the state through legislation in 1911. Although the paper printed articles that openly questioned the value of the legislature, it did provide favorable columns on the work of individual legislators and on those socialists in office or running for office. Ernst P. Marsh, the president of the Washington State Federation of Labor, had regular columns in the newspaper. A former shingle weaver by trade, he argued that legislation was meaningless without an organized working class. The paper voiced a brand of radicalism that criticized the state's legislature, supported socialism, and appealed to working-class consciousness.[3]

For many of the contributors to the *Timber Worker* an organized workforce may have included both male and female workers, but that was not extended to Asian workers, whether immigrant or native-born. Neither were some writers in the paper welcoming to immigrants from eastern and southeastern Europe. One of the greatest fears expressed concerned the opening of the Panama Canal and a subsequent rise in European immigration to the West Coast, which contributors argued would drive down wages and reverse the gains made by unions like the IUT. The workforce the IUT sought to organize, however, was becoming more ethnically diverse. Over the past several years, organizers and the rank and file of the shingle weavers were beginning to accept that diversity. Delbert Hubbell, member of the press committee for Local 26, in South Bend, Washington, writing on the issue of immigration to the West Coast, encouraged his fellow workers to extend "to the newcomers every possible protection of the international [IUT], helping to convert them into an enlightened, class-conscious organization, by keeping in view the motto of our official organ—Agitate, Educate, Federate—which will promote the reality of an early emancipation." Raynor and the press committee of Local 5 expressed in the paper similar sentiments concerning industrial unionism as a unifying force among a diverse workforce, which they experienced in their own local. The press committee wrote, "The industrial form of organization promotes the spirit of brotherly love; it wipes out racial distrust and antagonisms, develops class consciousness and solidarity, obliterates craft narrowness and craft lines and brings into existence one great harmonious family, where neither crafts, color, creed or nationality creates discord. Industrial unionism is humanizing; its effect is beautiful to behold."[4]

Fox along with other members of the IUT were excited about the union's convention, which began on 12 January and for the first time met as an industrial union. Sixty-nine delegates conferred at the Ancient Order of United Workmen Hall in Aberdeen, Washington, for five days. The delegates represented thirty-four locals along with several delegates-at-large and fraternal delegates that included Marsh and W. H. Kingery, a socialist state representative. Fox represented Tacoma's Local 16, a mixed local, and sat on two committees. On the first day, Brown, the vice presidents of the union, and organizers presented their reports to the delegates. The president's report contained a strong argument for the significance of the union's newspaper, which Brown believed could go places that an organizer could not, and could do so week after week. Although he thought the paper was well edited by Reid, Brown suggested that, with the increase in membership, the union had the means to hire someone to assist Reid as an associate editor. He also wanted the associate editor to act as an opinion writer to promote the union in a compelling manner. In Reid's secretary-treasurer report, he noted that circulation of the *Timber Worker* was up 300 percent from last year's *Shingle Weaver*. A. W. Swenson would take over the role of associate editor and editorialist of the union's newspaper. As a member of the International Typographical Union for twenty-three years, he had extensive trade union experience. Soon after the convention he began his work on the newspaper and would eventually have an editorial column titled "Short Jabs," in which he wrote short pieces on a wide range of topics.[5]

The most important development at the convention was support for the eight-hour day throughout the industry. By a roll-call vote, the delegates unanimously called "for the eight-hour day with [a] minimum wage of $2.25 per day in the timber industry." It was to go into effect on 1 May. Support for the eight-hour day had been building for years among the shingle weavers. Fox and other writers for the newspaper immediately began to agitate for the eight-hour day to be the standard workday after the convention. The common sentiment expressed was that eight hours was an adequate period of work, along with eight hours of rest, leaving eight hours for workers to raise their children, educate themselves, become more engaged with the world around them, or simply do as they pleased. Fox voiced his support for the reduced workday by arguing that every worker should "own his job as a birth right." Of course, this was in step with the syndicalist argument that workers should control the means of production through organized labor. Supporters also argued that such a measure would reduce unemployment. Too many out-of-work loggers and mill workers were forced to congregate, for example, on Washington Street in downtown Seattle to search for work at employment agencies or seek food at bread lines or soup kitchens. The eight-hour day would bring some rationality to the industry and reduce the chronic problem of overproduction of product, helping to stop the periodic shutdown of mills and logging camps that threw laborers out of work.[6]

A steady stream of articles began to appear in the newspaper supporting the reduction in the workday. Swenson and Fox continued to voice their support and to offer more rationales for the eight-hour day in their weekly columns. Members of the executive board, organizers, and Marsh met with members of locals to promote the workday demand, to answer questions by the union members, and to entice unorganized shingle and mill workers and loggers interested in the eight-hour day to join the IUT. Fox appeared with Marsh and Brown at an open meeting on 8 February at Liberty Hall in Everett. Fox, who was first to speak at the well-attended event, argued that "all comes to him that takes," for if workers in the timber industry waited for a reduction in the workday they would be working ten hours forever. He stressed that workers themselves needed to organize and enforce a shorter workday in the mills and the logging camps. At the conclusion of the meeting, forty loggers and mill workers applied for membership, bringing the number of recruits since the eight-hour day campaign began to 150. The Everett local's press committee noted that another 248 workers joined in Everett after the 8 February meeting. Local 2, though, was not the only local witnessing positive recruitment numbers. Throughout the spring, organizers and a number of locals' press committees published reports in the *Timber Worker* about the number of workers who joined the union during its campaign for the eight-hour day. Both Fox and Foster had the opportunity to participate in recruiting workers. Fox, who received official approval to organize for the IUT by President Brown, worked as an organizer out of newly acquired office space on Jefferson Avenue in downtown Tacoma. Foster worked as an organizer out of the new loggers' Local 45 in a basement office in Seattle on First Avenue, which had a reading room and was easily accessible to unemployed workers who frequented the Pioneer Square neighborhood.[7]

Although there was great enthusiasm among the IUT—especially among organizers Fox, Foster, Raynor, and C. J. Folsom, an additional AFL organizer for the union—to fight for the eight-hour day at the point of production, Kingery along with a number of other members of the Socialist Party in the state decided to drafted a universal eight-hour law. Now that the state had direct legislation available to voters, the socialists believed that they could circumvent the state legislature with such a proposal and bring it to the citizens for a vote. This unexpected development forced the union to decide between economic action or political action. Even though contributors to the *Timber Worker* and leaders of the union appearing at locals were making impassioned pleas for the membership to support the demand for the eight-hour day beginning on 1 May, a referendum vote on the demand could still take place. The union's constitution mandated a referendum vote if ten or more locals called for one on any resolution passed by the convention. Nine had already done so. Therefore, the executive board called a special convention to meet in Seattle on 26–27 February. At the convention, the delegates opted for the political action. According to Vice President Harry Call, a majority of the convention delegates decided "to advise all local unions to suspend all preparations for the 1st of May and devote all possible energy to the development of sentiment in favor of the 8-hour initiative measure to be voted on at the forthcoming election in November." Fox dissented but was willing to support the decision and encourage members to sign the petition that began circulating in February to get the measure on the ballot. As of early March, twenty-two thousand signatures had already been secured. Nevertheless, contributors to the newspaper argued that the only way to enforce the eight-hour day if it became law was by the unions in the state, which could call strikes, forcing employers to obey the law. Therefore, organization was still key to gaining the eight-hour day.[8]

The opportunity to take advantage of direct legislation motivated a variety of constituencies, frustrated by the legislative process in the state capital, to bring forward measures on the November ballot. Prohibitionists were successful in drafting a measure that would ban, statewide, the sale and manufacture of alcoholic beverages. At the conclusion of the legislative session in 1913, a joint legislative committee formed consisting of the Grange, the Farmers' Union, and the State Federation of Labor. The committee created seven initiatives, dubbed the "Seven Sisters." One of the measures proposed would prohibit employment agencies in the state from requiring workers to pay fees. If passed, "employment sharks" would be effectively eliminated in Washington. Another was a First-Aid Bill that would require employers to pay the first $100 for any worker injured on the job who required medical treatment. The rest of the cost would be borne by the state Industrial Insurance Commission. Given the frequency of accidents in the timber industry, the proposed bill enjoyed great support among the IUT, as did the banning of employment agencies, which preyed on shingle and mill workers and loggers who faced frequent layoffs in the industry. Reid and Swenson provided ample coverage of the petition signing process and encouraged workers to both register to vote and sign the petitions so that the measures would appear on the ballot. Many articles and editorials appeared to support political action that had a direct impact on union members. Illustrating the dangers of working in a lumber mill was a cartoon, titled "Safety First," that depicted four hands with missing fingers and thumbs. The West Coast cartoonist Alfred T. Renfro had several illustrations published that underscored reasons for supporting the initiatives. In one cartoon, an injured worker recuperates from an injury at home, surrounded by his weeping wife and children along with unpaid medical bills.[9]

Employers quickly coalesced into a near united front against the IUT and supported lobbying efforts to convince voters not to vote for the eight-hour universal law and most of the other measures. The editor of *The Timberman*, a West Coast lumber industry publication, argued that the eight-hour day was impractical in the logging camps due to the seasonality and weather conditions that affected operations. Mills, on the other hand, operated based on supply and demand, made the reduced workday unfeasible. In addition, if workers demanded an increase in wages to make up for the lost two hours of employment, that cost would have to be borne by consumers, which may motivate them to seek out other building materials. Finally, the industry as a whole was in terrible condition, especially in the Douglas fir region of the Pacific Northwest. *The Timberman* argued that the industry "at this time is probably at the lowest ebb in its history."[10]

After the first strike of the year in Everett, more strikes and lockouts followed due to open shop policies and wage reductions by employers at mills and logging camps throughout the region. Shingle mill owners in Willapa Harbor were soon purging IUT members from their mills as the owners sought to establish an open shop policy. The company had a significant contract with customers in San Francisco and other parts of California. Fox had strong contacts in the Bay Area and had written for *Organized Labor*, the California Building Trades Council's official publication. The union's executive board dispatched Fox to San Francisco to persuade the council to support the IUT if it were to declare the shingle manufacturers' product unfair to organized labor. After meeting with the council, he was able to secure its cooperation. Once Willapa Harbor shingle mill owners learned of this agreement, the IUT and the manufacturers reached a settlement and the open shop drive ceased. In early April, union members out of the Aberdeen local called a strike at the Coats-Fordney logging camps on Grays Harbor over wage reductions. Six hundred loggers participated in the strike. Even though employers sought scab labor at employment agencies in Portland, Tacoma, and Seattle, the union had pickets in place to try to persuade would-be strikebreakers from accepting employment in the logging camps. Foster helped to organize some of those pickets in Seattle and reported that the "Employers Association" had to give up recruiting scab labor after the employment offices stopped job placement efforts at the logging camps in Grays Harbor.

The union relocated the loggers' Local 45 to the corner of Occidental Avenue and Washington Street in the heart of the "slave market." Foster asserted that having a loggers' local on "skid row" was essential for the union to recruit new members, for thousands of unemployed loggers frequented that potion of downtown Seattle year-round. In his first report published in the *Timber Worker* from the new location, Foster claimed that the IUT "reading room is one of the best on the Pacific Slope. It contains an extensive file of labor papers and magazines of all kinds." Notices in the union newspaper encouraged workers to use the local as a social gathering place where they could meet members of the union, ask question about the union, and, if necessary, have their baggage stored free of charge. Creating solidarity was one of the key aspirations of the IUT locals. Given the industry's frequent layoffs, high turnover rates among the workers at mills and logging camps, and the fact that many of the laborers led a transient lifestyle, the local could be a secure and friendly oasis.[11]

Organizing new shingle and mill workers and loggers to the IUT was extremely difficult given the state of the industry. Brown noted in his April report to the membership that depression had a grip on the lumber economy. The union, however, was determined to resist any wage reductions. Only the shingle weavers had an actual wage scale that the IUT could defend, but a reduction in wages among mill workers and loggers of any kind would be resisted just the same. Some locals were successful in achieving a closed shop in some plants. The OK Mill near Machias, for example, produced a near complete union-made commodity. The work of Raynor out of Machias Local 5 had borne much fruit over the months as he organized both in mills and logging camps. In fact, in one of his reports he noted that at one logging camp two women working in the cook house inquired if they could join the union. Raynor's reply was, of course, that union bars "no one on account of race, color, creed, or sex" who works in the timber industry. They joined. In addition to AFL organizers Raynor and Foster, Fox, who relocated from Tacoma to Seattle to assist Foster at Local 45, received a general organizing commission from the federation in April. George Heatherton, formerly a member of the WFM, was also an AFL organizer for the IUT. Heatherton had an office at the Labor Temple in Vancouver, British Columbia, and AFL organizer Folsom traveled extensively throughout Washington and Oregon. Several of the vice presidents worked as organizers as well, such as Call in Bellingham and J. S. McDonald in Aberdeen. Both vice presidents frequently had their reports published, noting their visits to a variety of locals in their areas, dues collecting, and new members they were able to sign up. The union also had able organizers in Victor Zampatti, who worked out of Local 34 in Fort Bragg, California, and James Jondro, IUT vice-president, president of District 2, and lead organizer in Wisconsin. Northern

California, Wisconsin, and Michigan were extremely important areas for the IUT to extend beyond its Pacific Northwest stronghold.[12]

In late spring, Fox became associate editor, though Swenson still had his "Short Jabs" column in the newspaper. Fox wanted to make the *Timber Worker* different from what he considered typical labor papers. He had "a great dislike for the standard type of labor union journal devoted to drab, generally unimportant union matter [sic] of no educational value, and little read as a result." He was pleased with the feedback he received from his readers on his "Letters to Jack Lumber" and "On the Picket Line" columns. He was especially proud of the "Letters" column, which he believed exhibited "a crisp, snappy style" that "covered every phase of economic and political life as presented in the passing show and brought to Jack just what each incident meant to him." In fact, the column did have similar features to "The Passing Show" in *The Agitator* and *The Syndicalist*. He wanted the *Timber Worker* to be "both interesting and instructive." With "Letters to Jack Lumber," Fox employed an interactive, conversational style of editorializing that he had developed over the years in several different forums. Fox created the character of "Jack Lumber" to represent an average unorganized mill worker or logger, who held a variety of conventional ideas about unions, government, cultural traditions, capitalists, workers, and many other aspects of American society. Jack was not necessarily the most intelligent or well-educated worker. In fact, he could be quite dim-witted and naive. Nevertheless, he asked questions that Fox was all too willing to respond to in the form of a letter. In some respects Jack Lumber was similar to the featured character in Ernest Riebe's cartoon strip *Mr. Block* that began to appear in the IWW's western newspaper, the *Industrial Worker*, in 1912 until the newspaper folded the following year, though the strip continued to appear in Wobbly publications sporadically into the 1920s. Riebe used Mr. Block character to enlighten readers to the folly of trusting the basic attributes of American society. In Fox's letters to Jack, he achieved something similar. Writing a column rather than a cartoon strip allowed him to go into greater depth as he responded to Jack's questions.[13]

Periodically, Fox used his own personal experiences—whether actual, embellished, or completely fictionalized—to instruct Jack on the important role a union could play in a worker's life. In one letter, Fox empathized with Jack's ignorance and likened it to his own as a youth. He wrote that early in life he looked up to his father, a sober, hardworking section hand on the railroad, who went to church every Sunday with Fox's mother. His father always voted the straight Democratic ticket, never belonged to a union, and successfully paid off his mortgage on the family home. Nevertheless, he never rose above working a square-mouth shovel ten hours a day for $1.50. Fox wrote that he was proud of his father—that is, until he met Casey, the sewer digger, who became a mentor. He used Casey, an Irish immigrant, to explain how he became a class-conscious member of the working class and a dedicated union man. In his fictionalized encounter with the sewer digger, Fox learned that Casey cared little for government. Casey noted, "I don't care who is elected president of the United States: that doesn't affect sewer diggin'. The president can't raise my wages or prevent the boss from lowering it. But the union can. The president of the United States doesn't come around and say, 'How are you gettin' on Casey! Does the boss treat ye right? Have ye any complaint to make against him?' But the president of the union does." Casey goes on to ask, "What . . . makes a good American citizen if not a well-fed, well-clothed, well-housed, light-worked, independent workingman?" From Casey, Fox learned that "unionism is the highest form of citizenship, and the first duty of every working man is to be a union man." Fox told Jack that he took Casey's point of view to heart and resolved that he would become a union man and use all of his powers to persuade others to do likewise because it is the only way a worker could permanently improve his lot in life.[14]

Fox staked out his radical orientation early in his writing for the union paper. In one of his letters to Jack, he offered a scathing critique of patriotism, the democratic republican system of government, and the much praised ideal of American freedom. The Declaration of Independence, he noted, was sent "forth to the world as the voice of the oppressed defying the tyrant masters, black men were chattel slaves and white men were wage slaves in this country and the remarkable thing about it was the Declaration referred to neither of them." Once the revolution was won, with workers and small farmers doing most of the fighting, the patriots—behind closed doors—wrote up the Constitution. The new system of government, from the working-class point of view, merely changed the political bosses. Freedom in this country, Fox wanted Jack to know, is a farce: so long as a few individuals "own the wealth of the country and you and I must go to them and make terms for the right to exist on the earth, we have no freedom." Moreover, he argued, "There will be liberty in America when you and I establish it; not by changing the form of government but by changing the ownership of the job." The only way to make that possible was for workers to organize. Through the union, workers can establish changes in the workplace when it came to hours and working conditions. The union, he continued, "is the bulwark of liberty, because it is based on the job." He did not want his readers to put any faith in the government, for it was "an organization of property owners designed to protect their property." He noted that was why he wanted his readers to have a clear understanding of what government does when it comes to workers, which is that it oppresses them, as evidenced in recent strikes in Michigan, Colorado, and in other parts of the country. "I want to convince you at least, not by theory but by fact, that there is nothing in the patriotic liberty dope." "Liberty," he believed, "for the workers must come from their own efforts and the union is the organization through which they will gather strength and knowledge for the fight."[15]

Fox argued for a unified organized labor movement to achieve both immediate and long-term gains, but he did not extend that unified front to include the IWW. He frequently listened to Wobbly soap-boxers "knock" the IUT and the AFL on the streets of Seattle. He argued that if the Wobblies were true friends of labor, they would support the timber workers, regardless of affiliation, for their union was organized based on industry, just as the IWW maintained all unions should be. Fox defended his union's affiliation with the AFL and criticized Wobblies for arguing that the AFL was incapable of evolving. If that was so, how was the IUT's affiliation with the labor body possible? According to Fox, the IWW's dual union strategy was downright disastrous for organized labor, for it pitted workers against each other. Wobblies should be endorsing the effort to build an industrial union in timber. Fox was critiquing Wobbly orthodoxy but also the "slamming" of brother unionists. Given that Local 45 was on Washington Street and within earshot of constant Wobbly soap-boxing outside the window of their offices, Fox and Foster, who also penned articles in the *Timber Worker* critical of the IWW, decided to organize a debate between representatives of the IUT and the IWW. Foster volunteered to represent the IUT, and the union asked Wobbly James P. Thompson, a regular on the soapbox, to stand for the IWW. The debate was scheduled at the Seattle Labor Temple. Thompson, however, declined, claiming he thought Foster did not have the stature worthy of debating. Fox defended his friend and fellow organizer, noting that Foster was an experienced union man with a penetrating intellect and great knowledge of the labor movement in the United States and abroad.[16]

A feature of the newspaper that Fox had to deal with as associate editor was racist, xenophobic, and ethnocentric language used by contributors, who came from both the union leadership as well as the rank and file. Fox did not use racial epithets or indulge in fearmongering over newly arrived eastern and southeastern European immigrants. Reid, on the other hand, did use racist language at times and demonstrated a hostility toward "unrestricted European immigration." Fox did not criticize union officials or union members directly. He preferred to use his columns to educate his readers by offering an alternative perspective. Occasionally, he did use terms such as "dirty foreigners," "Mexican greasers," and "Japs," but always sarcastically. He would provide examples of how these supposedly "ignorant" and racially "inferior" Greek, Italian, Mexican, and Japanese workers instigated strikes and organized successfully for their own interests. He would contrast their direct action as workers with white workers—who thought of themselves as ethnically or racially "superior"—as compliant, docile, and accepting of their exploitation. In *The Syndicalist*, Fox was more explicit in his praise, for instance, of Japanese immigrant workers who organized among themselves in California to achieve better pay and improve their working conditions. He lauded the Japanese agricultural workers' temerity to demand from their employer a bathtub at their living quarters, something he thought white agricultural workers would never even consider. He ultimately blamed both the economic system and white racism that divided workers and undermined the inclusion of the Japanese into the ranks of organized labor.[17]

Fox had a noticeable impact on the culture of the newspaper after he became associate editor, evident in more articles condemning racism as well as pieces about and by women workers. The anti-racist articles usually were geared toward organized labor and the need for working-class unity. A short article by Jacques Loeb, the German-born biologist and physiologist, titled "The Fetish of Race" argued that labor unions were making a serious mistake by indulging in race prejudice toward Asians and African Americans. Moreover, Loeb believed that the promotion of "racial superiority" by whites in the United States could lead to war against the Japanese at some point. Another short piece, "Devil of Race Hatred" by the cartoonist

Art Young, a frequent contributor to *The Masses*, argued, "Until we learn to judge every individual on his own peculiar merits, we haven't taken a first good step toward social intelligence." In a piece quoting Peter Radford of the National Farmers' Union, Fox presented information about the toiling of hundreds of thousands of black women in the cotton fields of the South, whose lives, he noted, had changed little since the Emancipation Proclamation when it came to their working and living conditions. Fox provided statistical information about the increase in female employment. He noted that although white women had far more job opportunities than black women, their wages were poor, whether they were in professions or trades. Writing in support of women entering the labor force in greater numbers was the feminist and suffragette Anna Cadogan. In her article, she argued that "women should be self-supporting for the good of their souls," and she was especially encouraged by the increasing number of women engaged in the professions.[18]

Fox's anarcho-syndicalism was thinly veiled for readers familiar with that form of labor radicalism. It was highly unlikely that most readers would think of him as an anarchist, for he shared some of the same criticisms of the government, the legal system, and class oppression as other columnists in the *Timber Worker*, Everett's *Labor Journal* and the *Washington Socialist*, and the *Seattle Union Record*. Therefore, his overall perspective was not out of step with literature available for union members and workers in general who read such newspapers. It also was not uncommon for readers of these periodicals and even in the nonlabor press to read sympathetic columns on the Mexican Revolution and the revolutionaries imprisoned in the United States. Fox informed his readers that he was there, in January, along with several others to greet Ricardo and Enrique Magón and two other revolutionaries as they were released from McNeil Island Penitentiary. They had served two years, according to Fox, "for the atrocious crime of being Mexican revolutionists on American soil." Before they headed back to Los Angeles to resume work on *Regeneración*, they made a number of appearances in Seattle, Everett, and Tacoma. William Owen, who came north to greet his comrades at the gates of the prison, helped organized several of the engagements. Ricardo's English was less than fluent, though he did speak at the gatherings. Owen, however, could translate for Magón and the others and present his own remarks regarding the ongoing conflict in Mexico. In Tacoma, Hammersmark headed the local greeting committee, which included Gertie Vose of Home Colony.

Fox used his column to give voice to the revolutionary cause of Magón, the PLM, and those Mexicans who were not satisfied with post-Díaz governments. Much of his wrath, though, was targeted at American capitalists who were looting Mexico. Most Americans, Fox thought, seemed indifferent to what was taking place and the fact that the United States was prepared to invade the country. He took the opportunity to explain to his readers that Mexicans were fighting for "land and liberty." Moreover, he argued in his column that the United States was hostile to the Mexican revolutionaries because the federal government had become a counterrevolutionary force on the world stage, no different from the empires of Europe. Fox wanted his readers to appreciate the courage that Mexicans were demonstrating; furthermore, if the US military invaded Mexico, he felt that American workers should rise up and instigate "a new American Revolution [which] would be the most wonderful thing in the world—it would start the flame of liberty around the globe." A limited invasion did take place in Veracruz later in April over the Tampico Affair, resulting in the deaths of over twenty American servicemembers and several hundred Mexicans. Fox referred to this incursion as "murder and plunder by the U.S. in Mexico" and lamented the fact that while the Mexicans were willing to fight for their liberty and to take possession of the land, American workers, as members of the military, were willing to kill and die for imperialism.[19]

Fox wanted the *Timber Worker* to be an important resource for IUT members: educational, motivational, and above all read. In four pages, the paper could not provide all that a reader may have desired. The *Seattle Union Record* was a more comprehensive labor newspaper available for workers in the Pacific Northwest, but the *Timber Worker* was offered as one of the benefits that came with being a member in good standing with the IUT. Reid and Fox encouraged locals to offer more information about the goings on in their area and among their members. They responded with news regarding organizing efforts, conditions in mills and logging camps, and the state of the industry. Occasionally, locals published moving tributes to a loyal union member who had passed away. Given the transient nature of mill workers and especially loggers, Reid and Fox provided space for family members and friends to communicate with members, who may have had no permanent residence where they could receive mail. With "Among the Witsmiths," Fox brought a column of working-class humor to the newspaper in the form of jokes, wordplay, witty observations of social conventions, Scottish patter, repartee, and humorous stories. Another feature Fox brought to the paper was poetry. Almost every issue of *The Agitator* featured a poem, and once Fox became associate editor of the *Timber Worker* most issues ran a poem and sometimes two. The poetry most often focused on the plight of the working class, the power of organized labor, and with the advent of the First World War anti-war poems.[20]

Fox built on the existing militancy in the newspaper, which included his own writings as discussed above but also the reprinting of articles from other periodicals. With the *Seattle Union Record* and the *Labor Journal*, for example, both having a strong socialist influence and an open acknowledgment of class conflict, the *Timber Worker* was not out of step with other labor newspapers in the Pacific Northwest. Nevertheless, Fox featured literature by syndicalists, but he did not always refer to the writers as such. Foster, of course, was a member of the IUT and had a number of articles published as an organizer and an opinion writer. After he left the union, he continued to appear in the paper as a special correspondent writing mostly from Chicago. One piece in particular Fox published was Foster's "Militant Tactics for Thirty Years." In the article, Foster provides a brief overview of the origin of the revolutionary union movement, which he argued began in Chicago in the mid-1880s. The Chicago anarchists were that first militant minority who sought to radicalize the existing labor movement, making Chicago, for a time, the center of the most revolutionary labor movement in the world. He lamented the current labor movement there, which lacked that militant minority, and he lambasted radicals who preferred to philosophize and agitate in "Bughouse Square," a famed center of free speech in the city, rather than enter existing labor unions and do the hard work of turning conservative trade unions into a revolutionary force in society. He criticized these radicals for sneering at trade unions and their members while lionizing the IWW, which Foster argued was simply "straight-jacket unionism" that created "still-born unions."[21]

In addition, Fox published work by a number of young radical writers, such as Max Eastman, editor of *The Masses*, and John Reed, a frequent contributor to the magazine. Another radical writer Fox featured was the Danish-born Caroline Nelson, whose work could be found in a number of labor and radical journals. At this point in her career, she was based in San Francisco, a member and organizer for the IWW, and a member of the San Francisco Birth Control League. Fox reprinted a long excerpt from her pamphlet *Aggressive Unionism*, which he noted to his readers could be purchased for a dime from the publisher Hammersmark in Tacoma. Fox considered her pamphlet "an inspiration." The portion available for readers in the union paper focused on "building the new society within the old," which was a goal for both Wobblies and syndicalists. She presented a brief overview of the origins of labor unions as medieval guilds that contributed to the development of "free cities," an argument similar to that made by Kropotkin in *Mutual Aid*. Her analysis of the evolution of craft unions into industrial unions was in sync with the ideas of Fox, Foster, and the international anarcho-syndicalist movement in general. She presented an analysis of the ideas of Fernand Pelloutier, one of the key founders of the CGT in France. She noted that the "Syndicalist society" advocated by Pelloutier "will not settle into any unchangeable forms, but will always be able to adapt itself to the needs of the times, because its social basis will be a living, evolving organization." This, of course, was music to the ears of Fox in regard to the evolution of labor unions and the economic structure of society based on industrial unions. Nelson went on to criticize state socialists who barely focused on the freedom of individual workers, acting instead as cogs in an industrial machine controlled by capitalists. Little, she argued, would change if industries were controlled by the state. However, if workers could self-manage, they would be in control of labor systems and could transform the culture of work to make it more fulfilling and end the divisions between the skilled and unskilled trades.[22]

Fox maintained his connection to the anarchist movement throughout his involvement with the IUT. For example, he contributed to *The Revolutionary Almanac 1914*, edited by Havel, as well as to anarchist and syndicalist periodicals. He brought to the attention of the Freedom Group in London the evolution of the shingle weavers union into a progressive industrial union where he thought anarchists belonged. He sent the *Timber Worker* in exchange for *Freedom*, so that it could be available to IUT members and visitors to the union's reading room in downtown Seattle. As associate editor, Fox brought to readers excerpts and articles by anarchists, though he did not make their anarchism explicit. Fox published a long excerpt from de Cleyre's essay "Crime and Punishment," based on a speech she gave at the

Social Science Club of Philadelphia in 1903. In March 1914, the piece appeared in a collection of her poems and essays issued by Mother Earth Publishing Association. Fox assisted in raising funds for the publication for his friend and fellow anarchist who passed away in 1912. In his "On the Picket Line" editorial, he wrote glowingly of her attributes as a poet, writer, and thinker, claiming that through her writing "she was the very soul of labor itself." He provided a brief overview of the collection and how it could be purchased. Fox also published an excerpt from the anarchist Dyer D. Lum's *Philosophy of Trade Unions*. The essay was originally published, as a series of articles, in the *Bakers' Journal* in the 1890s, which was edited by the anarchist Henry Weismann, which the AFL then republished in pamphlet form, from which Fox gleaned an excerpt. Lum encouraged labor unions to make the practice of recruitment of nonunion workers a central part of union activity. They must be persuaded to join; therefore, education was paramount. This coincided with themes in Fox's writings and those of others in the newspaper. Fox obviously had the freedom to bring such voices to the *Timber Worker*. He wanted the newspaper to be a stimulating experience for workers, whether members of the union or not, since the paper was available at newsstands. The support he received for his work as associate editor was an indication that he was not too radical for either the union leadership or for the rank and file, as both officials and ordinary members commended him for his insightful essays and sometimes humorous writing style.[23]

When war broke out in Europe in August, Fox wrote to Jack that "the greatest slaughter the world has ever seen" had commenced. He did not bother with the political, diplomatic, and military alliances and policies that brought on the war. He preferred instead to critique the thin veneer of civilization that masks the savage underbelly and to attack those who exploit that savagery and keep workers in a deep state of ignorance. He argued that "patriotism, nationality, religion, the color line are all promulgated, fostered and kept at a fever heat so the workers of the world may be more easily kept apart and a sufficient number of them ever ready to fly at each others [sic] throats across imaginary boundary lines." Fox claimed that those who started the war had no problem with the killing that a modern conflict would bring, for they already accepted the daily death toll that workers experienced in industry. What the rulers—both capitalists and politicians—feared was the militant minority, who were "wise to their game."

The militant minority that consisted of socialists, syndicalists, anarchists, and unionists will cry out, "Down with all exploiters and parasites; down with war and its carnage; down with capitalism and its cruelty; away with imaginary boundary lines—there is no race but one, the human race; there is not religion but one. Humanity."

Fox was not a lone voice in the newspaper against the war and war preparedness. A series of anti-war and anti-preparedness articles written about the existing conflict in Europe either by contributors to the newspaper or reprints from labor publications and other periodicals throughout the country frequently appeared. Fox, though, was distinctive in connecting the war to the militant minority and to a lesser degree the great possibilities of a postwar labor resurgence. Again, Fox and the *Timber Worker* were not out of step with other labor and socialist newspapers in the Pacific Northwest or throughout the country in general. Anti-war sentiment and hostility toward preparing for war was prevalent throughout much of the labor movement before 1916, when the United States' entry into the conflict began to seem inevitable. Fox did publish Kropotkin's support of the Allied Powers, which generated a great deal of conflict within the international anarchist movement. Kropotkin's article appeared as a letter in London's *Freedom* in September and was then republished worldwide. Fox introduced Kropotkin as a scientist and revolutionary who offered a historical perspective on the origins of the war and what was at stake if the Allies succumbed to the Central Powers. Fox in one of his editorials did not think that Germany would prevail, though he never went as far as Kropotkin to openly support the Allies. He, like many anarchists in the United States and beyond, maintained an anti-war position.[24]

Over the course of the last six months of 1914 and into early 1915, Fox's influence on the *Timber Worker* was having an effect on the print culture of the newspaper, for it was taking on more attributes of *The Syndicalist* and *The Agitator*. It was becoming less newsy and more educational in nature, and it definitely reflected an anarcho-syndicalist sensibility that did not exist before Fox and Foster began writing for it. It had evolved into a wide-ranging labor newspaper that was supportive of syndicalism, industrial unionism, and socialism. The criticism of the Washington state legislature was as common as ever, though more articles questioning the political system as an institution, with an emphasis on union organization and direct economic action, became more prevalent. Single-column articles and reporting, though, were less frequent and more two-column essays appeared. Far more reprinted articles by radical writers unaffiliated with specific unions or who were outright advocates of syndicalism appeared as well. The types of racist and xenophobic articles published in 1913 and early 1914 were replaced by those condemning racism. More articles supporting greater labor unity and the role of women in the labor movement were published as well as more pieces written by women themselves. The newspaper maintained a staunchly pro-AFL and anti-IWW orientation. The libertarian nature of the AFL was promoted just as the disruptive nature of Wobbly activity was routinely denounced. Although the *Timber Worker* had become more distinctive in comparison to the *Seattle Union Record*, the *Labor Journal*, and the *Washington Socialist*, it was not entirely out of step with those publications that were easily purchased at newsstands or could be found in reading rooms or public libraries. One of the reasons the newspaper was becoming less newsy, specifically concerning the IUT and its locals, was the extreme difficulties the union faced. Frankly, there was less good news to report and the list of strikes and lockouts in the industry in Washington, Oregon, British Columbia, and California was growing longer.

While such actions took a considerable amount of the union's time, a good deal of attention was placed on the Seven Sisters and the eight-hour bill. Reid, Brown, Swenson, and other contributors to the newspaper, and to a lesser degree Fox, urged members and readers of the *Timber Worker* to sign petitions for all the initiatives. Rising in opposition was the Stop-Look-Listen League (SLLL), organized by E. A. Sims, a Port Townsend, Washington, Republican member of the state house and leading advocate for corporate fishing interests in the state capital, along with several Republican operatives. They encouraged voters not to sign the petitions. The SLLL ran advertisements in newspapers across the state, published pamphlets, and held meetings in many cities, denouncing the initiatives as an abuse of the new direct election process and the higher taxes the organization claimed would emerge if the initiatives passed. They eight-hour day, the group and their supporters argued in newspaper opinion pages, was completely unworkable in Washington, for the state relied heavily on extractive industries such as logging, fishing, and agriculture. Even after the petitions were delivered to Secretary of State I. M. Howell, the SLLL tried to have as many of the signatures rejected as possible in an effort to invalidate the process. At the organization's urging, Howell, who employed nearly two hundred clerks to review the petitions and other aspects of the proceedings, worked with the state attorney general to reject as many signatures as possible. In the end, the initiatives that were most significant to the IUT members and other workers in the state made it onto the November ballot. The league, though, would continue a campaign against the initiatives up to the day of the fall elections. Moreover, editorials in newspapers throughout the state spoke out against the initiatives, in particular the eight-hour day.[25]

The IUT countered the SLLL in the pages of the *Timber Worker*, but the union also had to wage a battle on the economic front against employers seeking to lower wages and in some cases purge union members from the mills. A Centralia strike was in its fifth week with no end in sight. The mill owners attempted to restart the mill but could not secure enough replacement labor and had to reclose. A union committee tried to meet with the mill owners but were coldly rebuffed. The mayor of the city as well as several ministers tried to mediate, but they were given no hearing by the mill owners. According to organizer Folsom, the new local sent "two thousand circular letters to farmers and tradesmen in the surrounding rural districts" that explained why the mill workers were on strike and appealed for some support in the form of food, clothing, or whatever people in the region could donate. Folsom used his column about the strike to remind IUT members of the need for a fund for a prolonged strike and lauded the courage of the strikers in Centralia who had no financial backing. The strikers, for their part, quickly learned how to maintain an organized picket line. Their IUT local established a commissary, which distributed support based on need rather than giving an equal amount to each striker, thereby ensuring that those members with families received more than single men. IUT locals donated food to the strikers, while others used social events to raise funds to send to Centralia. The Port Angeles local hosted a dance, which generated money that organizer Raynor was on hand to collect and send to the strikers.[26]

Later in October, the mill workers and loggers in Port Angeles had to contend with the Puget Sound Mills and Timber Company issuing an across-the-board wage cut of 10 percent for all employees regardless of skill. The company operated two large mills and logging camps and argued that the depression in the industry forced their hand. The only workers organized in the mills were shingle weavers. Almost every member walked out along with a number of nonunion workers. Unorganized loggers in the camps walked off the job site as well. Without access to the mainstream press to explain the position of the strikers, the Port Angeles local issued a circular to inform the public as to why a strike was necessary. At the beginning of the month the Silver Lake Manufacturing Company in Maple Falls, Washington, cut wages, prompting a walkout by workers there too, who were then locked out for not accepting the new pay scale. By the end of the month, the IUT had to deal with twelve strikes and lockouts in the state. Picket lines and efforts to dissuade scab labor from taking positions in the mills became a constant struggle for the IUT. Adding to the woes of the union were mills and logging camps closing down due to the market situation for lumber. This resulted in more unemployed lumber industry workers. Officials of locals along with organizers and Vice President Call had to resort to publishing the names of scabs be they nonunion workers or members of the IUT. The latter were expelled from the union. Reid and Fox did not enjoy publishing these announcements, but shaming workers seemed a necessary policy to maintain solidarity.[27]

To make matters worse for the union, the elections turned out to be a disaster for the progressive forces in the state and for those who believed political action could achieve results for the working class. The eight-hour measure was defeated by a large margin and only one of the original Seven Sisters passed—the abolition of private employment agencies. The Republicans scored a landslide victory. The progressive coalition of the state's labor federation, grange, and farmers' union—which had drafted the Seven Sisters and been a major political factor in the state for the previous four years—collapsed. According to the *Washington Standard*, the progressive vote fell by 50 percent. Perhaps due to prohibition being on the ballot, a more conservative electorate turned out on Election Day, which saw the highest voter turnout in the state's history. Moreover, a number of large employers in the mills and logging camps threatened to close operations if the eight-hour law passed, arguing that they could not compete with lumber being produced by companies in other states employing workers on a ten-hour basis.

After some reflection, articles appeared in the *Timber Worker* appraising the election results. Marsh reasoned that the forces arrayed against the initiatives and the eight-hour day had greater access to voters via the mainstream press. The constant drumbeat of anti-reform legislation in large and small newspapers across the state proved too difficult to combat. Even though Washington had seven socialist periodicals, according to historian Jeffrey Johnson, along with a number of labor newspapers and newspapers favorable to labor, their circulation was too small to reach a majority of the voters. Marsh, Brown, and others tried to persuade workers that through their unions they could increase their wages, but for many workers who only made two dollars a day for ten hours of labor feared that a reduced workday would leave then with too little to live on. Fox, who never thought achieving the eight-hour day through legislation was feasible, explained to Jack why that was the case. Employers obviously did not want the reduced workday because that would cut into their profits. The professional class who hired house servants would be voting against their own interests if the workday were reduced. Salaried workers perhaps feared a trimming of their earnings. Farmers, who in many instances were employers themselves, did not want state inference in the workplaces they controlled. Of the working class, those under twenty-one were unable to vote. Immigrants could not vote. Itinerant workers, who were a large segment of the workforce in extractive industries and had no fixed place of residence, were unable to vote. Other workers, Fox noted, were indifferent or fearful of lower wages. That left only a minority of voters for the eight-hour measure. However, Fox thought this could be a valuable lesson for Jack. He asserted that "there is only one method by which we have gained anything of material value, and this is organization and strike."[28]

For the rest of the year and into 1915, the union had to confront recalcitrant employers, city governments that favored employers over striking mill and shingle workers, and a growing unemployment problem. Centralia's local issued another circular to explain to the public the reasons for the strike. Coming to the aid of the company was the state's Merchants' and Manufacturers' Association. The group, working with the company, drafted an anti-picketing ordinance to put before the city commissioners. The local asked the city if representatives could be present at the hearing, but the mayor refused. The local was able to get into Centralia's *Daily Hub* a resolution stating that the proposed ordinance would violate the strikers' constitutional rights of free speech and free assembly. It was to no avail. The ordinance passed, but pickets continued to do their work in front of the company gates, leading to the arrest of twenty-nine strikers whose cases promptly went to trial. The arrested picketers demanded separate trials, which turned out to be a fiasco for the city officials, law enforcement, and the company. Hundreds of strikers and residents of the city turned out in subsequent days to picket the mill. The ordinance simply became unenforceable. The *Daily Hub* carried a number of stories favorable to the striking workers, noting that strikers and their families were needlessly suffering and that the city's business interests were undermined by a handful of men who refused to work out a solution with the workers.[29]

As the strikes and lockouts dragged on, the Port Angeles local set up a commissary, where two hot meals were served every day. Every evening, according to Raynor, dozens of men, women, and children took their meals there. In his article about the commissary, he wrote, "I see fifty members of the working class, my brothers and sisters of toil, assembled at a common table. I am taken back in imagination to the splendid co-operation, brotherhood and communism of the early Christians." In Centralia, the workers began to sell firewood at the commissary to bring in needed income. Some charitable donations arrived before Christmas for the children: the *Seattle Times* and some of the merchants in Centralia contributed candy, nuts, and fruit. Fox's former partner Esther donated stockings she was able to gather from her contacts in the garment industry in Chicago. Eventually, Brown had to make an appearance at one of the strikers' daily meetings. He announced that because the union's "treasury was rapidly being depleted" it could no longer support the strike. He told them that there was no shame in calling off the action. The workers, however, voted to persevere in their fight. Later in January, Marsh and the state labor federation tried to continue to support the workers in Centralia, if not in funds at least in morale support. In a similar manner and for similar reasons, the IUT pulled its support for the locked-out workers in Port Angeles. The workers, though, continued to maintain their picket line and commissary, and refused to accept the company's wage scale. Unfortunately, the strikers and locked-out workers could not endure their situation indefinitely. The following spring the strike was called off in Centralia and some of the shingle weavers in Port Angeles returned to work at the mill or in other mills that began to slowly open up in other parts of the state. Workers were forced to accept whatever wages employers offered.[30]

Against this backdrop, the IUT's convention took place on a cold, gray January morning in Anacortes, Washington, at the Eagles Hall. The attendees were from western Washington, British Columbia, and Wisconsin. It was telling that a majority of the locals did not send delegates. Fox represented

Local 45. The attendees passed a series of resolutions. The most difficult resolution for Fox emerged out of his own committee. It resolved that given the *Timber Worker*'s drain on IUT finances the number of issues published per month needed to be reduced. It was thought by the committee that funds could be better spent on supporting striking members.[31] From the president, vice presidents, and organizers' reports to the convention, several common themes emerged. The industry was depressed. The expected opening of logging camps and mills in the spring did not happen. Those that did open tended to run at low production levels, and wage reductions were implemented in many regions. In this atmosphere, recruiting loggers and mill workers was extremely difficult, whether in Washington, Oregon, California, Wisconsin, Michigan, or British Columbia. District vice presidents all noted that many workers expressed interest in joining the IUT, but most would not follow through. Raising funds to fight the ongoing strikes and lockouts was proving quite difficult, for the union did not have an adequate strike fund. Although the situation for the union seemed bleak, most attendees took heart in the possibilities that 1915 could offer. Moreover, everyone seemed to believe that the timber industry was bound to revive in the spring. In fact, every vice president requested organizers to be sent to their districts as soon as funds were available.[32]

In the issue that contained the proceedings of IUT convention the *Timber Worker* announced that it would become a biweekly publication; however, after the 15 February issue appeared, no more issues followed. The *Labor Journal* and the *Seattle Union Record* became the primary news outlet of the IUT. For Fox, the demise of the *Timber Worker* brought an end to one of the most significant writing experiences of his life. Never before and never again would he have the opportunity to be a member of an industrial union and have a prominent position as an editorialist, reporter, and associate editor for that union's newspaper. Even though he had two columns in most issues of the newspaper beginning in late 1913 and continuing into early 1915, he found other venues for his labor journalism after joining the IUT, such as the *American Federationist*, in which he wrote reports on the activities of the IUT. Fox's "Dear Jack" columns and "On the Picket Line" editorials were reprinted in *Painter and Decorator*, *Seaman's Journal*, *Railway Carmen's Journal*, *American Photo Engraver*, *Sheet Metal Workers' Journal*, and *Journeyman Barber*, among others. Fox's work in the *Timber Worker* was republished in *Organized Labor* and the *Seattle Union Record*. Both publications carried his piece on labor spies and how they operate in unions. Fox went into a detailed explanation of how such operatives or "stoolpigeons" infiltrate a union to create "disruption," identify organizers to employers, and reveal sensitive union information, all while being paid by a detective agency or directly by an employer. The editor of *Organized Labor* urged subscribers to "read every word of it."[33]

Despite Fox's presence in the IUT as an anarcho-syndicalist along with other syndicalists in unions in trades and industries in other states, as a whole the syndicalist movement was flagging. It was becoming a disconnected association of militants in parts of the Midwest and West Coast without success anywhere else in the country, and the SLNA barely functioned outside of Chicago and a few midwestern cities. *The Toiler*, in its last issue, announced "an informal Syndicalist conference," with Max Dezettel encouraging syndicalists throughout the country to attend. With the *Timber Worker* on hiatus the second half of January, Fox was free to attend following the IUT convention. The small gathering of syndicalists, primarily from Chicago, Kansas City, Omaha, and St. Louis, met to assess the movement. The delegates decided to create a new organization along the same lines as the SLNA, but with a national board headquartered in Chicago and a newspaper, the *Chicago Labor News*, with Dezettel serving as editor. Fox along with Jack Johnstone, Jack Carney, Joseph Manley, and others were elected by conference delegates to the executive board, and Foster became the secretary of the International Trade Union Educational League (ITUEL). The *Seattle Union Record* published the ITUEL "Manifesto" later in the spring, which invited "all militant union men and women to join with" the new organization to revitalize the labor movement, stay clear of "dual industrial unions," and work to amalgamate trade unions into larger labor associations that could naturally evolve into industrial unions. Although the ITUEL planned to produce a number of pamphlets, only Foster's *Trade Unionism: The Road to Freedom* was to appear later in the year.[34]

Although boring within AFL unions was still the syndicalists' primary strategy, the IUT, one of the most promising opportunities for the movement, was in such a weakened condition that employers took full advantage and moved against the industrial union's largest local. In Everett, shingle mill owners posted a notice that a wage cut of 20 percent would go into effect on 1 March. Local 2 voted to strike on 22 February, which began the biggest action in IUT's short history. Employers were able to obtain an injunction against the union's picketing effort, but the IUT ignored the order and picketed anyway. With many of the mills idle for lack of labor, only two mills could continue to operate. Employers erected barricades surrounding the mills, a common practice that was put in place in Centralia and Port Angeles as well. Conflict ensued among pickets, scabs, and employers' hired gunmen resulting in riotous events in late April. Brown, having previously been against cooperative enterprises to produce shingles or lumber, was able to secure several idle mills in Everett for union members to operate. In other parts of the state and region, the IUT was engaged in more strikes than at the end of the previous year. Some were settled in the union's favor, such as in Grays Harbor and Doty, but others were lost, including the strike in Everett. In the mill owners' defense, they claimed that the timber industry was driving their need to lower wages, though Marsh in an article in the *Labor Journal* pointed out that a number of mills operating in Washington were paying the union scale of wages. Nevertheless, more strikes and lockouts continued as the year wore on. In all, the IUT would fight fifty-five strikes and lockouts and lose most of them. Making the situation worse in Washington for the IUT and organized labor in general was anti-union legislation emerging from a more conservative state legislature after the devastating elections for progressives and socialists the previous fall. One of the most significant anti-labor bills was an anti-picking ordinance that prohibited picketing within five hundred feet of businesses in labor disputes.[35]

By the time the AFL convened its annual convention in November, the IUT was in serious distress. Its membership was in the hundreds at best, mostly shingle weavers. Therefore the industrial union had to surrender its charter at the convention. In 1916, however, the shingle weavers were able to rise from the ashes of the IUT and establish the International Shingle Weavers' Union (ISWU). By April, the ISWU held a well-attended convention of close to thirty delegates at the Labor Temple in Seattle and could boast of twenty-four locals in Washington, Oregon, California, Wisconsin, and Michigan. At the ISWU convention, the delegates voted in favor of establishing trade agreements with employers in the hope of minimizing strikes and lockouts. Brown again was elected president, and one of the vice presidents was Marsh. The non–shingle weaver locals, now stranded, did not completely disband. Those that continued to maintain their locals cooperated with each other to rebuild as an industrial union of mill workers and loggers, which they were able to do as the new International Union of Timber Workers in January 1917 at their convention in Aberdeen. In the spring, the Washington State Labor Federation endorsed the new IUT and around the same time it received a charter from AFL.[36]

7. An Anarcho-Syndicalist Adrift

E ARLY IN 1915, FOX WAS PREOCCUPIED WITH HIS WORK WITH THE IUT and the newly founded ITUEL. In addition, he continued to have his articles published in the labor and radical presses and traveled back and forth between Seattle and Home with forays to the Midwest. The New York Free Speech League, which had taken up Fox's case after the ruling by the Washington State Supreme Court, continued the appeals process. The case eventually made its way to the United States Supreme Court in mid-January. New York attorney Gilbert F. Roe represented Fox for the Free Speech League. He made similar arguments that James J. Anderson made at the first trial, and the prosecuting attorneys made similar arguments to the earlier trial as well. The court issued its decision on 23 February, unanimously upholding the lower court ruling. Justice Oliver Wendell Holmes Jr. wrote the court opinion, arguing that "by indirection but unmistakably, the article encourages and incites a persistence in what we must assume would be a breach of the state law against indecent exposure." Rather than criticism of the law, however, the court ruled that Fox's article was an "incitement to crime." Holmes concluded the opinion by stating "Of course we have nothing to do with the wisdom of the defendant, the prosecution, or the act. All that concerns us is that it cannot be said to infringe on the Constitution of the United States." After reading the court's decision, Fox was also able to read a critique of that decision in the *Central Law Journal*, which argued that the state law did not clearly indicate when an individual crosses the line and violates the law. The journal's editor was disappointed that the federal Supreme Court did not seem to think that was an issue. The justice's final comments and the sentiments of the law journal editor were of little consolation for Fox, for he was going to have to serve his two-month prison sentence.[1]

Neither Fox's lawyer nor IUT president J. G. Brown were not prepared to end the fight. In May, they both sought to lobby Governor Ernest Lister to issue Fox a pardon. Anderson wrote a lengthy appeal in which he explained the history of the case and the court proceedings. He argued that the appeals process only ruled on the constitutionality of the law and not on the facts of the case, unlike the jury trial. However, the jurors, Anderson asserted, were prejudiced against Fox because of the community in which he lived. Anderson went on to note that that prejudice had "died out." His argument supporting the notion that prejudice was involved in Fox's conviction was based on the fact that numerous other publications in the state "have criticised laws, courts and judges in terms many times more offensive." Fox's publication, though, was singled out "while greater offenders are allowed to go unmolested." Anderson made a similar argument at Fox's trial, and in his letter he included a copy of "The Prude and the Nudes," asking the governor to consider for himself if such "an American citizen should be incarcerated in jail on such a flimsy pretext." He also reminded the governor that Fox had already spent more than a week in jail during his trial. Included in Anderson's appeal was a petition requesting a pardon, circulated by Brown among labor leaders in Seattle, which included signatures from Harry Ault of the *Seattle Union Record*, Alice Lord of the Waitresses' Union, Frank W. Cotterill of the Seattle Building Trades Council, and members of the IUT.[2]

Governor Lister sought out the opinions of Judge W. O. Chapman who presided over the case, and attorney A. O. Burmeister, one of the prosecutors. Chapman thought he was vindicated by both the state and federal courts and that Fox's sentence was light, taking into account considerations favorable to him. He had "no feeling against Mr. Fox, who seems to be a rather quiet, inoffensive man," but he believed that the punishment would force Fox to think twice before authoring a similar article. Nevertheless, Chapman would not criticize the governor if he were to pardon

Fox. Burmeister wrote two letters, one to the governor and one to the governor's secretary, marked "personal." In his first letter, he noted that he "never considered the defendant in any way a vicious character" but claimed that the people of Home "caused us much trouble in the way of law violations." Fox, he believed, was the leader of the colony and that his conviction had curbed the colony of lawless behavior. Of course, that was not true, as nude bathing continued as the years went by. Burmeister indicated that he did not have any objection to the governor pardoning Fox. In his second letter, which he asked the secretary to bring to the governor's attention, Burmeister thought it would be "inexpedient and unwise from a political standpoint for the Governor to pardon the defendant." Fox and his Home community members were "all anarchists, either revolutionary, or otherwise." They deserved the condemnation of "the better class of citizenship" and would not provide any political assistance to the governor. He thought that Fox should serve at least a portion of his sentence.[3]

After deliberating on the matter for several weeks, Lister decided not to issue Fox a pardon. He thought that to ignore the court rulings would be unfair to the process and that Fox should serve at least a portion of his sentence. He wrote to both the deputy prosecuting attorney of Pierce County and Anderson about his decision. Word eventually reached Home on 25 July. The community had gathered for their weekly dance at Liberty Hall that Sunday evening when they learned of the governor's decision. Fox, who was present when the news arrived, received several cheers from his comrades as a champion of free speech and a free press. The following day, with a crowd of colonists by his side at the community wharf, Fox was taken into custody by Deputy Sheriff Fred Shaw, who escorted him to Tacoma where he was to serve out his sentence in the Pierce County Jail. Fox donned county prison clothing and adjusted to life in jail for the next two months in the dank basement below the county courthouse. By all accounts, Fox was a model prisoner. While he passed his time interacting with his fellow inmates—largely working-class men such as himself—and reading whatever material he could procure, Anderson and Brown worked to get him released. Brown wrote to Clarence Parker, head of the state's Industrial Insurance Commission, to familiarize him with Fox's case and make him aware that the petition sent to the governor bore "the name of practically every officer of the labor movement in" Seattle. Anderson wrote to the governor, reminding him that he was open to Fox serving only a portion of his sentence. Lister at this point decided to issue a full pardon to Fox, just shy of his last two weeks in jail.[4]

A cold and winding Saturday evening greeted Fox as he emerged from the county jail on 11 September. He said nothing to reporters who gathered at the courthouse. It is highly likely that Samuel Hammersmark greeted him upon his release and invited him to stay at his apartment in Tacoma that first night of freedom. The following morning Fox took the steamer *Tyconda* to Home, where he was met by his close friends in the community. His stay at Home would have been brief for he needed to attend to his duties with the IUT in Seattle. The industrial union in which he placed so much faith lay in tatters. Fox found work as a machinist in Tacoma, a short steamship ride from his house in Home. Over the next couple of years he worked in Seattle, Chicago, and Pittsburg as a machinist as well and as a general organizer for the AFL. He wrote dispatches for the *American Federationist*, particularly on the labor situation in Seattle and Tacoma. He penned articles for the shingle weaver page of the *Seattle Union Record*, which was the new official organ of the ISWU. Moreover, Fox wrote "a weekly article for a syndicate of the labor press."[5]

Although Fox had focused much of his energy on the syndicalist movement and the IUT in recent years, his connection to the anarchist movement was still strong when he emerged from his jail cell. In late November, he spent time with Alexander Berkman and Eric B. Morton during the former's lecture tour of the Pacific Northwest. Fox maintained an active correspondence with anarchists in different parts of the country, some of whom were close friends. In one letter, he affectionately referred to Berkman as the "Kosher kid" and Morton as the "dillicate Norwiegan [*sic*]." The movement itself seemed vibrant, at least on the surface, particularly among Mexican, Spanish, Italian, and Jewish immigrant communities especially among Yiddish speakers. The noticeable exception were Germans, whose heyday was in the 1880s; by 1900 the number of German anarchists had gone into decline as they made up an ever smaller percentage of immigrant communities. Native-born children of these German anarchists, most of whom had become anarchists after settling in the United States, did not follow in their parents' footsteps. Native-born American anarchists, those immigrants who had adopted English as their primary language, and those who maintained their native language to promote anarchism, maintained a strong presence as the libertarian wing of the socialist movement in the country.

Native-born and immigrant anarchists along with those who were sympathetic to a libertarian socialist worldview numbered in the thousands during the first decade and a half of the twentieth century. New York City had become a central hub of anarchism, with Boston, Paterson, Barre (Vermont), Chicago, San Francisco, and others also maintaining active anarchist affinity groups. Anarchists were often involved in strike activity, primarily as speakers and with some limited organizing on the behalf of unions. They frequently organized defense committees and fundraising for workers on trial or imprisoned. Anarchists also were at the forefront of social and cultural reforms, especially in terms of gender equality, birth control, and free speech. Moreover, anarchists, except for a few who supported the Allied Powers, were adamantly anti-war and spoke out against preparedness for the United States' possible entry into the war. The number of anarchist publications in circulation, however, paints a different picture. The high point of anarchist periodicals in circulation peaked around 1910. According to historian Kenyon Zimmer, given that anarchists did not have lists of party members such as the SPA or membership lists that trade unions and industrial unions would keep, the circulation of anarchist periodicals provides an important means by which historians can determine the number of anarchists and those sympathetic to the cause.[6]

In early 1916, Emma Goldman considered the number of English-language anarchist periodicals in circulation to be a literary renaissance for the movement. Her publication, *Mother Earth*, was in its tenth year. Published out of Minneapolis, Herman Kuehn's *Instead of a Magazine* leaned anarchist individualist along the lines of Benjamin Tucker's *Liberty*, which ceased publication in 1908. The International Propaganda Group of Chicago published *The Alarm*, in the spirit of Albert Parsons's publication, with Theodore Appel serving as editor. Hippolyte Havel edited *Revolt: The Stormy Petrel of the Revolutionary Movement* in New York with the assistance of Harry Kelly. And former editor of *Mother Earth* Alexander Berkman edited *The Blast* with the assistance of Margaret Fitzgerald and Morton in San Francisco. Robert Minor, who transitioned from socialism to anarcho-syndicalism, would become a significant contributor to the publication as an artist and writer. These periodicals seemed to bode well for the promotion of and reception to anarchist ideas. The Chicago Propaganda Group considered their publication's primary purpose to bring "the ideas of Anarchism before the working class." Anarchist communist in orientation, the Group argued that social revolution was the only means by which the capitalist system and the state could be overthrown. The shock troops of the revolution were workers employing "direct action . . . in their struggle for emancipation." Havel echoed these sentiments with his publication. He considered *The Alarm* to be "a live weekly revolutionary organ" that would bring "news from the firing line" by people engaged in the struggle. Berkman became concerned that the revolutionary movement had waned since he was released from prison. On speaking tours, he found workers and "social rebels" fatigued by "narrow party lines" and antiquated methods. He believed that revolutionaries such as himself needed to harness that dissatisfaction and growing militancy to revitalize working-class radicalism. His goal for his publication was to be a "revolutionary labor weekly."[7]

Although *Mother Earth* was the premier English-language anarchist journal in the country, Kelly thought that at ten cents a copy and without advertisements when it was first being published it could not be "an organ of the working-class." In other words, he thought it was too expensive for the wageworkers, who in many cases made less than three dollars a day. Nevertheless, issues significant to the working class and support for the radical element of the labor movement, the IWW in particular, were always the publication's domain. Other working-class-oriented anarchist publications had come and gone over the years, *The Agitator* and *The Syndicalist* being just two of them, but anarchists who saw workers as a major element of any revolutionary movement believed that such outlets were always necessary. Appel, Havel, and Berkman saw that as their calling at mid-decade. Fox felt the same way as both an enthusiastic supporter of the anarchist press and a contributor to anarchist publications. He wrote for both *The Alarm* and *Revolt*. In *The Alarm*, he had a rewrite of one of his "Letters to Jack Lumber" published that was anti-war and called on workers to fight the industrial war at home. In another article, titled "The Cry of Alarm," Fox demanded that readers rise up against the conditions that working people were forced to accept by the capitalist system, to be agitators, to preach "the glorious gospel of Discontent," and to bring to an end the industrial carnage that working people experienced every day in the "mines, factories, and workshops." He wanted the publication's readers to "enlist under the folds of the scarlet banner of Social Revolution . . . Enlist in the great modern war of Man against Mammon." It was time, he argued, for "the final blow that will free the world from war and militarism, from exploitation and tyranny of every kind." He wrote a very similar piece for *Revolt*, calling on readers to "sing the song of Revolt" and to become engaged in the struggle for emancipation.[8]

Fox, though, had concerns about the health of anarchist movement. Not only was it not growing in numbers of adherents, but it seemed disconnected from the working class, despite the appearance of these new publications. Immigrant working-class anarchists were somewhat segregated, largely due to language barriers, from the rest of the English-speaking working class. Regardless of language used, Fox did not think that publications alone were sufficient to bring about a militant, revolutionary consciousness among workers nor were they sufficient to bring about social revolution. That had to come from within the working class itself, and the only way to achieve that was to work within the labor movement rather than outside of it. Earlier in his life, it was not uncommon for Fox to work with fellow anarchists in the labor movement. By the mid-1910s, however, he found most of the anarchists still active to be comrades from years earlier rather than a younger generation. Syndicalism seemed to offer a resurgence of militant libertarian labor activity, but it was not bearing the fruit that he and William Z. Foster had hoped. Fox was encouraged by Berkman's *The Blast*, for as a militant labor publication it could continue to bring anarchist and syndicalist ideas to the West Coast and beyond. In a letter to "The Blast-ed Three" he included a short poem:

Here's to THE BLAST; may it blow
'Till the flame of Freedom envelopes the earth
And the last limb of tyranny's laid low.

Despite his enthusiastic support for *The Blast*, *The Alarm*, and *Revolt*, he knew more was necessary and brought his concerns to Berkman. He argued that they "were following the beaten path of propaganda without getting anywhere" and suggested to Berkman that an anarchist convention be called to discuss the problem of the stalled progress of the anarchist movement. He thought by bringing anarchists from across the country together "a change in tactics" could be achieved. Berkman agreed that Fox brought up an important matter. "But," quoting Berkman, "it cannot be decided by shouting at a convention. A convention is only good for those who believe in majority rule." Fox thought that this was a major disagreement between "two anarchist workers." He supported majority rule while Berkman did not. Berkman held a more rigidly anarchist ideological position that consensus decision-making was the only legitimate path anarchists could follow. Fox, on the other hand, held that majority rule was necessary for concerted action. His extensive experience within the labor movement led him to the conclusion that majority rule was necessary to move forward and was something on which anarchists needed to compromise. Fox had had too many experiences over the years among anarchist discussion groups where much was said but then little was acted on. More disconcerting for Fox was Berkman's response to his suggestion that anarchists "direct more attention to the unions." Berkman argued that "anarchists can help revolutionize the unions much better from outside than from within." Fox believed that Berkman was operating on theory that was not informed by experience. He argued that "to get the full confidence of union men you must be one of them. Comradship [sic] on the picket line is a mighty binding force that brings workers closer together and more ready to listen to each others' views. There the rebels can explain the true meaning of the strike for what it is, a preliminary skirmish, to be followed by the bigger battle later that will eliminate the bosses and make an end to the need for strikes." Fox thought that had Berkman not spent fourteen years in prison for his attempted assassination of Henry Frick and instead been "in active factory and trade union activity" he would have a more realistic appreciation for workers in general. Moreover, Fox believed that laborers needed to be radicalized in large numbers before any significant change could happen, "and the place to arouse them to action [was] in their unions." He had great hope for organized workers because "a union card in his pocket is proof that he has taken the first step towards his emancipation from 'ruggid [sic] individualism.'"[9]

The promising prospects for anarchists in early 1916 did not last long, especially for their publications, which suffered from weak support and hostility from postal authorities. Havel made repeated requests for more subscribers and for delinquent readers to pay up. To make matters worse, the Postal Service deemed *Revolt* unmailable under "section 211 of the Criminal Code." The letters Havel received from Postmaster E. M. Morgan did not specify what element of the section the publishers violated. Regardless, the periodical folded. *The Blast* also had issues suppressed because it carried articles on birth control and one titled "Villa or Wilson—Which is the Bandit?" The publication continued on, but Berkman and his associates needed to continually request that subscribers to pay their past-due balances and that casual readers subscribe. Appel and his associates were finding it increasingly difficult to produce *The Alarm* and to get it into the hands of workers. They had hoped to distribute their newspaper "in the shops, in front of factories and at all occasions where the workers who do not know our ideas, gather." Instead, given the Group's members need to earn a living, issues were piling up on their bookshelves. The publication had 750 subscribers, but that was not enough to keep the publication afloat. It suspended operations in September 1916. The Group and Havel worked together in 1917 to produce the *Social War*, which was published in Chicago over the course of 1917.[10]

After the sinking of the British passenger ship *Lusitania* in 1915 by a German U-boat, which killed over one hundred Americans, the United States moved closer to war. Even though President Woodrow Wilson won reelection partly on the slogan "He Kept Us Out of War," in 1916 war preparedness, which anarchists, syndicalists, socialists, and militants in the labor movement all rallied against, swept across the country. Radical publications of all stripes voiced their opposition, with anarchist publications using some of the most extreme rhetoric. Public meetings, demonstrations, and a variety of anti-preparedness activities unnerved elements of the public, especially the daily press. In this atmosphere, a wave of anti-anarchist hysteria in the papers appeared in the wake of a mysterious illness that affected a banquet at the University Club in Chicago in honor of the Archbishop George Mundelein. Governor Edward Dunne was in attendance along with two hundred other guests. More than one hundred at the dinner became sick from what turned out to be arsenic poisoning. Although some became violently ill, no one died. Investigators concluded that Jean Crones, a chef at the club, was an anarchist and responsible for poisoning the soup served to guests. As a nationwide search for the suspect was underway, Berkman professed in *The Blast* that he did not know if Crones was an anarchist but he thought his actions could be warranted, given that the archbishop and governor were representatives of church and state, which were "inimical to the best interests of the people." Crones's real name was Nestor Dondoglio, a Galleanist—an insurrectionist anarchist faction, led by Luigi Galleani, who published *Cronica Sovversiva* in Barre, Vermont. Dondoglio eluded police with the help of comrades and died a dozen years later in Connecticut.[11]

With the passage in Congress of the National Defense Act of 1916, which President Wilson signed into law on 3 June, cities across the country rallied to the call of war preparedness. In San Francisco, supporters organized a massive Preparedness Day Parade on 22 July 1916. The parade had over fifty thousand participants with thousands of spectators watching the procession. A bomb planted on Steuart Street denotated a little after 2:00 p.m. The explosion killed ten people and wounded forty more. Immediately, police suspected anarchist involvement and arrested labor radicals indiscriminately. Soon charges were filed against Thomas J. Mooney and his wife Rena, Warren K. Billings, Edward D. Nolan, and Israel Weinberg. According to Fox, who read newspaper accounts and maintained his correspondence with his comrades in California, "The anarchists sprang at once to the defense and organized a committee with Bob Minor in charge." The offices of *The Blast* were raided by the police on multiple occasions because of articles supporting the accused. Federal officials barred several issues from second-class delivery, essentially suppressing them. Berkman, suspecting that the police wanted to link him to the bombing, left for New York. He was instrumental in organizing labor support in New York. Fox noted that "he rallied the Jewish unions, whose eager response was a splendid addition to their long record in defense of class war prisoners." Ultimately, Mooney and Billings were convicted, while the cases against the others fell apart. Although they initially received death sentences, Mooney and Billings eventually had their sentences commuted to life in prison. The real bomber or bombers were probably members of the Gruppo Anarchico Volontá in San Francisco. The attack had a chilling effect on the anarchist movement as other publications were suppressed by federal authorities and anarchists of all stripes were under surveillance by law enforcement.

The repression of anarchists, socialists, Wobblies, and labor radicals would increase significantly in 1917 and 1918 with the passage of the Espionage and Sedition Acts. The anarchist movement and the IWW in particular would be driven to the breaking point by 1920. Even Home was not exempt from federal attention. In summer 1918, an agent of the Bureau of Immigration made a fact-finding trip to the colony. He found little that was noteworthy about the community as a threat to national security, but his lurid description painted the colony as a hangout of undesirables. The agent also noted that the village had harbored participants in the Los Angeles Times Building bombing and supported revolutionaries such as the Magón brothers and other members of the PLM. In addition, several individuals who had spent time at Home were under surveillance by law enforcement, including Fox's good friend Alex Snellenberg. He was arrested in 1919, though the indictment was eventually dropped. Fox's writings were part of a federal investigation as well, though he himself never faced charges. Nevertheless, he actively followed these disturbing events and the increased repression of radicals by federal authorities. During the trial of David Caplan, one of the suspects in the Los Angeles Times Building bombing, Fox's name came up. Oscar Engvall—testifying for the prosecution—noted that Fox and Caplan had asked about dynamite at the Home Grocery Company that Engvall managed. He also claimed that he had seen Caplan reading pamphlets on dynamite in Fox's home. Nothing came of the testimony for Fox, though Caplan would be found guilty of second-degree manslaughter and face years in prison.[12]

At Home Colony, Fox had to deal with the changing nature of his beloved community. Even though he had spent the last few years engaged in activities that forced him away from the community for long stretches of time, he still participated in the MHA and in fact served as its president in 1916. In the pages of *The Blast*, Fox requested that anyone interested in joining a "cooperative society" contact him at Home, Washington. He emphasized starting a poultry business on a large scale to entice those interested in relocating. Theodore Van Beek, a retired sea captain, began such a business at Home and it proved to be quite profitable. By mid-decade, many Home residents raised poultry, especially for eggs, which could be sold in neighboring villages, towns, and in Tacoma. Joe's Bay Trading Company, a cooperative store, owned by thirty farmers (some Home residents and some not) was managed by Abe Cohn. The company was situated on the community's wharf and did extensive business with surrounding communities, especially with the bay islands. In many respects Home had taken on attributes similar to other villages situated on the extensive coastline of Puget Sound. Many of the residents had well-developed gardens, fruit orchards, and berry fields and raised a variety of farm animals. The bay was a rich source of fish and shellfish that members of the community harvested on a regular basis, with smoked salmon being a particular favorite. Liberty Hall remained a center for community meetings and for a variety of public events, and it could be rented out by people from other villages in the area. The community's population had grown over the years and now comprised families, couples, and single individuals, in all numbering perhaps four hundred. Home had a thriving school and even had a baseball team that hosted visiting squads and traveled to play others in the region.[13]

Although most of the "prudes" had left the community several years earlier, Home's population had become quite diverse when it came to ideology. Due to the change in the bylaws of the association, those who considered themselves to be anarchists and decided to sell their property did not necessarily inquire if the buyers were a good fit for the community's libertarian nature. Consequently, anarchists were only one contingent among many at mid-decade. Some villagers were socialists, others progressives, some single taxers, others belonged to the two main political parties, and some were apolitical. The community had a local of the Socialist Party in 1915 and by 1918 it had a War Savings Society. In summer 1916, a rift emerged between recent settlers and those who were long-term residents. The association's officers had met to consider disposing of several items of community property. Those opposed to the actions by the association's officers filed a lawsuit to restrain them. Named in the suit was Fox, George Allen, and other officers and individual community members including Lewis Haiman. In December when the officers planned to meet, the plaintiffs were able to secure a restraining order in Pierce County Superior Court to bar Fox and his fellow officials from the proceedings. Early in January, the group hostile to the association's officers met in Liberty Hall, which now included some long-term members of the community, and elected Thomas J. Mullen as association president along with a slate of other officers. Soon thereafter another group met to elect their own set of officers, including Fox as president. The two sets of association officials appeared in court in January in which questions of who was actually a member of the association came into play and the plaintiffs accused Haiman of altering association documents. In February the judge issued a ruling that stripped from Haiman, Allen, and a number of others the right to serve as association members because they had disposed of property which they received when joining the community. Court proceedings continued in the spring without a permanent resolution. Nevertheless, the Fox faction continued to meet as did the Mullen faction, making it difficult for Cohn to know which set of association officials he should pay rent to for the trading company. Sadly, due to the conflict much of the community's common areas—the wharf, seawall, sidewalks, cemetery, and Liberty Hall—were falling into disrepair as the two factions divided the citizenry.[14]

Of course, the situation at Home was distracting for Fox as he continued his writing career, which had become more narrowly focused on the labor movement since the founding of *The Syndicalist*. When living at Home, he worked as a staff writer for the *Seattle Union Record* covering labor activities both local and national. When working as a machinist in Chicago or Pittsburg, the paper referred to him as a special correspondent. The *Chicago Labor News* was a frequent publisher of Fox's writing. Dezettel was so impressed by his work that he suggested Fox may one day be an editor of the *American Federationist*. Dezettel's newspaper was the "official organ" for fifty union locals and trades councils in Chicago and the ITUEL's "principal national voice." Other labor papers carried his writing either as reprints or as featured pieces. One of his first articles for the *Chicago Labor News* was an overview of the history of the eight-hour-day movement in the United States, Great Britain, Canada, Australia, and New Zealand. He continued to write anti-war pieces and reiterated his concern that preparedness efforts only increased the chances of actual war. His argument was in line with much of the left in the country as well as with the ITUEL's official policy as expressed at the organization's 1916 conference in Kansas City.

After the US declaration of war, the left's attitude toward the war began to change, though most anarchists, socialists, and labor radicals continued to condemn it. Nonetheless, Dezettel encouraged Fox to buy war bonds, though there is no indication that Fox did so. Even Foster sold war bonds at one point, but Fox stayed true to his anti-war stand. In his "Flag Waving Patriots" article for the *Chicago Labor News*, he introduced a new feature to his labor articles with "Henry Dub" and the "Union Man." Fox most certainly borrowed Henry Dub's name and some of his characteristics from the cartoonist Ryan Walker's character Harry Dubbs. Walker's work was featured in a number of socialist and labor periodicals in the 1910s and two collections of his cartoons were published as books. In Fox's articles, Dub is similar to Jack Lumber. With this device, Fox could point out Dub's lack of knowledge and underdeveloped critical thinking skills. Dub, of course, was supportive of the war and saw positive consequences to the country's participation, particularly in regard to women entering trades that were traditionally the domain of men. These women were doing their patriotic duty according to Dub. The union man had no problem with women working for wages, whether repairing railroad cars in Tacoma or operating elevators in New York. Nevertheless, according to the union man, the claim of "flag waving patriots" that there was a shortage of men for jobs was a means by which employers could secure cheaper labor. These same patriots were raising prices on goods throughout the country to capitalize on the war effort. In short, behind the flag waving was an effort to generate greater profits.[15]

In another series of exchanges between Dub and the union man, Fox also continued to criticize the IWW. Dub asked why the union man did not support the IWW. The response was a typical one for Fox, who could point out that Wobblies were unsuccessful at organizing lasting industrial unions and proved to be a disruptive rather than a uniting force in the labor movement, and that much of their activity was theoretical and political, especially in regard to their free speech fights. He used the events in Everett, Washington, to explain to Dub that the Wobblies' free speech fights did little for labor. The shingle weavers were in the midst of a great strike in the city. The Wobblies, at first, seemed interested in assisting the shingle weavers. However, their presence devolved into a free speech fight, a political rather than an economic struggle. Although laudable in that labor must have its free speech rights protected, the conflict had little to do with the immediate needs of the striking weavers, according to Fox. After being viciously thrown out of the city in late October, the Wobblies returned on 5 November 1916 on the steamship *Verona*. When the ship attempted to dock, sheriff deputies and members of the city's Commercial Club met it with a hail of gunfire, resulting in the Everett Massacre. The union man had nothing but condemnation for the murders and injuries that the Wobblies experienced and applauded western labor organizations for rushing to the legal defense of the IWW members jailed in Everett. In another article, Dub asked the union man about Frank Little, who was lynched in Butte, Montana. Dub thought that Little must have been a "desperado" to receive such treatment. The union man countered that Little was nothing of the sort. Fox wrote, "He was a peace-loving American, an idealist, striving to aid his fellow workers in their efforts to hold their own against one of the largest and most powerful trusts in the world—the copper trust; and his murder was the most cowardly, the most bloodthirsty, outrageous ever committed in the interest of organized capital."[16]

Violence was an ever-present element in the struggle between labor and capital as far as Fox and many labor radicals were concerned. The Everett Massacre and the murder of Frank Little were but two examples that Fox could bring to his readers' attention. Yet violence also was an inherent element of the work that laborers did in the "industrial age" in which so many machines could kill and maim. Fox was a witness to that violence most recently with his work in the IUT. Violence between labor organizations and between striking workers and scabs was present in Fox's articles over the years as well. Racism as a factor in that violence, particularly between white and black workers, was something that Fox and many of his fellow militant labor radicals seemed to have had a difficult time conceptualizing. For many radicals, class was the overriding framework through which they viewed conflict, and Fox was no exception. While he went out of his way to point out to his readers that ethnocentrism and racism divided the working class to its detriment, he rarely confronted the racism that was deeply rooted in much of the white working class of his era. In one exchange between Dub and the union man, Dub asks, "What does it mean, the killing and burning of colored men?" Dub continued that the white man "affects to be the very apex of civilization, still, in a sudden outburst of passion, he turns savage and destroys his brother of a different colored skin. What does it mean, I ask?" The union man explains "that man is still a savage under the veneer of civilization, and that under great provocation, he throws off the mask and becomes the animal of a hundred thousand years ago." Before the union man gets to the crux of the question about the savage behavior of white workers toward black workers, he explains what civilization would mean for the working class. The union man lays out a vision of the good life for workers and their families that included no more than eight hours of wage work a day, plentiful food, warm clothing, a spacious house, an automobile, and an annual vacation. Workers created these material comforts and consumer items, the union man asserted, why should they not have them? Without realizing it at the time, Fox was describing the material comforts that much of the white working class was able to attain by the 1940s and 1950s, primarily through the power of the labor movement.

In 1917, when Fox's piece was published in the *Chicago Labor News*, those good things in life were out of reach for most of the white working class. The union man then turned to the "great provocation." Although Fox does not specify an exact conflict, he refers to African Americans being used as strikebreakers. White workers, the union man notes, have no legal recourse to stop the importation of scab labor. Fox was sympathetic to black workers. He argued that even though they were being manipulated by employers, they were improving their economic condition by taking such jobs, especially in northern cities. White workers saw themselves, according to the union man, as being replaced by black workers, which was the "great provocation." The union man argued at the end of the piece that "not until society is more just and equitable in the good things of life . . . can we justly expect the [white] workers to be civilized." Fox was essentially arguing that capitalism created these combustible conditions that led to racial violence. Decades later when many white workers attained a better quality of life, African Americans were still the victims of terrible violence by working-class white mobs in Chicago, Detroit, and other cities. Not once in the article did Fox call on white workers to make common cause with black workers or criticize trade unions for not welcoming black workers into their ranks. He condemned the violence but not the racism.[17]

Fox rarely wrote about African Americans in comparison to Mexicans and Japanese. He did feature an African American in a parable that was published in the *Chicago Labor News*, "The Flies and the Hornets." He told the story of meeting a black mule driver who was so adept at using a whip that he could kill flies one by one with it if he chose to do so. Fox called the man "Sam" because that was the name you used when referring to a "colored man whose name we do not know, just as we call the Chinese 'John,' the German 'Fritz,' and the Irishman 'Pat.'" While traveling with the mule driver, Fox witnessed Sam's expertise with the whip as he killed flies with ease while perched on the wagon seat. At one point in their journey they came close to a hornets' nest. Fox asked if Sam was willing to use his excellent skills to strike a hornet as he had demonstrated striking flies. Fox explained that he would write of his exploits and would make him the envy of the sporting world. Sam turned to him and was surprised that Fox would suggest such a thing. Flies, Sam reasoned, had no rights worth respecting. They worked for no one but themselves and cared little of other flies. Sam noted, "But when it comes to ho'nets, boss, dat's different . . . Ah respect thah right an; show mah respect by passin' 'em by without so much as raisin' mah whip." Fox was puzzled by Sam's reasoning, asking him if was because the flies had no stinger that he would kill them for sport and not the hornets. Sam explained, "It's not the sting that makes one respect the rights of the ho'net . . . Them 'are ho'nets has a union; they is shu' organized. If I hits one with mah whip all the udders come right aftah me jus like I had hit them all. They fights for each udder, they 'fend each udders rights." Fox asked, 'Suppose us working men were all organized like that each upholding the rights of the others, what would happen?" Sam replied, "What would happen boss? Why, everybody would 'spect our rights just as I 'spect the ho'nets."

Fox, of course, was using stereotypical black English of the era when quoting Sam. He did something similar with Casey the sewer worker, with his heavily Irish accented English. In addition, they both had menial jobs and lacked formal education, though they possessed wisdom. Although Casey was a union man and clearly a member of the white working class, Sam used the phrases "us working men" and "our rights," which could have been Fox's way of subtly including Sam and black workers in the greater working class. The prism through which he viewed his world was class and class struggle. Race and even gender were subsumed by class. Goldman and other anarchists were similar in this regard, particularly in terms of race, as scholars such as Kathy Ferguson have suggested. Of course, some of Fox's white contemporaries could see racism in a much clearer light. His friend James Morton was a champion of African American civil rights, author of *The Curse of Race Prejudice*, and a collaborator with the National Association for the Advancement of Colored People. In the same year that Fox's article on working-class racial conflict appeared, Martha Gruening had an essay published in *Mother Earth* that explicitly called to attention the cruel racism evident in white mob violence in East St. Louis. Later, communists would display a much better recognition of racism within the ranks of labor and call for its eradication.[18]

Fox's labor writing coincided with a growing number of labor bulletins, newspapers, and journals in the 1910s. City labor papers were something Fox was familiar with from his youth in Chicago where the labor press was quite vibrant compared to other cities. His writing appeared in labor publications across the country, either as reprints of his work or as articles written specifically for that publication. Bringing to his readers commentary on a variety of issues related to working-class interests had been central to his life as a writer dating back to the 1890s. As the number of English-language anarchist publications went into decline in the second half of the 1910s, Fox focused more on getting his work into the labor press. Although payment for his writing was not very lucrative, it did supplement his income while he worked as a machinist in Chicago, Tacoma, Pittsburgh, and possibly Philadelphia. He wrote several articles championing the labor press, seeking to provide a counternarrative to what workers would read in mainstream outlets. Few such papers had a labor reporter, and city daily newspapers usually sided with employers in labor disputes. Exceptions existed, of course—for example, Fox thought the labor reporter for the *Seattle Daily Times* was fair-minded.

Generally speaking, though, Fox argued that the labor press was an essential part of the labor movement. In fact, he thought that a labor newspaper was "as important as the union itself." The daily papers of America's cities, according to Fox, were a business that rarely told the truth because it did not pay as well as fabrication or serving the interests of capital. The owners and editors of daily newspapers had no commitment to presenting to readers the truth, especially when it came to the issues significant to the working class. In addition, he asserted that the press molded public opinion to the interests of the capitalist class, for "the newspapers represent the dominant idea of our times," in a word, "Business." The labor question, for example, was always viewed through the lens of business interests rather than the workers' interests. If the mainstream press supported "social justice" then it would be a fact. However, that was unlikely to happen. Therefore, Fox believed it was "the duty of organized labor to establish a people's press, free from the corruption of big business." Fox asserted that the working class had grown discontented with weekly or monthly labor papers and was ready for a daily paper that could counter the daily papers' biased attitude toward labor. The *Seattle Union Record* carried several articles by Fox in late 1917 and early 1918 on the topic as it related to a daily labor newspaper. Efforts by organized labor in the city coalesced into a united effort to transform the *Seattle Union Record* from a weekly into a daily. At meetings held in the Seattle Labor Temple sponsored by the Daily *Union Record* Booster Committee of the Central Labor Council, support for such an endeavor seemed imminent as thousands of paid-up subscriptions were on hand to begin a daily after the first of the year. The campaign bore fruit when the newspaper issued its first daily addition in April 1918.[19]

Fox's primary activity continued to be writing while he supported him-self as a machinist, but his work as an anarcho-syndicalist with the ITUEL faded as the organization itself began to falter. In early 1917, it was really only active in Chicago with a scattering of affiliated militants in parts of the Midwest and Far West. The organization's numbers never even equaled those of the SLNA despite Foster traveling extensively to boost for the ITUEL. By the spring, the organization no longer existed. In the summer Foster, who worked in Chicago as a railcar inspector for the Soo Line, came up with the idea of organizing workers at the packing houses. The meatpack-ing industry was doing quite well after the United States entered the First World War. It expanded and hired more workers, making the workforce even more diverse with a variety of immigrants from Europe and African Americans from the South. He brought his idea to the Chicago District Council of the Railway Carmen, which was controlled by former members of the ITUEL. They endorsed his proposal and he then took his idea to the Chicago Federation of Labor, which also approved an organizing effort. Soon Foster was meeting with a number of locals and the campaign was on its way, with the Stockyards Labor Council serving as the primary organ-ization for the movement. The council specifically targeted the largest segment of the workforce: immigrant and black laborers. Despite great difficulty in overcoming racism, ethnocentrism, employer intransigence, and skepti-cism from local leaders and the AFL leadership, by 1918 the effort achieved great success. Although Fox was periodically in Chicago, he did not par-ticipate in the organizing effort directly. He wrote an article, though, for the *Chicago Labor News* in which he took J. Ogden Armour to task for not being able to answer a basic question posed to him during his testimony at a Commission on Industrial Relations hearing. He was asked if workers who averaged twelve dollars a week could live on that wage. He could not answer the question or subsequent ones about the wages, working, or liv-ing conditions of his employees. Fox then proceeded to explain to his read-ers the extreme wealth of the packinghouse owners in comparison to the poverty of the laborers. He extrapolated on the class divide in the meat-packing industry to the country as a whole and argued that the wealthy and the largest corporations had a "union" to maintain their control of the economy. Fox returned to a common refrain in his piece by calling on workers to counter the organization of employers with one of their own and to "organize into trade unions or be forever slaves."[20]

At the beginning of 1918 Fox still considered himself an anarcho-syndicalist, and as such he was committed to the boring within strategy. He was aware of the Non-Partisan League (NPL) and found it be similar to the syndicalist movement in that league members were boring within political parties, primarily the Republican Party, in North Dakota, Minnesota, and other states in the Midwest and Far West to move those parties to embrace policies in the interests of farmers. When Fox was in Chicago in January 1918, he learned that the NPL needed organizers to work among farmers, which sounded interesting to him. Perhaps he desired a change from urban life and working in shops and factories as a machinist. The league also had a reputation for radicalism, opposition to the US involvement in the European war, and, in North Dakota, a copesetic relationship with IWW farmworkers. Moreover, the league, after Congress's declaration of war, was harangued in the press. And some league members were physically assaulted. Fox sent a letter of application for the position to the NPL headquarters in St. Paul. In order to be hired, he had to take a course in farm economics as preparation for work as an organizer. He reasoned that "a farm organizer should know something about farming in its relation to the food trust that buy the produce; and how to combat the racket that farms the farmer from daylight till dark." Though syndicalists had no policy against organizing farmers (unlike the IWW), it was hardly their focus, making Fox rather unique in this endeavor. The correspondence course Fox took, designed by the socialists Arthur and Marian Le Sueur, educated students to the basic elements of farm economics, which included "markets, bookkeeping, wages, mortgages, tenancy, consumption, and taxation." Also, the history and development the "cooperative movement" was heavily emphasized. Fox did exceedingly well in the course and infused many of his responses with the commonalities industrial laborers and farmers faced in a capitalist economy. In one of his responses, he noted that both farmers and city workers were producers of wealth and "by the organization and co-operation of these great bodies the problems of both will be eventually solved."[21]

Before he departed for St. Paul, he received a letter from Marian Le Sueur asking him if he would be interested in working in the "Publicity Department." She was aware of his journalistic background and wrote that "the average newspaper man is not much good for this job. If he is in the newspaper game long enough to be really adept, he has prostituted himself too long to be of any account." He wrote back accepting the offer and looked forward to communicating with farmers and explaining to them their need for organization. When he arrived at the NPL headquarters, he was impressed by the modern office building and the ongoing campaign in sixteen states. Fox worked on the *Non-Partisan Leader*, the primary periodical for the league, which the league leadership had relocated from Fargo, North Dakota, to St. Paul in early 1918. Fox's other duties included "furnishing copy" for small-town newspapers that were either controlled by the NPL or highly sympathetic to the league. Fox also wrote letters to the editor for league members in several states who subscribed to other newspapers. The prewritten letters, which were copied by the member and sent off to the publication, touted the league and its accomplishments, especially in North Dakota, and addressed specific issues that farmers faced in that member's town, region, or state. The department issued a large number of pamphlets that Fox helped with, and he was quite pleased by the "pile of propaganda" they produced.[22]

Along with his duties for the NPL, he continued to publish in the *Seattle Union Record*. In April, he attended a three-day convention in St. Paul, which ended in a rally of several thousand farmers and workers. Representatives of the NPL and organized labor in the state drew up a platform of common interests to present a united front economically and politically that would "clean up the state of Minnesota and make it safe for democracy." The NPL endorsed a slate of candidates "composed of farmers and union workers." He noted for readers the program of the NPL that called for "the people" to "own the railroads, flour mills, grain elevators, packing houses, cold storage houses," and in addition supported legislation that would benefit workers that included free employment bureaus, old age pensions, and the eight-hour day. Fox went on to note how both farmers and workers were exploited by "big business" and had to organize and work together. He closed his article by arguing "Labor united is good. Farmers united is good. But united labor and united farmer united together is great. It is unconquerable. It will win. It will make America a real democracy." The following month he had another article published in the Seattle paper that again made the case for workers and farmers to cooperate to further their common interests. He summarized the *Biennial Report of the Railroad Brotherhoods' Legislative Board*, which called on workers to make common cause with farmers and explained that workers and farmers were not natural enemies but natural allies. The report echoed the NPL argument that the "middle man" and systemic inefficiency were the major reasons for the high cost of production, whether that was for wheat or for farm machinery. Fox quoted a portion of the report that argued that organized labor should follow the lead of the NPL and enter the political field. The report emphasized the power the NPL had exhibited in North Dakota and the league's spread throughout the country, especially in Minnesota. Moreover, the report argued that the legislative record demonstrated that little had been enacted in the interests of organized labor and that as long as workers only focused on the "industrial field . . . their gains will be thwarted through the legislative and judicial power of the state." Fox stressed this point, asserting that "labor has got to control political power in the proportion it attains economic power." In other words, political power and economic power went hand in hand. Fox's articles were welcomed by Harry Ault, who would be a founding member of the Farmer-Labor Party at its convention in Chicago in 1919.[23]

Fox had made a remarkable conversion in the spring of 1918. He was now making an argument that socialists and other labor advocates had been making for years. Foster and other syndicalists and anarchists would make a similar conversion a year or two later. For example, Hammersmark would become the secretary treasurer of the Cook County Farmer-Labor Party in 1920. There probably was no one event or influence that changed Fox's thinking, but rather a host of experiences over the preceding years. After he left Chicago and relocated to the Pacific Northwest, his work with labor militants of a variety of stripes in the IUT opened him up to different points of view regarding strategies to further the interests of labor and fundamentally change the economic system. It was clear to him that the anarchist movement was in decline even before the onslaught of oppression anarchists experienced at the hands of federal and state governments once the country entered the war in Europe. His syndicalist comrades continued to fight on the economic field and score some victories, the Chicago packinghouse organizing effort being the most recent. However, the syndicalist movement that Foster had spearheaded and Fox readily joined had dwindled to a handful of militants. And even though most Wobblies would not consider themselves syndicalists, they had a great deal in common with syndicalism, especially in their direct, economic action and refraining from engaging in political activity. They were being crushed by the federal government's persecution under the Espionage and Sedition Acts. Without political power, labor, especially labor militants and radicals, were at the mercy of governments that, in Fox's words, were controlled by the "employing class." For Fox, something needed to change. He still held on to his belief in a new social order in which workers—and he now included farmers—would control the means of production and distribution. The appropriate vehicle for that had not manifested itself to him yet. Although he enjoyed his work with the NPL and was witnessing the very beginnings of a farmer-labor party movement in Minnesota, he declined an offer to transfer to North Dakota and work on an NPL-affiliated newspaper. He decided to return "to Puget Sound where the weather was more kind to me, and where I had so many friends."[24]

When Fox returned to Washington in the fall of 1918, he found work in the Ames Shipyard in Seattle and rented a room on Yesler Way, near Pioneer Square. He lived near the headquarters of the ISWU, though the leadership had changed. Brown had become a general organizer for the organizing drive of iron and steelworkers led by Foster and would later serve as the campaign's secretary-treasurer. Fox was able to reconnect with Ault and the staff at the *Seattle Union Record* as well as other comrades in the region. His longtime friend Snellenberg, who now considered himself a "philosophical anarchist," operated the Occidental Sheetmetal Works in the city. Hammersmark, though, had relocated to the Midwest to organize with the Chicago Federation of Labor and in fact participated in the massive steel strike that took place in September 1919. Employment was plentiful in the city when Fox arrived, and the shipyards were teeming with workers in the production of vessels for the war effort. Many nonunion workers joined unions once they were hired in the shipyards, which made for a near 100 percent unionized workforce. The shipyard unions were affiliated with the Metal Trades Council, which took on the task of negotiating wage increases. Employers were prepared to increase the pay of mechanics, such as Fox, but not for the less skilled workers. The council, however, was committed to wage increases for all workers, regardless of trade, as the shipyards had proven quite profitable for the owners. The intransigence of the employers led to a shipyard workers' strike on 21 January 1919 and eventually a general strike in the city on 6 February. For Fox, this would be the largest and last strike in which he would be participate.[25]

Fox at Home, 1919. Courtesy University of Washington Libraries, Special Collections, UW 2915.

The Steel Strike Committee, Pittsburg, 1919. Foster is seated at the table with his arms folded. Courtesy Bettmann via Getty Images.

Fox, though, did not think the Seattle General Strike was revolutionary. Nevertheless, it was part of an international strike wave in that year that included actual revolutionary uprisings. A careful reading of newspaper accounts in the *Seattle Union Record* and in the "Minutes of Meetings of the General Strike Committee and Its Executive Committee" suggests that the goals of the strike were rather limited and far from revolutionary.[26] Nevertheless, many in the city, especially political leaders, members of the middle class, and some workers, thought a revolution was underway. Newspapers from across the country sounded the alarm of the first example of a soviet in America. Most workers in Seattle were either calm to jubilant and set about adjusting to the new reality in the city.. The strike shut down much of Seattle from 6 February to 11 February, after which the city reopened under the leadership of the General Strike Committee, comprising 330 representatives from 110 unions. The city's hospitals were unaffected, government employees continued to work, and a number of other key elements of the city continued to function. The committee made sure that essential services were there for people, especially food distribution. Milk deliveries were made available for families and meals were provided for workers in cafeterias. The committee also enlisted a security force that

Fox referred to as "Labor's War Veterans Guard." They did not carry weapons but did keep the peace. Both the chief of police and the commander of the Thirteenth Division, called up to address the unrest that never materialized, were impressed by the peaceful nature of the strike and the drop in daily police cases. For Fox, the strike was an incredible example of worker solidarity and the possibility of what a worker-controlled society could achieve: "As an expression of Labor solidarity the five day Seattle General Strike was a complete success. American Federation of Labor, Industrial Workers of the World, and Japanese workers laid down their tools to the last man and woman; and behold we witnessed for the first time in history a closed city, a city without business and without traffic, accept such as carried the meaningful sign 'Exempt by order of the Strike Committee,' the new ruling body now seated in the Labor Temple and elected by the votes of the workers in their union halls." The fact that the center of economic power in the city, for at least a few days, was located in the Labor Temple reinforced for him the "supreme power in any city" if workers took control. He thought that the strike in Seattle was an instructive example to workers everywhere, but especially in the United States, that they had power to create a new society that functioned by and for the working class. The key ingredient to that power was solidarity, which began to break down within a few days. The extensiveness of the strike was primarily due to unions and locals striking in sympathy with the shipyard workers. However, the *Seattle Union Record* suspended publication for several days, which removed a significant source of information for workers. The *Strike Bulletin*, which provided favorable coverage of events, was not well distributed throughout the city and the major daily newspapers—the *Seattle Star, Post-Intelligencer,* and *Seattle Daily Times*—tended to run negative to outright hostile strike coverage. As the coalition of unions and locals waivered, Ault and other labor leaders made impassioned pleas to keep the action going. In the end, the strike was eventually called off. Yet, the striking workers believed they had achieved something extraordinary. Like other workers, though, Fox had to go back to work in a city that returned to a semblance of normality.[27]

Fox was happy to have made the move back to the Pacific Northwest to be near friends and comrades and to participate in and witness such a major strike. However, he had grown tired of bachelor life and "was beginning to think about getting married again." He parted ways amicably with Esther several years earlier and had maintained a connection to his daughter, Rebecca, and former stepchildren, Sylvia and David. Working as a machinist and AFL organizer in Pennsylvania a couple of years earlier, Fox remembered a woman he had met and "greatly admired," Cora Petersen, whom he had encountered in Philadelphia. Fox thought that perhaps she might accept his proposal. She was born and raised on the Danish island of Bornholm in the Baltic Sea but had relocated to Copenhagen to study the delicate craft of hand-painting porcelain, especially fine china. Later she moved to Berlin, where her skills were highly marketable. In 1905 she immigrated to the United States, and when Fox planned to propose to her she was working at "an epileptic sanitarium." She accepted his proposal and came to Seattle, where they were married in June. Unfortunately, the city's postwar economy, like much of the country, was experiencing a recession. In Seattle, a variety of industries were negatively impacted, especially the shipyards. Fox along with hundreds of other mechanics lost their jobs. He still had his house and waterfront property in Home and suggested they relocate there and begin a poultry business. She agreed and they moved into his small home and began to construct "a 100 × 20 foot chicken house." A number of his neighbors helped with the construction and provided food for the work crew. Fox was struck by the community's neighborliness and cooperative spirit.

Home as a colony, however, was nearing its official end. In November 1918, twelve community members set in motion a lawsuit to dissolve the MHA because of members they considered to have usurped control of the association. Along with dissolution of the association they sought a receiver appointed by the court. Dozens of residents testified for or against the plaintiffs in Judge Ernest Card's courtroom in Tacoma. He rendered a verdict in September 1919 agreeing with the petitioners that the association had been usurped and that the bylaws of the community had been inoperative for years. He ordered the association dissolved and appointed Charles W. Johnson as the permanent receiver. It took a couple of years for Johnson to complete his work, but in May 1921 Judge Card accepted Johnson's report and the MHA was no more. Of course, the community did not disappear with the dissolution of the association. Home had perhaps several hundred residents, though many still had to leave for Tacoma or other locations for employment while others made a living with small businesses. Many in the community still held a variety of radical political views and maintained connections to comrades in other parts of the country and world. With the

Cora, seated, circa 1915. Courtesy University of Washington Libraries, Special Collections, UW 28601z.

end of the association, the community became much less contentious. The poultry business turned out to be modestly lucrative for Jay and Cora, just as it had been for others in the community. Fox attended the annual American Poultry Association convention that took place in Seattle in August 1921 and became a member. Profit, though, was not the ultimate motive for the couple's entry into the business. Fox noted, "With us the purpose was not to make money but to arrange our lives so to get the most comfort and enjoyment out of it."[28]

8. A Communist at Home

Fox's INTELLECTUAL LIFE AND WRITING CAREER DID NOT END when he and Cora relocated to Home. Fox maintained a keen interest in the labor movement, the Farmer-Labor Party (in Washington and nationwide), and Foster's new effort to radicalize AFL and independent unions with the formation of the Trade Union Education League (TUEL) in 1920. World-changing events that Fox followed with great interest were the Russian Revolution, the country's subsequent civil war, and the establishment of the Soviet Union. Unlike the Mexican Revolution that Fox had championed, the revolution in Russia eventually established a socialist nation-state, ostensibly a worker-controlled society. Years later, in his unpublished memoir, he wrote, "I was aroused by the fact that the Bolsheviks were doing that which I never imagined would happen in my time. They were doing my job, realizing my dream of a classless world where all would belong to all." Moreover, he wrote, "It now became my duty as a revolutionist to watch the evolution of the new order as it progressed, notice how the people reacted and to encourage the pioneers who were performing the World moving task." Early on anarchists, socialists, and labor militants worldwide welcomed the revolution in Russia. Fox and other radicals thought a revolution may grow out of the war in Europe, though few expected to see it take place where it did. Berkman writing in *Mother Earth*, like Fox, thought that the Bolsheviks were the "pioneers of the Social Revolution." Goldman agreed that "the Boylsheviki Revolution" was "the beginning of the real Social

Revolution." Robert Minor would journey to Russia in 1918 as did several anarchists, either freely or due to deportation in the case of Goldman, Berkman, and others in 1919. Early on, Bolshevik polices had an anarchist communist quality that would be quite seductive to the movement—namely, opposition to parliamentarianism, expropriation of bourgeois property, direct action, control of the means of production, and support for the soviets or councils of workers and peasants. Foster was moved by the revolution as were other labor militants, including Wobblies such James Cannon, Ralph Chaplin, and Bill Haywood, the general secretary of the IWW, though they initially had reservations about the Bolsheviks and political action. Nevertheless, it would not be long before many labor militants would begin to embrace political organization rather than an exclusive focus on economic action, with the Communist Party in Russia serving as a guiding light.[1]

As enthusiastic as many on the left were about the revolution in Russia and other parts of Europe after the First World War ended, few were willing to immediately join the young communist parties in the United States. The Farmer-Labor Party picked up support of labor radicals along with more moderate labor activists. The growth of the British Labour Party had become an important model for political action favorable to the interests of labor. Foster, by 1920, had moved to support a farmer-labor party movement and toured the western states promoting it. More important to Foster was getting the TUEL off the ground. It was his third effort to radicalize the AFL through a boring within strategy. Starting with only a handful of militants, syndicalists, and anarcho-syndicalists—"live wires" to use his term—the TUEL would grow in time. Foster, though still a syndicalist at heart, scoffed at labor radicals who had become communists. The early communist movement in the country had a harsh view of trade unions and even the more progressive industrial unions, viewing many of them as hopelessly conservative along the same lines that many anarchists had criticized the labor movement in previous years.

Foster's reading of Vladimir Lenin's *"Left-Wing" Communism: An Infantile Disorder* had a dramatic impact on him, confirming that radicalizing the existing labor movement was central to achieving revolutionary change and that dual unionism was a dead end. Communists, under Lenin's leadership, rejected dual unionism and embraced boring within, which of course changed the communist policy toward existing labor unions. Fox read the book as well in 1921 and it had a similar impact, bringing him closer to the communist movement. Foster left for Russia as a correspondent for the *Federated Press Bulletin* in 1921 and sent back dispatches chronicling his observations and interviews. After his return to the United States, he wrote about Russian society as it was being transformed by the revolution. It is highly likely that Fox was a subscriber to the publication and read these accounts firsthand, though given his friendship with Foster he may have communicated directly with him about his experiences in Russia after his return. Foster's time there was profound. He attended the first congress of the Red International of Labor Unions (RILU) and the TUEL became an affiliate. Syndicalists and anarchists from around the world were invited to the congress including the IWW. At the congress, the RILU embraced the policy of boring within existing labor unions, which Wobblies largely rejected, though a number would eventually leave the IWW and become communists. The syndicalist and anarchist movements—mostly from Latin countries—divided over membership in the RILU, which included engaging in political action. At the first RILU congress, they voted against the close working relationship between the Communist International and the RILU, preferring the RILU to be independent. Nevertheless, prominent syndicalists, such as Pierre Monatte and Tom Mann, saw the communists as the new dynamic movement that would emancipate the working class. The communists seemed to be a third option in contrast to reformist democratic socialism and anarcho-syndicalism, which had not born any tangible fruit in comparison to what the Bolsheviks had achieved in Russia.[2]

After returning from Russia, Foster focused his energies on building the TUEL, which included a growing number of labor radicals, former members of SLNA, ITUEL and IWW, and socialists and industrial unionists such as Brown, who would be a key leader of the Farmer-Labor Party. The new publication to promote the boring within venture was the *Labor Herald*, which first appeared in March 1922. The magazine, edited by Browder, featured a number of contributors who ranged from socialists to unionists to communists. It had the quality of a radical labor journal, reminiscent of syndicalist periodicals from a few years earlier, though with a key difference in that the periodical advocated for political action. In the first issue, the American labor movement was criticized for its lack of development in comparison to Great Britain and Germany. The labor movement's continued devotion to craft or trade unionism rather than industrial unionism received special attention. Mann authored a piece in the first issue updating readers on the labor situation in Great Britain. Moreover, the inaugural issue called on the militant minority in the labor movement to get busy and organize and radicalize existing labor unions. The publication was endorsed by the editorial staff of *The Worker*, the official organ of the Workers' (Communist) Party, which also published a series of articles by Foster promoting the TUEL. The merging of the communist movement and the radical labor movement as a coordinated effort was underway. At its high point, from 1922 to 1924, the TUEL had several hundred dedicated members and was a truly nationwide organization. Although Fox had retired from active involvement in the labor movement as an organizer or labor journalist, he contributed to the *Labor Herald* and authored a TUEL publication. He was comfortable with the goals of the boring within strategy, and even though he was not a communist in the early 1920s there were elements of the movement that made sense to him: its character had a firm trade and industrial union orientation with a syndicalist and of course a revolutionary flavor. He considered this younger, more militant minority to be a successor to his efforts over the last thirty years.[3]

An early theme in the *Labor Herald* was amalgamation. Foster penned an article on the subject in the railroad industry, whose labor unions were divided along a multitude of trades and crafts. He elaborated on the topic with the first pamphlet issued by the TUEL, *The Railroaders' Next Step—Amalgamation*. Fox brought a historical perspective to his support of amalgamation by arguing that when labor unions first came into existence more than fifty years earlier, manufacturing was on a relatively small scale in comparison to its current state. The labor unions of the time could cope with a cutthroat capitalist era that pitted one manufacturer against another. However, with time, smaller manufacturers were absorbed by large corporations, concentrating great economic power. The AFL's industrial departments were a half measure to address the changing economic landscape, but Fox asserted that the federation's response was weak and ineffective. The next step was "the amalgamation of all unions in each industry into one union." For Fox, "the industrial union is as necessary today as the craft union was forty years ago."

In his writing for the periodical, he could share with readers his experiences as a worker and trade union member. For example, he wrote of his experiences as a "metal mechanic" in early 1890s in Chicago. He participated in organizing the first Metal Trades Council in the city. It was an effort to coordinate the various metal trades unions with one voice in negotiations with employers. Incorporating trades into one organization was a slow process. Just getting "helpers" into the blacksmiths' union and other trade unions was a challenge. A motivating factor to bring less skilled workers into the union was the fear of other workers within the industry remaining on the job while the skilled members of a trade union were on strike. Therefore, the skilled trade union members agreed to absorb helpers into their union rather than having a separate union in the same industry, who could potentially "scab" on those that were striking. Although he acknowledged that the metal trades had made some progress, he conceded that more was necessary. Fox noted that the internationals among the metal trades needed to be unified into one industrial union if they were to continue on a path to greater power in the face of employers.[4]

Fox's thoughts on industrial unionism culminated in a league pamphlet, *Amalgamation*, which was published in June 1923. It was well-publicized in the pages of the *Labor Herald* as a long-awaited booklet on the subject. He began his study with a vision of society without masters or slaves, employers and employees, rich or poor, but a "civilized society" without conflicting economic interests. First, he presented a brief history of capitalism in the United States and the rise of corporations, which he argued were "industrial unions of capitalists." Fox tapped themes he explored in his previous writing in newspapers and journals as he elaborated on capitalist control of the educational system and religious institutions. He proceeded to treat the rise of the labor movement in conjunction with the development of capitalism, and he outlined how capitalists outpaced workers in organization and an understanding of how best to advance their interests at the expense of labor. He lambasted the contemporary leadership of the AFL for undercutting any truly progressive ideas to take shape in the federation, let alone anything radical. When he reached the topic of craft unionism, he explained how "there are too many unions and not enough unionism." He lamented the fact that labor in the beginning of the 1920s was still organized on a nineteenth-century basis in too many sectors of the economy. When he began to treat the process of amalgamation, he synthesized a variety of articles in the *Labor Herald* to explain how amalgamation would transform the labor movement and labor organizing in a host of industries. He called for change to come from below where the TUEL operated. The resistance to change came from the leaders who saw the loss of their positions if amalgamation took hold, though he did not let those who were committed to craft autonomy off the hook. Their selfish focus on their own craft blinded them to an antiquated labor movement strategy. Nevertheless, Fox stressed that amalgamation was not complicated and in fact was clearly an inevitable, evolutionary step. He used the metal trades as his example of how the amalgamation process would affect an industry as it evolved from trade unions to an industrial union with departments. He pointed to the German model for a metal workers' union, which had over a million members, the largest such industrial union in the world. He concluded his pamphlet by explaining the goals of the TUEL as a revolutionary organization and its support for a workers' republic as well as the need to build up a militant labor party. Fox gave several lectures, some as far away as San Francisco, on the topic of amalgamation and a labor party under the auspices of the TUEL.[5]

One distinguishing characteristic of Fox's writing in the pages of the *Labor Herald* was his style. Unlike other contributors to the periodical, his articles were more accessible to an average reader, someone who was new to the concept of a "militant" or to the TUEL. He also used humor in a way that few other contributors did, especially Foster, whose prose, though filled with passion and conviction, could be overly pedantic. Fox incorporated an attribute similar to his earlier writing by injecting queries to him by friends or acquaintances, whether real or imagined, which he could then respond to in an essay on a particular topic. A. B. Callaham or "Cal," a resident of Alaska who practiced law, and for a time edited the socialist *Sunday Morning Post* in Juneau and occasionally wrote for the *Seattle Union Record*, was a friend of Fox's who stayed with the couple at Home in the summer of 1922. On his way back to Alaska, on a Seattle steamer heading north, he wrote a letter to the couple. He was looking forward to reading the next issue of the *Labor Herald*, which featured a new article by Fox. He noted, "It is damning Jay's stuff with faint praise to say that for me his style has more charm than any other labor writer, for the average labor [writer] dispises [sic] language as bourgeoise conventionality, and hasn't any [charm]."

Underscoring Cal's comments were several articles of Fox's in which he started by acknowledging that the piece originated with a question posed to him. In one example, a friend wrote, "Why a trade union educational league?" and suggested that the country's educational system was sufficient "without you brothers handing us out some new-fangled stuff to torture our tired brains about." Fox responded, "First, he is a victim of capitalist propaganda—the most pernicious pest the world has ever known. Second, he dislikes to use his brain—a plague second only to the other." Fox proceeds to explain the class system at work in the country, though the press, educators, politicians, and many others denies that it even exists. He used the 1922 coal miners' strike to illustrate the class divide, with employers who owned the mines (the jobs) supported by the courts, newspapers, and capitalists, and the workers on the other side, supported only by their family and friends. He then proceeded to explain the usefulness of TUEL, for it offers "a simple explanation of things as they exist and have existed for hundreds of years." He asked his friend to look around him to see who owned the wealth in the country and who created that wealth. Workers needed to use their "tired brains" because capitalists were certainly using their own. The TUEL wanted workers, through industrial organization, to take control of the industries in the country. He continued, "And it is in our opinion that the burden of liberating labor lies in its own hands and no where else." After reading a letter from a friend who expressed his support for "Organized Labor" and the right of workers to strike but did not think it was right to prevent workers from taking striking workers' jobs, Fox wrote, "I was a bit riled and felt like batting my friend on the bean. Distance preventing the use of the bat I was compelled to resort to the highbrow stuff." He then proceeded to explain the brutal history that striking workers experienced and how over time society and the law accepted the right of workers to strike. Yet, the job, "owned" by another man, forced the worker to beg for a living. True, the worker currently had no legal right to a job. However, Fox reasoned that more and more workers were coming to realize that they should "own" the job through their industrial union "as a birthright."[6]

Although Fox for years had supported efforts within the AFL to reform and move toward industrial unionism, it had become clear to him that the leadership was hopelessly conservative and downright reactionary. The fact that Gompers easily won reelection as president year after year demonstrated how intractable the federation had become to meet the changing nature of the American economy. The heady days of the war years that culminated in union membership in 1920 of over five million had fallen precipitously by 1923. The progressive coalition within the postwar federation did not have the strength that the socialist bloc of the prewar years had, and Gompers was successful at dividing any unified opposition. In addition, employers had initiated open shop drives in multiple industries at the beginning of the decade, putting unionists on their heels. The anti-radicalism and pervasive Americanism that swept the country after the war infiltrated the federation just as it had other institutions.

Fox noted in one of his essays that he recently had a conversation with a friend at the University of Washington. This friend had read a few labor journals, trade union constitutions, and AFL convention proceedings, but he was unsure where the labor movement was headed. Fox replied that "we are standing perfectly still." The labor bureaucracy impedes any progress, and amalgamation was treated only with distain. He suggested that were his friend to attend a federation convention and he would mistake it for a conference of the National Manufacturers' Association. Labor leaders had become satisfied with the status quo and had no inter-est in change that could negatively affect their secure jobs. Transforma-tion of the AFL would have to come from below, Fox asserted, when "the workers take a hand in their own affairs and elect men and women right out of the factories to the conventions." In many respects, Fox was echo-ing points made by Foster in his TUEL pamphlet *The Bankruptcy of the American Labor Movement.*[7]

Fox returned to some familiar themes and history lessons in his *Labor Herald* essays such as his loathing of compulsory arbitration, which forced workers to stay on the job or risk prosecution for striking. He provided a historical perspective on Labor Day when it was more than a day of lei-sure, and on laws that affected labor, especially the Sherman Antitrust Act. He began the latter subject with a quote from Clarence Darrow: "I don't care who makes the law if you let me interpret it." Here, Fox could explain to readers how a law that was meant to restrict the creation of monopolies was used against labor unions, the ARU in particular. He took his analysis of the law into subsequent uses that impaired labor unions to the point where he concluded that strikebreaking had become a function of govern-ment. Resurrecting Henry Dub in this essay, Fox noted that even he knows "that labor has no friends outside of its own ranks." In yet in another essay, he used the striking coal miners in Washington, who he had great affec-tion for, due to their membership in District 10 of the UMW, which had supported the IUT several years earlier. Their strike, he argued, was under-mined by the craft unions that continued to transport "scab" coal. Unified labor action was the only hope against a unified employer front run out of "Wall Street," according to Fox.

A labor party was a new theme in his writing, which would have been unthinkable to him ten years earlier. However, at this point in his intellectual evolution, he championed the concept and noted the significant development of the British Labour Party, which had 143 members in the United Kingdom's House of Commons, second only to the Conservative Party. He called on those supporting their own version of a labor party to end their petty fixation on an ideal and to ally with others into one unified party. He castigated Gompers and AFL leadership for standing in the way of a labor party and pointed out that the two main political parties only served the interest of capitalists. He noted that "the time is rotten ripe for a union of unions that will represent the workers industrially" and for "a party of parties, a great Labor Party, that will rally the workers under its banner and conjointly with the industrial unions make the supreme effort in a united front for freedom of labor from the thraldom [sic] of capitalism." His article was published before the July 1923 farmer-labor party convention in Chicago. The gathering was designed to ally the Workers' (Communist) Party, a progressive farmer-labor party advocated by the Chicago Federation of Labor (CFL), and other labor representatives. Over six hundred delegates attended, but the unity effort failed, largely because of pressure from the AFL leadership, the Railroad Brotherhoods, and other labor organizations taking an anti-communist stand. Foster blamed John Fitzpatrick, president of the CFL, who withdrew along with his allies from a united labor party that would have brought together progressives, socialists, and communists. It also precipitated a break between the TUEL and the CFL. Foster and his allies soldiered on with the formation of the Federated Farmer-Labor Party, but in the end it was a stillborn affair.[8]

Despite the movement for a labor party growing among the ranks of radicals and the creation of new militant cadre to push for industrial unionism, the labor movement was in retreat as the decade unfolded. In his final article for the *Labor Herald* Fox acknowledged that union membership nationwide was on the decline. The most vital issue for labor—he implored his readers—was organization. Millions of workers were without organization and more workers were leaving unions than were joining them. Fox placed much of the blame on Gompers and the conservative leadership of the AFL. At the AFL convention in Portland, Oregon, in 1923 Gompers claimed that union members who were out of work could not pay their union dues and therefore had to leave their union. Fox argued that this was true for some union members; however, many unions, such as the machinists' union, had provisions for members out of work so that they could maintain their good standing. Fox pointed to the recent mass organizing drives among packinghouse workers and steelworkers, which had brought thousands of workers into the labor movement. Similar organizing drives were of great necessity, but the labor bureaucracy appeared to stand in the way. Fox did not make note of the postwar economic downturn as a factor in plummeting union membership numbers. By 1924, economic prosperity— though spread unevenly—was returning to the country, which in some respects undermined the TUEL's radicalism. Moreover, collaboration efforts among unions of skilled workers and employers became a general trend as a means of trade union survival. The TUEL held a large second convention in September 1923, but it did not have another for four years. Efforts to purge militants from the ranks of AFL constituent unions proved successful and by mid-decade TUEL members were in essence working outside the labor movement rather than boring within it. Foster, writing years later, thought that the TUEL had become too closely identified with the Workers' (Communist) Party and thereby alienated itself from workers who were open to a more aggressive unionism but suspicious of or outright hostile to communism.[9]

Fox along with many former anarchists, anarcho-syndicalists, left-wing socialists, Wobblies, and militant labor activists became communists in the late 1910s and through the mid-1920s. Fox joined the Workers' (Communist) Party in 1924, though he did not make that public until the following year. As the radical element he identified with carried on the struggle during a very difficult decade for radicalism that would not see a strong resurgence until the advent of the Great Depression, Fox took a break from the struggle. Both Jay and Cora were workers who were used to laboring six days a week, but raising chickens required a daily commitment. In addition, Fox had written extensively for the *Labor Herald* and his pamphlet was the longest piece of writing he ever published. The couple decided to leave Home for an extended period. They sold their flock and spent a year working and traveling the West Coast, primarily in California where Cora had relatives and Fox had friends and comrades, especially San Francisco. There was nothing unusual about the two of them working and traveling by automobile. With inexpensive used cars and trucks available, individuals, couples, and families could seek out employment, traveling from worksite to worksite and living out of their vehicles. Families of "fruit tramps" had become a major feature of the West Coast harvest labor supply for employers, largely replacing the nearly all-male workforce that that got around on freight trains. Fox was able to procure "an old buick that some smart lad had hinged the back of the front seat so it could lay back to connect with the rear seat so to make a bed." Fox built a shallow wooden cabinet and attached it to the running board of the automobile to store food and cooking utensils. The couple stopped in Oregon to visit a close friend of Cora's and then continued on to the Bay Area, stopping at campsites along the way, which offered few if any amenities. In San Francisco, Fox was familiar with the "high spots" having lived there a number of years ago. After the sightseeing, they settled into working. Fox was able to secure employment at a shipyard and Cora, who had skill as a seamstress, found work at "a swanky gown shop." Several months later, they decided to see more of the state and drove along the coastal roads to Los Angeles, where Fox had several friends. On their return trip to Washington, they traveled on inland roads and visited Cora's relatives in the San Joaquin Valley. After a year of tramping the West Coast, they arrived back at Home, where Cora worked as an egg candler at Home's cooperative store and Fox operated the chicken "ranch."[10]

Fox and other former anarchists made the transition to become communists, each in their own way. His friend and comrade Samuel Hammersmark worked closely with the TUEL in Chicago and followed Foster's lead into the Workers' (Communist) Party. He was instrumental in getting the communist *Daily Worker* off the ground in 1924. Minor had been skeptical of the Bolshevik government but publicly explained his conversion in the pages of *The Liberator* in 1920. He became a prolific writer in communist periodicals for the next two decades. Other anarchists, however, stayed true to their ideology. Fred S. Graham (Shmuel Marcus) published a pamphlet, *Anarchism and the World Revolution: An Answer to Robert Minor*, to refute Minor's analysis of the Bolsheviks and their "workers' state." In late 1924, Hippolyte Havel and the *Road to Freedom* Group published a new anarchist periodical called the *Road to Freedom*. After the repression that anarchists experienced during the war years and the Red Scare of the postwar period, which silenced most of their periodicals, anarchists wanted to return to publishing an English-language journal. The *Road to Freedom* was similar to anarchist journals of the past in that it adhered to anarchist communism; however, Havel and the Group encouraged all anarchists, whether communists, syndicalists, or individualists, to feel welcome in contributing to the publication. Many of the articles were geared toward the working class and cautioned workers from being seduced by socialist, communist, and other political parties. They counseled readers to take the path of social revolution and employ the general strike, a libertarian rather than an authoritarian means for overthrowing the existing system. The publication paid special attention on the situation in the Soviet Union in which those who criticized communist policies experienced horrific repression, imprisonment, and even execution.

After supporting the Bolsheviks early on, anarchists had become greatly disillusioned, including Goldman and Berkman. Their writings and speeches, along with those of other witnesses who spoke out against Bolshevik brutality, turned anarchists against the authoritarian regime as it developed in Russia. The failed Kronstadt Rebellion in 1921 represented the last effort to maintain the independence of the soviets from the Bolshevik government. Moreover, with the conclusion of the civil war, the Communist Party implemented the Dictatorship of the Proletariat, which further moved anarchists to be openly anti-Bolshevik or anti-communist. For both Goldman and Berkman, the slaughter of the Kronstadt rebels ended their support for the Bolsheviks. Goldman's *My Further Disillusionment in Russia* appeared in 1924, the second volume of her experiences and analysis of the Soviet Union, in which she notes the effect that the Bolshevik suppression of the Kronstadt rebels and the persecution of Russian anarchists had on her. While seeking asylum in Great Britain, she continued to write critically of the Soviet government and gave speeches condemning the repression in Russia. Her work was picked up by the press throughout the United States. In 1925, Berkman's *The Bolshevik Myth* demonstrated clearly the Bolsheviks' oppression, which he witnessed firsthand. Both Goldman and Berkman as well as most anarchists still supported the revolution in Russia; however, they concluded that the communists had usurped it for their own ends.[11]

It was in this context that Fox felt compelled to publicly declare his support for the Bolshevik seizure of power and the Soviet Union and explain why he had become a communist. His essay "From Anarchism to Communism" appeared in the *Workers Monthly*, which resulted from the merger of the *Labor Herald*, *The Liberator*, and the *Soviet Russia Pictorial*. First, Fox set out to explain the origin of his radicalism when as a teenager he "imbibed the teachings of Anarchist Communism" from Albert Parsons and the other "Chicago Anarchist Martyrs." He accepted the view that by using the ballot it was not possible to overthrow the capitalist system, and that only by radicalizing trade unions could a social revolution take place. Practical experience over the years made him question some aspects of anarchism. For instance, if a social revolution did take place, how was it going to be protected from those who would seek to destroy it? Anarchism, Fox reasoned, did not have a satisfying answer for the charge that "organized defense would constitute a revolutionary government and Anarchists were opposed to any kind of government." He thought that anarchist principles needed to be modified, though only those anarchists with trade union experience seemed to agree with him. As he followed the events in Russia, particularly the civil war, he saw the Red Army protect the "Workers' Republic" from its enemies. Even though he was troubled by some of the Bolsheviks' repressive policies, he thought that to attack them was to attack the revolution itself. Having never been part of a social revolution, he doubted that he would have held to anarchist theory when practical necessity would have forced him to modify his principles. He believed that the Communist International was paving the way for the emancipation of labor worldwide, and he wanted to be part of that liberation.

Fox thought that communists were the most committed agitators working within the labor movement, seeking to radicalize it along the lines he had advocated over the course of many years. He defended the Dictatorship of the Proletariat as the only means to prevent "parasites" from having any power to undo the revolution. He argued that "the Soviet System of representation is much more representative than bourgeois 'democracy.'" Moreover, he accepted the theory of the state withering away once society had "readjusted on a Communist basis" with no economic classes. At that point, the state could be discarded. Clearly Fox had read Vladimir Lenin's *The State and Revolution*, for some of the examples in his piece were derived from his personal copy of Lenin's work, underlined with his distinctive blue pencil marks. At the end of his article, he unleashed a vicious attack on Goldman, arguing that she had no standing in the labor movement, and that while she had been a revolutionary earlier in her career she had shifted to lectures on "ethical subjects and literature." Her attacks on the Russian

Revolution and the Soviet Union were downright traitorous and had culminated in her becoming "a revolutionary scab" by Fox's estimation.[12]

It was not long before Fox was openly criticized and condemned by
anarchists, especially in the pages of the *Road to Freedom*, by two of his
oldest anarchist comrades. Havel noted that for three decades Fox had
been in the anarchist movement yet seemed to have not understood anarchist theory. He continued, "Fox does not seem to comprehend that the
controversy between Bolshevism and Anarchism two opposite theories of
life are being fought out—the difference between liberty and authority."
Havel went on to charge that Fox always hid his "anarchism" whenever in
the pay of the AFL and claimed that Fox may have never been an anarchist.
As for his attacks against Goldman, Havel asked, Who is the traitor? Goldman, who supports the revolution in Russia but condemns the "small sect
which destroyed the Soviet idea of revolutionary Russia and suppresses
every manifestation of the Soviet spirit"? Or Fox, who rejected his libertarian past and had gone over to the authoritarians? A more detailed excoria-
tion of Fox followed written by Harry Kelly. He examined Fox's career over
the previous decade and found that the former anarchist had been searching for an ideological home. He wrote, "So after skating around for a number of years trying to find where he belongs, brother Fox lands with both
feet in the 'Workers' Party.'" Kelly proceeded to challenge each major point
made in Fox's article. While Fox tried to explain the necessities behind the
controversial policies of the Bolshevik government, Kelly took each one
apart, charging that Fox seemed to have no idea how oppressive the Soviet
state had become and how counterrevolutionary it was from an anarchist
perspective. Kelly thought it strange than an anarcho-syndicalist who had
read Kropotkin's *Conquest of Bread* would question how production and
distribution would be organized when the famed anarchist had already
laid out a strategy that did not involve a government of any kind. Moreover, Fox, who had extensive experience with trade and industrial unions,
did not seem to see their role in defending the revolution. And he seemed
to accept the Red Army as the protector of the revolution, without any
reservations. Kelly also chided Fox for not questioning information coming out of the Soviet Union, when it was not difficult to see that all of it was
censored by the communists. Fox's support for the Communist International, which ostensibly called for the emancipation of the world's workers,
gave them no independent voice, and those who spoke out in Russia were

jailed or worse. Even though both Havel and Kelly made excellent critiques of Fox's support for the Bolsheviks, they did not seem to understand that his motives were tied to his commitment to the labor movement. Havel never played a serious role in labor organizing or in the labor movement in general, and Kelly had stopped active participation in 1904. Nevertheless, they were holding firm to the notion that the ends can never justify the means, a conviction that most anarchists held dear, as would have the anarchist Fox of years ago.[13]

Writing years later as a communist in his unpublished memoir, he commented on his detractors who attacked him for leaving the anarchist cause, which was in peril by the mid-1920s. He maintained that he "did not desert the cause" when he embraced the communist movement. Fox wrote, "I could not desert a cause that is a vital part of my intellectual life." From his point of view, he was not "swerving an inch from [his] original purpose." He was still devoted to the emancipation of the working class and the destruction of capitalism, but his path toward that end had changed. Anarchism had simply become "outmoded and ineffective," even before the repression of the war and postwar years. He wished that his former anarchist comrades would join him in this more labor-focused revolutionary effort because he believed the communists were a new version of the militant minority. He argued that anarchists who worked in the labor movement had a more realistic conception of anarchism than did the idealistic theorists. It was this group of anarchists "who developed the idea of revolutionary trade unionism." It was true that anarchists or anti-statist revolutionaries played an important role in Europe, especially France, in advocating for a revolutionary trade unionism and revolutionary industrial unionism. In the United States, the IWW was at the forefront of that effort. Yet it was inaccurate of Fox to make such a distinction between anarchists who were theorists and those who were active participants in the labor movement. Even though neither Havel nor Goldman had extensive labor movement experience, other theorists did. Carlo Tresca, for example, had a long history of labor movement activity as well as being an anarchist theorist, editor, and writer. In addition, Rose Pesotta became an anarchist in the mid-1910s and joined the International Ladies' Garment Workers' Union (ILGWU) in 1914. For years, she belonged to the ILGWU while writing for both Yiddish and English-language anarchist and union publications, including *Der Yunyon Arbeter* and *The Road to Freedom*.

Nevertheless, by the mid-1920s anarchists were moving in a much different direction in comparison to communists. With some notable exceptions such as the Anarchist Red Cross and some trade union activity, many anarchists had turned inward. Publications espousing anarchist theory, history, and a critique of society at home and abroad continued to be an important feature of the movement, but anarchist colonies and the Modern School became a growing aspect of anarchist activity during the 1920s and 1930s. Although anarchists in the colonies maintained an outwardly positive conviction that their intentional communities were successful, privately they expressed some concern about the difficulty of living an anarchist life. Anarchists, however, were taking a long view of transforming society into libertarian socialist reality. As early as 1915, Berkman thought that if social revolution meant "a fundamental reorganization of life" then it would require "the gradual—primarily individual—substitution of new values for old ones." Therefore, education—whether that of children or the readers of anarchist literature—became the most important activity for anarchists. In a series of letters between Kelly and Berkman, Kelly thought that they had kept their movement "pure" by refusing to throw themselves in with the Bolsheviks. That choice, however, left the movement, in Kelly's words, "small and tattered." To be committed to the anarchist cause, he believed one had to be "an ascetic" and avoid temptations that could lead one into compromising one's values and beliefs.[14]

The communist movement that Fox put a great deal of faith in was experiencing its own difficult situation at mid-decade. The conservativism of the 1920s and relative economic prosperity had undermined recruitment into the communist movement at the same time that TUEL members were purged from trade unions. Moreover, factionalism between those committed to the importance of trade unionism and those committed to the importance of the party further weakened the movement. Exacerbating the situation were American communists competing for support from the shifting communist party line out of Moscow. In the state of Washington, the party experienced a similar trajectory with communists being forced out of the Seattle Central Labor Council and party membership declining. As the decade ended communism in the Pacific Northwest as well as nationally began to show signs of growth. With the advent of the Great Depression, the American Communist Party would have a new lease on life and communists would become some of the most dedicated trade union and industrial union activists of the 1930s. For Fox, these were issues he followed in the *Daily Worker* and other periodicals he subscribed to as he managed his poultry business. In addition, he began work on a history of anarchism in which he was far kinder to Goldman and acknowledged her indispensable role in the US movement. Fox had a wealth of personal knowledge and a vast collection of anarchist and other radical periodicals and correspondence to draw on as sources for his book.

Meanwhile, while working as an egg candler at the community's cooperative store, Cora became interested in returning to her craft as a ceramic artist. Fox built a studio for her so that she could go back to painting. Samples of her work were sent to Tacoma and Seattle and soon she was receiving orders for hand-painted fine china. Working with Cora as an egg candler was Edward Padgham, an immigrant and cooper by trade back in England, who boarded with the couple. With the economic downturn of the Depression years, the bottom fell out of the poultry business and Fox was forced to close his "ranch." He sold his flock at a loss and was without a job. Cora and Padgham lost their jobs at the cooperative store as well as most of the poultry businesses closed. Her ceramic work, however, proved essential for the couple's financial survival. Taking "advantage of the crash in building material," Fox decided to put his carpentry skills to good use and built a six-room "modern home." Once the poultry business rebounded, Cora and Padgham were able to work as egg candlers again. Moreover, in the 1940s, Cora secured a contract with a ceramic company in Berkeley, California. In addition, she taught painting classes for a small fee. Her income supported Fox in his retirement as well as Padgham, who suffered from a physical disability that prevented him from working as he continued to stay with Jay and Cora.[15]

Fox maintained his connection to the Communist Party in the 1930s as the organization rebounded. He was modestly active in District 12, which included Washington, Oregon, and Idaho. At its high point in 1939, the party counted more than 3,500 members. Communists at the outbreak of the Great Depression were particularly skilled at organizing the masses of unemployed in key cites in Washington as well as nationally and played an important role in labor organizing. For several years the party reversed itself and created dual unions, with limited success. Oddly, their industrial unions bore a great similarity to the IWW's efforts from years earlier. However, the party stopped its dual union strategy and worked within existing unions, helping to expand labor union membership. The unions that affiliated with the new Congress of Industrial Organizations (CIO), a breakaway from the AFL, proved receptive to communists as long as their focus was on labor organizing. Communists participated in several major industries in Washington including the longshoremen's union. In the timber industry, communists played a role in the International Woodworkers of America (IWA), formerly the Federation of Woodworkers.

In the 1930s, the IWA issued a newspaper with the same title that the IUT used, the *Timber Worker*, which published several of Fox's "Letters to Jack Lumber." In these pieces, Fox revived his folksy style with a combination of wit and radicalism. He wrote in support of the timber workers breaking free from the carpenters' AFL-affiliated union and their dismissing Red-baiting tactics, designed to dissuade timber workers from joining the CIO. Fox congratulated Jack for being with a union that chose to affiliate with the new labor federation, which Fox believed was a "family of progressive industrial unions . . . the high hope of the American labor movement." The IWA, like many progressive labor unions, supported the loyalists in the Spanish Civil War. Several IWA members served in Spain fighting the fascists, and in the pages of the *Timber Worker* the justification for taking the side of the pro-republican coalition was to support democracy. Fox also wrote letters to the *Tacoma Daily Ledger* defending the Communist Party and its activities from attacks in the newspaper and elsewhere. He also wrote letters to the editor to correct newspaper accounts that Home was no longer a haven for radicals, as they still existed in the community. Communists were at the forefront in protecting the rights of people of color and women, both nationally and in the state of Washington. Fox attended meetings of the Communist Political Association of Piece County, which hosted discussions of the "problems [faced by] Negroes, women, veterans, youth, farmers, Filipinos, and American-Japanese." Fox's attitudes on race and gender were changing in his later years, probably as a result of the communist literature he read and the communist discussion groups he participated in. He was coming to see that oppression was not only a result of class but of race and gender as well.[16]

Fox maintained his friendships with a number of anarchists who had become communists, but also with socialists, progressives, and a variety of individuals who populated the left end of the political spectrum. In the mid-1930s, Foster and Esther paid a visit to Jay and Cora. Foster was suffering physically and mentally from his 1932 presidential campaign and a trip to the Soviet Union, which he returned from in early 1934. While on the West Coast, Esther thought it would be a good break for Foster to reunite with his old friend and rest in Home. Fox had plenty of room for the couple in his newly built house. The community was an inviting place for both Foster and Esther, both having fond memories of their time there. Fox may have given Foster a copy of his history of anarchism manuscript to read then or sent it to him after the couple returned to New York. Foster wrote out a number of suggestions to improve the book, and to avoid any hurt feelings he related his own experience with reviews of his work before publication. He thought that Fox's book had great merit but that some chapters and passages should be added, especially regarding the "McNamara case," the "Magoon [sic] Brothers and the Mexican revolution." Most telling was Foster's urging that Fox have a strong concluding chapter on the "rising 'crescendo' for the Communist Party." Otherwise, Foster thought Fox's "book appears as pro-Anarchist." He also wanted Fox to make sure that he included a "Marxist viewpoint on Anarchism."[17]

In Fox's later life, he served as a resource for those interested in the history of the most radical elements of the American labor movement. For instance, he wrote for the *Daily Worker* about his experiences as a youth in Chicago. In one article, he explained what he witnessed at the McCormick strike in 1886. His account documented the events that led to several workers being killed and others wounded in the conflict between police and strikers. That incident, of course, precipitated the Haymarket gathering that proved so decisive in the history of anarchism and the labor movement as a whole. In 1939 he began his memoir, at the urging of Foster, who was a little tired of hearing about Fox's carpentry skills and the ongoing work on his house. Foster thought he had a long experience in the most radical elements of the labor movement and that his life story would be "more permanent" than a house. However, work on both manuscripts was postponed by a serious illness that forced Fox to undergo stomach surgery, though his recovery period allowed him to resume writing and maintain his correspondence. One correspondent in particular was Ewing C. Baskette, a lawyer by profession and a librarian at the University of Kentucky. He worked as public defender, participated in the Scottsboro Case, and defended radicals, most notably Ray Becker, an African American communist in Georgia. Baskette became deeply interested in the history of the struggle for civil liberties. He contacted Fox in the early 1940s to ask whether he had copies of anarchist literature he would be willing to share. He was interested in *The Agitator*, *The Demonstrator*, anarchist pamphlets, and any other radical writings Fox may have had. Baskette was a friend of Theodore Schroeder, who may have suggested that he contact him. Fox sent a large cache of books, pamphlets, and newspapers in 1943. Baskette would eventually amass the country's largest private collection of radical literature, especially focusing on free speech and civil liberties. In 1959, the University of Illinois at Urbana-Champaign would purchase his archive.[18]

With the outbreak of another world war, Fox was convinced that another revolution would follow, one that would "complete the job" of the first. In a letter to Schroeder, with whom he had maintained a correspondence, he predicted that the workers of Europe would rise up against the Nazis and the Allies as well. Like most communists, he believed that Nazism was the "last stage of capitalism." Capitalism's demise, though predicted by communists during the worldwide Great Depression, of course did not happen; the global war, communists thought, would surely bring it down. Fox, moreover, believed that the oppressed peoples of the British Empire would likewise revolt once the war concluded. These predictions did not come to pass, though decolonialization did take hold in the postwar period. For Fox and Cora, they occasionally spent time in Seattle to take a break from work at Home. Fox farmed a small plot of land on their "homestead" while Cora worked again as an egg candler and painted porcelain and china. Fox did suffer from some reoccurring illnesses and a cataract in one of his eyes, which prevented him from working on his manuscripts. Fox was old enough to receive a Social Security payment each month, which was important for the couple's income. Despite Fox's eyesight (a condition he would eventually treat), he continued to have his writing published, mostly, notably in the *Daily Worker*, *Labor Unity*, and the *People's World*, a communist periodical founded in 1938 and published in San Francisco.

Most of his published writing in his later years involved his experience in labor union activity and his eyewitness account of Haymarket. In addition, he maintained correspondence with friends in different parts of the country, especially Chicago, and he occasionally gave public talks and even later in his eighties considered "restarting perhaps a lecture career." Remarkably, some of his anarchist literature was published in a periodical out of Mumbai (Bombay), India, by the Libertarian Socialist Institute. In corresponding with members of that organization, he thought that perhaps they could publish his book on anarchism, though he believed they probably did not have the financial resources to do so. Fox was proud of his anarchist past and enjoyed the attention it bought him. His conversion to communism held firm to his last years, despite the oppressive environment of the Red Scare of the 1950s. In fact, he had an outline on the front porch of his house of a hammer and sickle, which made it clear to any visitors which side of the Cold War he was on. He lamented the situation his comrades were in after the passage of the Smith Act, which practically made membership in the Communist Party illegal.[19]

Fox's beloved Home continued to be of interest to visitors long after its activist heyday came to an end. He was not the only aging radical; several others continued to live in the little village, and visitors from Tacoma and Seattle occasionally visited to learn about its past from those who lived through its famous (or infamous) periods. Fox and his fellow villagers enjoyed the pilgrimages, the ability to make new friendships, and the attention these visitors brought to their community. For example, the *Northwest Enterprise*, a newspaper published in Seattle that focused on promoting the accomplishments of African Americans in the Pacific Northwest and that also had a progressive civil rights agenda, sponsored an excursion that featured music, dancing, and a picnic at "Old Home Colony." In 1937 Stewart Holbrook, timber worker turned author and regional historian, wrote a three-part series on the history of Home Colony for *The Oregonian*. Though writers had visited the community before and chronicled their observations, Holbrook's narrative may have been the first attempt to tell the full story of the colony from its initial settlement up to the 1930s. He focused on Home's radicalism and the challenges it faced in its first years. Fox and other anarchists and radicals were featured, along with visitors such as Goldman, Haywood, and Foster. Controversies involving the "Nude and the Prudes," free love, and the community's newspapers received ample coverage.

Other visitors had more nefarious purposes. Frank Pease, who had written for *The Agitator* years earlier, spent time at Home and ingratiated himself with the residents. He seemed like a progressive, open-minded man, worldly and compassionate. When the Second World War broke out, he abruptly left the colony. It was later discovered he was an intelligence officer in the army.

He issued a report about Home in which he described it as an "old time get-away for reds, <u>real</u> ones: dynamiters, riot-provokers, slackers, anti-military propagandists, and all around 'unAmericans.'" He presented a short history of Home when it was an anarchist colony and described Fox as one of the leaders. Pease had met Detective Burns, who was "morally certain" that Fox threw the bomb at Haymarket.

Terry Pettus, editor of *People's World*, visited Home in the early 1950s and wrote an article on Fox, "Sixty-Four Years a Union Man." Pettus presented a brief overview of Home's history and Fox's experiences as a union worker, organizer, anarchist, editor, and communist, especially his friendship with Foster and his work with him in the SLNA. Holbrook would return to Home and write another, largely sympathetic series of articles in the late 1950s for a new generation of readers. He went over much of the same history and noted that few of the radicals were still alive. Fox was essentially the last, whom Holbrook referred to as an "old anarchist, perhaps the last of his kind." Holbrook hoped that historians would discover the history of Home. One eventually did research and write a thorough history the colony, Charles LeWarne, whose chapter on the colony in *Utopias on Puget Sound, 1885–1915* has been a significant resource to researchers on Home. More recently, Justin Wadland wrote his own insightful history of the colony, *Trying Home: The Rise and Fall of an Anarchist Utopia on Puget Sound*.[20]

Late in life Fox tended to his garden, continued to work on his history of anarchism and on his memoir, and enjoyed his life with Cora and his friends in the community. However, he never completed either of his manuscripts. His struggles might be explained by the fact that he had never written any long pieces comparable to his friend Foster. *Amalgamation*, a sixty-four-page pamphlet, was his longest published work. He was most adept at writing periodical articles of five hundred to a thousand words. Moreover, in the surviving portions of his history of anarchism, Fox seemed to have been unable to write a repudiation of the movement and add a celebratory ending focused on the Communist Party, which Foster had advised him to do. Perhaps that is why he did not seek support for his book from International Publishers, a publishing company closely associated with the Communist Party, and instead wondered whether the Libertarian Socialist Institute in India would publish it. Even though he was a communist,

Fox at Home, date unknown. Courtesy University of Washington Libraries, Special Collections, UW 28603z.

anarchism, as a theory of society with a distinct history, still resonated within him. On 8 March 1961, Jay Fox passed away. A grand funeral with a headstone did not interest him, for he preferred something simple and modest. His body was cremated and his ashes spread in the couple's rose garden. Here, he could eternally rest on the banks of the tranquil waters of Puget Sound in the village he called Home.

NOTES

ABBREVIATIONS

Berkman Papers, IISH   Alexander Berkman Papers, Microfilm, International
Institute of Social History, Amsterdam

CCC, WSHS   Cooperative Colony Collection, Washington State
Historical Society, Tacoma

Fox Papers, Gonzaga   Jay Fox Papers, Special Collections Department, Foley
Center Library, Gonzaga University, Spokane,
Washington

Fox Papers, WSU   Jay Fox Papers, Manuscript, Archives, and Special
Collections, Holland Library, Washington State
University, Pullman

Gov. Lister Papers, WSA   Governor Ernst Lister Papers, Washington State
Archives, Olympia, Washington

Haiman Papers, UW   Lewis Haiman Papers, 1971, Special Collections,
Suzzallo and Allen Libraries, University of Washington,
Seattle

Kelly Papers, UM   Harry Kelly Papers, 1924–1951, Special Collection
Archival and Manuscript Collection, University of
Michigan, Ann Arbor

Labadie Papers, UM   Joseph Labadie Papers, Special Collections Research
Center, University of Michigan, Ann Arbor

Schroeder Papers, SIU   Theodore Schroeder Papers, 1842–1957, Special Collection Research Center, Southern Illinois University,
Carbondale

Silverberg Papers, UW   Darby N. Silverberg Papers 1983, Interview, 1983, Special
Collections, Suzzallo and Allen Libraries, University of
Washington, Seattle

1 *Free Society*, 13 November 1898; Jay Fox, untitled manuscript, Box 1, Folder 1, Jay Fox Papers, Special Collections Department, Foley Center Library, Gonzaga University, Spokane, Washington (hereafter Fox Papers, Gonzaga); Jay Fox, untitled manuscript, Jay Fox Papers, Private Collection of Ross K. Reider, scanned copies in author's possession (hereafter in author's possession); *Daily Worker*, 29 April 1936; *Chicago Times*, 1 May 1886; *The Argus*, 3 May 1886; James Green, *Death in the Haymarket: A Story of Chicago, the First Labor Movement and the Bombing that Divided Gilded Age America* (New York: Anchor Books, 2006), 145–46.

2 *Free Society*, 13 November 1898; Jay Fox, "The McCormack Massacre," Folder 1, Box 1, Fox Papers, Gonzaga; Jay Fox, untitled manuscript, in author's possession; *Daily Worker*, 29 April 1936; *Free Society*, 13 November 1904; *Chicago Daily Tribune*, 4 May 1886; *The Argus*, 5 May 1886; Green, *Death in the Haymarket*, 170–71; Paul Avrich, *The Haymarket Tragedy* (Princeton, NJ: Princeton University Press, 1984), 180–89; Carolyn Ashbaugh, *Lucy Parsons: American Revolutionary* (Chicago: Charles H. Kerr Publishing Company, 1976), 74–75; Henry David, *The History of the Haymarket Affair: A Study in the American Social-Revolutionary and Labor Movements* (New York: Collier Books, 1963), 164–65.

3 Quintin Hoare and Geoffrey Nowell Smith, eds. and trans., *Selections from the Prison Notebooks of Antonio Gramsci* (New York: International Publishers, 1992), 3–23; David Collins, "Jay Fox: The Life and Times of an American Radical" (MA thesis, Eastern Washington University, 2016), 15–16.

4 Caroline Cahm, *Kropotkin and the Rise of Revolutionary Anarchism, 1872–1886* (Cambridge: Cambridge University Press, 1989), 8–13; Tom Goyens, *Beer and Revolution: The German Anarchist Movement in New York City, 1880–1914* (Urbana: University of Illinois Press, 2014); Kenyon Zimmer, *Immigrants Against the State: Yiddish and Italian Immigrants in America* (Urbana: University of Illinois Press, 2015).

5 David Montgomery, *The Fall of the House of Labor: The Workplace, the State, and American Labor Activism, 1865–1925* (New York: Cambridge University Press, 1987), 2; Dorothy Sue Cobble, "Pure and Simple Radicalism: Putting the Progressive Era AFL in Its Time," *Labor: Studies in Working-Class History of the Americas* 10 (Winter 2013): 61–87.

6 Kenyon Zimmer, "Anarchist Newspapers and Periodicals, 1872–1940," Mapping American Social Movement Project, University of Washington, Seattle; Kathy Ferguson, "Anarchist Printers and Presses: Material Circuits of Politics," *Political Theory* 42 (2014): 395; Jon Everett Bekken, "Working-Class Newspapers, Community and Consciousness in Chicago, 1880–1930" (PhD diss., University

of Illinois, 1992), 13–14, 30–68; Linda J. Lumsden, *Black, White, and Red All Over: A Cultural History of the Radical Press in Its Heyday, 1900-1917* (Kent, OH: Kent State University Press, 2014).

7 Sigurður Gylfi Magnússon, "The Life is Never Over: Biography as a Microhistorical Approach," in *The Biographical Turn: Lives in History*, ed. Hans Renders, Binne de Haan, and Jonne Harmsma (London: Routledge, 2017), 42–52.

8 Hutchins Hapgood, *The Spirit of Labor* (1907; repr., Urbana: University of Illinois Press, 2004), 290.

1. BECOMING AN ANARCHIST

1 Jay Fox, untitled manuscript, Box 1, Folder 1, Fox Papers, Gonzaga; Mary M. Carr, "Jay Fox: Anarchist of Home," *Columbia* 4 (spring 1990), 3; Robert A. Slayton, *Back of the Yards: The Making of a Local Democracy* (Chicago: University of Chicago Press, 1986), 10.

2 Fox, untitled manuscript, Fox Papers, Gonzaga.

3 Fox, untitled manuscript, Fox Papers, Gonzaga.

4 Fox, untitled manuscript, Fox Papers, Gonzaga; Jay Fox, untitled manuscript, in author's possession.

5 Fox, untitled manuscript, in author's possession; Melvyn Dubofsky and Foster Rhea Dulles, *Labor in America: A History* (Wheeling, IL: Harlan Davidson, 2004), 130–31; Ashbaugh, *Lucy Parsons*, 70–71; Jacqueline Jones, *Goddess of Anarchy: The Life and Times of Lucy Parsons, American Radical* (New York: Basic Books), 90–94; Alan Calmer, *Labor Agitator: The Story of Albert R. Parsons* (New York: International Publishers, 1937), 62–63; Green, *Death in the Haymarket*, 109–10, 126, 158–59; Avrich, *Haymarket Tragedy*, 91–92.

6 Bruce C. Nelson, *Beyond the Martyrs: A Social History of Chicago Anarchists, 1870-1900* (New Brunswick, NJ: Rutgers University Press, 1988), 38–51, 66–76; Lucien van der Walt and Michael Schmidt, *Black Flame: The Revolutionary Class Politics of Anarchism and Syndicalism* (Edinburgh: AK Press, 2009), 131–32; Green, *Death in the Haymarket*, 96–101; *The Alarm*, 1 November 1884; Cahm, *Kropotkin and the Rise of Revolutionary Anarchism*, 71–72, 213–30; Jones, *Goddess of Anarchy*, 80–81, 120–21; James R. Barrett, *William Z. Foster and the Tragedy of American Radicalism* (Urbana: University of Illinois Press, 1999), 60.

7 Green, *Death in the Haymarket*, 89, 97, 169–71, 179–80; Fox, unpublished manuscript, in author's possession; *Our World*, 27 April 1951; Ashbaugh, *Lucy Parsons*, 50–54; Jones, *Goddess of Anarchy*, 132–33; Jay Fox, "Two Talented Women: Lucy Parsons and Lizzie Holmes," Box 1, Folder 20, Fox Papers, Gonzaga.

8 David, *History of the Haymarket Affair*, 172–75; Avrich, *Haymarket Tragedy*, 199–203; Green, *Death in the Haymarket*, 183–84; Timothy Messer-Kruse, *The Haymarket Conspiracy: Transatlantic Anarchist Networks* (Urbana: University of Illinois Press, 2012), 17; Fox, untitled manuscript, in author's possession; Jay Fox, "I Was at Haymarket" (*Our World* newspaper clipping), Box 1, Folder 12, Jay Fox Papers, Manuscript, Archives, and Special Collections, Holland Library, Washington State University (hereafter Fox Papers, WSU).

9 Green, *Death in the Haymarket*, 134–35, 184–87; Fox, untitled manuscript, in author's possession; Fox, "I Was at Haymarket"; Jay Fox to Theodore Schroeder, 29 November 1951, Correspondence, Theodore Schroeder Papers, 1842–1957, Special Collection Research Center, Southern Illinois University, Carbondale (hereafter Schroeder Papers, SIU).

10 Fox, untitled manuscript, in author's possession; James R. Barrett, *Work and Community in the Jungle: Chicago's Packinghouse Workers, 1894–1299* (Urbana: University of Illinois Press, 1987), 122–25; Craig Phelan, *Grand Master Workman: Terence Powderly and the Knights of Labor* (Westport, CT: Greenwood Press, 2000), 65; Louise Carroll Wade, *Chicago's Pride: The Stockyards, Packingtown, and Environs in the Nineteenth Century* (Urbana: University of Chicago Press, 1987), 246–48; Leon Fink, *Workingmen's Democracy: The Knights of Labor and American Politics* (Urbana: University of Illinois Press, 1985), 133.

11 Fox, untitled manuscript, in author's possession; David, *History of the Haymarket Affair*, 106, 180–84, 190–96, 399–400; Green, *Death in the Haymarket*, 207; Jones, *Goddess of Anarchy*, 183–93; Joseph R. Conlin, *The American Radical Press, 1880–1960*, vol. 1 (Westport, CT: Greenwood Press, 1974), 26; Avrich, *Haymarket Tragedy*, 318–19; Philip S. Foner, ed. *The Autobiographies of the Haymarket Martyrs* (New York: Pathfinder, 1993), 27–57.

12 Fox, untitled manuscript, in author's possession; Fox, "I Was at Haymarket"; *The Agitator*, 15 November 1910; Green, *Death in the Haymarket*, 263–76; David, *History of the Haymarket Affair*, 379–91.

13 Fox, untitled manuscript, author's possession; *The Labor Herald*, June 1922, 26; Jay Fox, "The American Railway Unions," Box 1, Folder 7, Fox Papers, Gonzaga.

14 Fox, untitled manuscript, in author's possession; Fox, "American Railway Unions"; Philip S. Foner, *History of the Labor Movement in the United States*, vol. 2, *From the Founding of the A.F. of L. to the Emergence of American Imperialism* (New York: International Publishers, 1998), 247–57.

15 Nick Salvatore, *Eugene V. Debs: Citizen and Socialist* (Urbana: University of Illinois Press, 1982), 119–21; Foner, *Labor Movement*, 2:257–58; Fox, untitled manuscript, in author's possession; Fox, "American Railway Unions."

16 Fox, untitled manuscript, in author's possession; Fox, "American Railway Unions"; Foner, *Labor Movement*, 2:263–65; Salvatore, *Eugene V. Debs*, 129–30; Carr, "Jay Fox," 4; *Railway Times*, 15 June 1894.

17 Salvatore, *Eugene V. Debs*, 127–38; Foner, *Labor Movement*, 2:267–78; Fox, untitled manuscript, in author's possession; Fox, "American Railway Unions."

18 Salvatore, *Eugene V. Debs*, 138, 153–54; Jay Fox, "Debs and Social Democracy," Box 1, Folder 3, Fox Papers, Gonzaga; Foner, *Labor Movement*, 2:276; Jay Fox, "Tramping on a Bicycle," Box 1, Folder 4, Fox Papers, Gonzaga.

19 Fox, "Tramping on a Bicycle."

20 David V. Herlihy, *Bicycle: The History* (New Haven, CT: Yale University Press, 2004), 280–82; Fox, "Tramping on a Bicycle."

21 Herlihy, *Bicycle*, 5, 204–5; Fox, "Tramping on a Bicycle."

22 Fox, "Tramping on a Bicycle."

23 Fox, "Tramping on a Bicycle."

24 Fox, "Tramping on a Bicycle"; Candace Falk, ed. *Emma Goldman: A Documentary History of the American Years*, vol. 1, *Made for America, 1890–1901* (Berkeley: University of California Press, 2003), 520, 536–37, 546; Harry Kelly, "Roll Back the Years: Odyssey of a Libertarian," chapters 4–6, Harry Kelly Papers, 1924–1951, Special Collection Archival and Manuscript Collection, University of Michigan, Ann Arbor (hereafter Kelly Papers, UM); Paul Avrich, *An American Anarchist: The Life of Voltairine de Cleyre* (Princeton, NJ: Princeton University Press, 1978), 104–6; *Liberty*, 22 May 1886; *The Firebrand*, 25 August 1895; *Mother Earth*, April 1913, 50–54.

25 Jay Fox, untitled manuscript, Box 1, Folder 2, Fox Papers, WSU; *Mother Earth*, April 1913, 50–54; Falk, *Emma Goldman*, 1:38–39, 527–28, 536–37, 565; George Woodcock, *Anarchism: A History of Libertarian Ideas and Movements* (Harmondsworth, UK: Penguin Books, 1975), 419–21; Avrich, *American Anarchist*, 107–12.

26 Fox, untitled manuscript, Fox Papers, WSU.

27 Fox; Matthew Thomas, *Anarchist Ideas and Counter-Cultures in Britain, 1880–1914* (Burlington, VT: Ashgate, 2005), 84–85.

28 Fox, untitled manuscript, in author's possession; Avrich, *American Anarchist*, 107–20.

2. WRITING ANARCHY

1 UK and Ireland Outward Passenger Lists, 1860–1960, Liverpool, July 1897, https://www.ancestry.co.uk/search/collections/2997/; Nelson, *Beyond the Martyrs*, 211–21; Ashbaugh, *Lucy Parsons*, 168–75, 183, 206; Falk, *Emma Goldman*, 1:344, 498, 552; *Free Society*, 13 November 1904, 5 December 1897, 13 November 1904.

2 Terry Perlin, "Anarchist-Communism in America, 1890–1914" (PhD diss., Brandeis University, 1970), 111–14; Goyens, *Beer and Revolution*, 61, 80; *The Rebel*, 20 September 1895.

3 A. Isaak, "Origin of Anarchism," Box 1, Folder 43, Fox Papers, Gonzaga; *The Demonstrator*, 7 December 1904; Falk, *Emma Goldman*, 1:500, 516, 535, 536, 548, 551–52, 565; Mari Jo Buhle, Paul Buhle, and Dan Georgakas, *Encyclopedia of the American Left*, 2nd ed. (New York: Oxford University Press, 1998), 244; *The Firebrand*, 14, 18 July 1895, 4, 11, 18 August 1895.

4 *Chicago Daily Tribune*, 28 September 1897; Falk, *Emma Goldman*, 1:288, 502, 575–76; Ashbaugh, *Lucy Parsons*, 200–201; *Free Society*, 14 November 1897; Salvatore, *Eugene V. Debs*, 164.

5 *Chicago Daily Tribune*, 14, 17 September 1897; Jay Fox, "Debs and Social Democracy," Box 1, Folder 3, Fox Papers, Gonzaga; Priscilla Long, *Where the Sun Never Shines: A History of America's Bloody Coal Industry* (New York: Paragon House, 1991), 155–56; Elliott J. Gorn, *Mother Jones: The Most Dangerous Woman in America* (New York: Hill and Wang, 2001), 77; Salvatore, *Eugene V. Debs*, 165–69; Falk, *Emma Goldman*, 1:575–76; Charles LeWarne, *Utopias on Puget Sound, 1885–1915* (Seattle: University of Washington Press, 1995), 129–38.

6 *Free Society*, 2 January 1898; Falk, *Emma Goldman*, 1:577–78; David DeLeon, *American as Anarchist* (Baltimore: Johns Hopkins University Press, 1978), 103–4.

7 Falk, *Emma Goldman*, 1:572–73, 576–77; Nelson, *Beyond the Martyrs*, 105–9; Goyens, *Beer and Revolution*, 34–46; Avrich, *American Anarchist*, 129–33; *Free Society*, 28 May 1899, June 6, 1899; *Chicago Daily Tribune*, 7 September 1897.

8 *Free Society*, 28 August 1898, 11 September 1898, 13 November 1898, 6 May 1900, 31 March 1901, 28 July 1901, 1 September 1901; Jay Fox, "Labor's Discontent," copy of a lecture given to the Chicago Society of Anthropology, in author's possession; Philip S. Foner, *History of the Labor Movement in the United States*, vol. 3, *The Policies and Practices of the American Federation of Labor, 1900–1909* (New York: International Publishers, 1964), 78–86; LeWarne, *Utopias on Puget Sound*, 224; Jay Fox, "Off to Home Colony," Box 1, Folder 5, Fox Papers, Gonzaga.

9 *Free Society*, 3, 17 March 1901, 14 July 1901.

10 Nelson, *Beyond the Martyrs*, 40–51; Lucy Parsons, ed., *Life of Albert R. Parsons: With Brief History of the Labor Movement in America: Also, Sketches of the Lives of A. Spies, Geo. Engel, A. Fischer and Louis Lingg* (Chicago: Lucy E. Parsons, Publisher, 1903), 24–26; *The Torch*, August 1894; *Free Society*, 28 August 1898, 13 November 1898; Davide Turcato, "European Anarchism in the 1890s: Why Labor Matters in Categorizing Anarchism," *Working USA: The Journal of Labor and Society* 12 (September 2009): 455–56; Van der Walt and Schmidt, *Black*

Flame, 16; *Free Society*, 14 April 1901; Robert Graham, ed., *Anarchism: A Documentary History of Ideas*, vol. 1, *From Anarchy to Anarchism (300 CE to 1939)* (Montreal: Black Rose Books, 2005), 93–96, 189–93.

11 *Free Society*, 31 March 1901; Jay Fox, "Peter Kropotkin and Anarchism," in author's possession; George Woodcock and Ivan Avakumovic, *The Anarchist Prince* (New York: Schocken Books, 1971), 49–91; Dubofsky and Dulles, *Labor in America*, 162; Jay Fox, "President McKinley Is Shot," in author's possession; Paul Avrich, *Anarchists Portraits* (Princeton, NJ: Princeton University Press, 1988), 100; Neil V. Salzman, *Reform and Revolution: The Life and Times of Raymond Robins* (Kent, OH: Kent State University Press, 1991), 90–91; Nelson, *Beyond the Martyrs*, 237; Hapgood, *Spirit of Labor*, 415.

12 Isaak, "Origin of Anarchism"; *Free Society*, 12 May 1901; Paul Avrich, *Anarchist Voices: An Oral History of Anarchism in America* (Princeton, NJ: Princeton University Press, 1995), 160–62; *The Lakeside Annual Directory of the City of Chicago. 1901* (Chicago: Chicago Directory Company, 1901); Fox, "President McKinley Is Shot"; Falk, *Emma Goldman*, 1:464, 510, 534; Steven Kent Smith, "Abraham Isaak: The History of a Mennonite Radical," *Mennonite Quarterly Review* 65 (October 1991): 449; William Z. Foster, *From Bryan to Stalin* (New York: International Publishers, 1937), 59; Barrett, *William Z. Foster*, 61–62.

13 *Free Society*, 10 February 1901, 12 May 1901, 1, 8 September 1901; Isaak, "Origin of Anarchism."

14 Ashbaugh, *Lucy Parsons*, 210–11; Fox, "President McKinley Is Shot"; Isaak, "Origin of Anarchism"; Smith, "Abraham Isaak," 453–54; Falk, *Emma Goldman*, 1:525.

15 *Chicago Daily Tribune*, 7, 8 September 1901; *Free Society*, 6 October 1901; *The Public*, 12 October 1901; Isaak, "Origin of Anarchism"; Fox, "President McKinley Is Shot"; Falk, *Emma Goldman*, 1:512–13.

16 M. J. Heale, *American Anticommunism: Combating the Enemy Within, 1830–1970* (Baltimore: Johns Hopkins University Press, 1990), 41–42; *Chicago Daily Tribune*, 8–17 September 1901; Avrich, *American Anarchist*, 133–36; Falk, *Emma Goldman*, 1:473, 512–14; Daniel Bessner and Michael Stauch, "Karl Heinzen and the Intellectual Origins of Modern Terror," *Terrorism and Political Violence* 22 (2010): 152; LeWarne, *Utopias on Puget Sound*, 180–81; Goyens, *Beer and Revolution*, 100–101; Emma Goldman, *Living My Life* (New York: Alfred A. Knopf, 1934), 297–300.

17 Fox, "President McKinley Is Shot"; *Free Society*, 6 October 1901; *Chicago Daily Tribune*, 10, 14 September 1901; Falk, *Emma Goldman*, 1:512–13.

18 Fox, "President McKinley Is Shot."

19 Jay Fox to Theodore Schroeder, 24 February (no year), Schroeder Papers, SIU; Fox, "President McKinley Is Shot."

20 *Free Society*, 6 October 1901, 6, 22 June 1902, 9 November 1902; Goyens, *Beer and Revolution*, xii; Falk, *Emma Goldman*, 1:471–77; *Chicago Daily Tribune*, 8–15 September 1901.

21 Fox, "President McKinley Is Shot"; Jay Fox, *Roosevelt, Czolgosz and Anarchy* (New York: New York Anarchists, n.d.), 2–13.

22 *Free Society*, 5 January 1902; *Discontent*, 5 February 1902, 19 March 1902; LeWarne, *Utopias on Puget Sound*, 182–83.

23 Heale, *American Anticommunism*, 45; William Preston Jr., *Aliens and Dissenters: Federal Suppression of Radicals, 1903–1933* (Urbana: University of Illinois Press, 1994), 31–32.

24 Goyens, *Beer and Revolution*, 187–93; *Free Society*, 18 May 1902, 15 June 1902; *New York Tribune*, 4 April 1902; Thomas, *Anarchist Ideas*, 156, 158–60; Heale, *American Anticommunism*, 45; Candace Falk, ed., *Emma Goldman: A Documentary History of the American Years*, vol. 2, *Making Speech Free, 1902–1909* (Berkeley: University of California Press, 2005), 471–72, 545.

25 Goyens, *Beer and Revolution*, 184; Alan Trachtenberg, *The Incorporation of America: Culture and Society in the Gilded Age* (New York: Hill and Wang, 1982), 87–88; Ronald Takaki, *A Different Mirror: A History of Multicultural America* (Boston: Little, Brown, 1993), 285–88; Falk, *Emma Goldman*, 2:533, 551–52; *Free Society*, 4 January 1903, 1, 15 March 1903, 3 January 1904; Goldman, *Living My Life*, 296; meeting announcements indicating Jay Fox as a featured speaker, Box 1, Folder 17, Fox Papers, WSU.

3. LABOR'S REVOLUTIONARY POTENTIAL

1 Jay Fox, "Elected a Business Agent," in author's possession; *International Wood-Worker*, March 1903, 33; *Machine Wood-Worker*, December 1891, 5; *American Wood-Worker*, May 1895, 3, 5.

2 *Directory of Unions Affiliated with the Central Federated Union of New York* (New York: Central Federated Unions of New York, 1904), 41; *International Wood-Worker*, July 1903, 27–28, October 1903, 173–74, March 1904, 124–25; *The Carpenter*, October 1903, 4–6; *International Wood-Worker*, August 1903, 80; Frederick Shipp Deibler, "The Amalgamated Wood Workers' International Union of America: A Historical Study of Trade Unionism in Its Relation to the Development of an Industry" (PhD diss., University of Wisconsin, 1912), 161–94; *Free Society*, 10 March 1901.

3 "The Radical Club" (leaflet listing featured speakers) and "Chicago Martyrs Memorial Meeting" (leaflet), Box 1, Folder 17, Fox Papers, WSU; *Liberty*, 1 April 1902; Jay Fox, "Anarchist Communism: The Society of the Future," in author's possession; Jay Fox, "Social Democracy and Anarchism," in author's

possession; Jay Fox, "The Decline of Anarchism," Box 1, Folder 2, Fox Papers, Gonzaga; Zimmer, *Immigrants Against the State*, 15–48.

4   *Free Society*, 26 January 1902, 3 August 1902, 13 March 1904, 28 August 1898; *Liberty*, 1 May 1902; Kelly, "Roll Back the Years," chapter 17, Kelly Papers, UM; *The Torch*, August 1894.

5   *Free Society*, 3, 10, 24 August 1902, 7 September 1902, 19 October 1902.

6   *Free Society*, 25 May 1902.

7   Jay Fox, untitled manuscript, Box 1, Folder 21, Fox Papers, Gonzaga; *Free Society*, 3 January 1904, 21 February 1904, 13 March 1904, 19 June 1904, 20 November 1904.

8   Falk, *Emma Goldman*, 2:55, 476; Paul Avrich and Karen Avrich, *Sasha and Emma: The Anarchist Odyssey of Alexander Berkman and Emma Goldman* (Cambridge, MA: Harvard University Press, 2012), 187; *The Demonstrator*, 1 November 1905; LeWarne, *Utopias on Puget Sound*, 197.

9   *The Demonstrator*, 6 December 1905; *The Liberator*, 8 October 1905; Ashbaugh, *Lucy Parsons*, 219–20; Jones, *Goddess of Anarchy*, 270–71; *Proceedings of the First Convention of the Industrial Workers of the World* (1905; repr., New York: Merit Publishers, 1969), 127–30, 595; Falk, *Emma Goldman*, 2:55; Salvatore Salerno, *Red November Black November: Culture and Community in the Industrial Workers of the World* (Albany: State University of New York Press, 1989), 70, 82, 87–88; Brigitte Koenig, "Law and Disorder at Home: Free Love, Free Speech, and the Search for an Anarchist Utopia," *Labor History* 45 (May 2004): 211–12; Charles Govan to Joseph Labadie, 11 January 1906, Joseph Labadie Papers, Special Collections Research Center, University of Michigan, Ann Arbor (hereafter Labadie Papers, UM); Zimmer, *Immigrants Against the State*, 91; Carr, "Jay Fox," 5; LeWarne, *Utopias on Puget Sound*, 206.

10   *The Lakeside Annual Directory of the City of Chicago, 1905* (Chicago: Chicago Directory Company, 1905), 778; Hapgood, *Spirit of Labor*, 285–91; Hutchings Hapgood, *An Anarchist Woman* (New York: Duffield and Company, 1909), 173–74, 193, 387–88, 438.

11   *International Wood-Worker*, July 1904, 311–12, July 1905, 206–7.

12   Foner, *History of the Labor*, 3:418–24; Philip S. Foner, *History of the Labor Movement in the United States*, vol. 4, *The Industrial Workers of the World, 1905–1917* (New York: International Publishers, 1965), 23–24; *Proceedings of the First Convention*, 82–83; Melvyn Dubofsky, *We Shall Be All: A History of the Industrial Workers of the World* (Chicago: Quadrangle Books, 1969), 76–80; Montgomery, *Fall of the House of Labor*, 22–24; *The Demonstrator*, 3 May 1905; *International Wood-Worker*, July 1905, 207; Jay Fox, "A Revolutionary Union," Box 1, Folder 16, Fox Papers, Gonzaga.

13 *Proceedings of the First Convention*, 117–30, 147–57, 612; Salerno, *Red November Black November*, 69–90; *The Demonstrator*, 2 August 1905; Avrich, *Haymarket Tragedy*, 73–74.

14 *The Demonstrator*, 6 September 1905; James Green, *The World of the Worker: Labor in Twentieth-Century America* (Urbana: University of Illinois Press, 1998), 61; Dubofsky and Dulles, *Labor in America*, 191.

15 *The Demonstrator*, 17 January 1906; *Proceedings of the First Convention*, 3–6, 82–83, 117–30; Foner, *History of the Labor Movement*, 4:65–66; Dubofsky, *We Shall Be All*, 95–96.

16 *To-Morrow: A Rational Monthly Magazine*, April 1906, 73–77; Parker H. Sercombe to Freedom Group, 27 June 1908, in author's possession.

17 *Mother Earth*, May 1907, 124–28, 157–58; *The Demonstrator*, 15 May 1907; David Miller, *Anarchism* (London: J. M. Dent & Sons, 1984), 128–29; Maurizio Antonioli, *The International Anarchist Congress: Amsterdam, 1907*, trans. Nestor McNab (Edmonton: Black Cat Press, 2009), 5–19.

18 *Mother Earth*, June 1907, 178–81, October 1907, 307–19; Goldman, *Living My Life*, 401–4; Antonioli, *Anarchist Congress Amsterdam, 1907*, 5–19, 23–29, 32–34, 42–47, 51–54; Graham, *Anarchism*, 1:206–11; van der Walt and Schmidt, *Black Flame*, 181–83; Miller, *Anarchism*, 127–34.

19 Jay Fox, *Trade Unionism and Anarchism: A Letter to a Brother Unionist* (Chicago: Social Science Press, 1908), 5–8.

20 Fox, *Trade Unionism and* Anarchism, 9–16.

21 "Freedom Archives," Box 407, folder "Pamphlet Sales 1904–1909," International Institute of Social History, Amsterdam, Netherlands; *Mother Earth*, September 1907, 292–93; LeWarne, *Utopias on Puget Sound*, 207; *Mother Earth*, October 1908, 326–27; *Voice of Labour*, 18, 25 January 1907; meeting announcements indicate Jay Fox as a featured speaker in Boston and New York, Box 1, Folder 17, Fox Papers, WSU.

22 *The Demonstrator*, 21 August 1908, 19 February 1908; Kenyon Zimmer, comp., "American Anarchist Periodicals Circulation Data, 1880–1940," 2014, www.academia.edu.

4. THE AGITATOR AT HOME

1 LeWarne, *Utopias on Puget Sound*, 112–13, 164, 206; Jay Fox, "Off to Home Colony," Box 1, Folder 5, Fox Papers, Gonzaga; Carr, "Jay Fox," 5–6.

2 Carlos Arnaldo Schwantes, *The Pacific Northwest: An Interpretive History* (Lincoln: University of Nebraska Press, 1996), 308–9; Fox, "Off to Home Colony"; Jay Fox, "Organizing Timberworkers," Box 1, Folder 13, Fox Papers, Gonzaga.

3 Fox, "Off to Home Colony"; LeWarne, *Utopias on Puget Sound*, 193; United
   States Census 1910 Home, Washington; United States Census 1910, San
   Francisco, California, Assembly District 32; Lewis Haiman, interview, Lewis
   Haiman Papers, 1971 Special Collections, Suzzallo and Allen Libraries,
   University of Washington, Seattle (hereafter Haiman interview, Haiman
   Papers, UW); Darby N. Silverberg, interview, Darby N. Silverberg Papers 1983,
   Interview, 1983, Special Collections, Suzzallo and Allen Libraries, University of
   Washington, Seattle (hereafter Silverberg interview, Silverberg Papers, UW);
   Sylvia E. Retherford, "Early Business in Home, 1983," Evadna Cooke, "The Best
   Time Ever," A. F. Cotterell, "From Handwritten Pages by Mrs. De Crane,"
   Cooperative Colony Collection, Washington State Historical Society, Tacoma
   (hereafter CCC, WSHS); William J. Burns, *The Masked War* (1913; repr., New
   York: Arno Press, 1969), 81.
4 *The Agitator*, 15 November 1910, 1 February 1912; Avrich, *Anarchist Voices*, 333;
   Fox, "Off to Home Colony"; Jay Fox, "Home: A Radical Community," Box 1,
   Folder 25, Fox Papers, Gonzaga; LeWarne, *Utopias on Puget Sound*, 208.
5 Falk, *Emma Goldman*, 2:40–42; *The Agitator*, 15 November 1910, 15 November 1911, 1 December 1911, 1 November 1912.
6 Dave Roediger and Franklin Rosemont, eds., *Haymarket Scrapbook* (Chicago:
   Charles H. Kerr Publishing Company, 1986), 175–251; LeWarne, *Utopias on
   Puget Sound*, 188; *The Demonstrator*, 6 November 1907; *The Agitator*, 1 December 1911; *Industrial Worker*, 9 November 1910, 9 November 1911.
7 *The Agitator*, 15 November 1910.
8 *The Agitator*, 15 January 1911, 15 February 1911, 1 March 1911, 1 April 1911, 1
   June 1911; Goyens, *Beer and Revolution*, 34–51; Zimmer, *Immigrants Against the
   State*, 37.
9 *The Agitator*, 1 January 1911, 15 March 1911, 1 April 1911; Avrich and Avrich,
   Sasha and Emma, 191–92; Joseph R. Conlin, ed., *The American Radical Press,
   1880–1960*, vol. 2 (Westport, CT: Greenwood Press, 1974), 394–97.
10 *The Agitator*, 15 November 1910; Paul Avrich, *The Modern School Movement:
   Anarchism and Education in the United States* (Princeton, NJ: Princeton Univer-
   sity Press, 1980), 23–24, 51–52, 63; Candace Falk, *Emma Goldman: A Documentary
   History of the American Years*, vol. 3, *Light and Shadows, 1910-1916* (Stanford,
   CA: Stanford University Press, 2012), 741; Harvey O'Connor, *Revolution in
   Seattle: A Memoir* (New York: Monthly Review Press), 85.
11 Dubofsky, *We Shall Be All*, 173–75; Patrick Renshaw, *The Wobblies: The Story of
   the IWW and Syndicalism in the United States* (Chicago: Ivan R. Dee, 1999), 87;
   Falk, *Emma Goldman*, 3:713–14; *The Agitator*, 15 June 1912, 1 April 1912.
12 Justin Wadland, *Trying Home: The Rise and Fall of an Anarchist Utopia on
   Puget Sound* (Corvallis: Oregon State University Press, 2014), 83–84; LeWarne,

Utopias on Puget Sound, 212–14; *The Agitator*, 1 July 1911; Eugene Travaglio, "The Trials of a Noble Experiment," Folder 9, CCC, WSHS.

13 Wadland, *Trying Home*, 88; LeWarne, *Utopias on Puget Sound*, 215; Heale, *American Anticommunism*, 63; *Tacoma Daily News*, 26 August 1911; *The Agitator*, 1, 15 September 1911, 1 October 1911, 1 November 1911; *Industrial Worker*, 2 November 1911; *Mother Earth*, October 1911, 231–32, December 1911, 293, March 1912, 28–29.

14 Pierce County, Superior Court, Criminal File 21895, State of Washington v. Jay Fox; *Tacoma Daily News*, 10 January 1912; *The Agitator*, 15 January 1912, 15 February 1912; LeWarne, *Utopias on Puget Sound*, 215–17; Wadland, *Trying Home*, 91–95; Nathaniel Hong, "Free Speech Without an If or a But: The Defense of Free Expression in the Radical Periodicals of Home, Washington, 1897–1912," *American Journalism* 11 (Spring 1994): 149–50.

15 *Tacoma Daily News*, 13 January 1912; *The Agitator*, 15 January 1912, 15 March 1912; *Mother Earth*, October 1911, 231–32, February 1912, 382; *Industrial Worker*, 7 September 1911; Free Speech League, *The Free Speech Case of Jay Fox* (New York: Free Speech League, 1912); *The State of Washington vs. Jay Fox, Appeal from the Superior Court for Pierce County* (Tacoma, Washington: Allen and Lamborn Printing, 1913), 8–9; State v. Fox, 71 Wash. 185, 127 Pac. 1111 (1912); Hong, "Free Speech," 150–51; LeWarne, *Utopias on Puget Sound*, 217–18; Wadland, *Trying Home*, 95–97; Goyens, *Beer and Revolution*, 100–101.

16 *The Agitator*, 15 February 1912, 1, 15 March 1912, 1 April 1912; David Burns, *The Life and Death of the Radical Historical Jesus* (Oxford: Oxford University Press, 2013), 82–125.

17 *The Agitator*, 1, 15 December 1910, 1 January 1911, 1, 15 February 1911, 1 March 1911; Ira L. Plotkin, *Anarchism in Japan: A Study of the Great Treason Affair, 1910–1911* (Lewiston, NY: Edwin Mellon Press, 1990), 2–3, 21–31.

18 *The Agitator*, 15 January 1911; Falk, *Emma Goldman*, 2:553, 3:710–11; Ward S. Albro, *Always a Rebel: Ricardo Flores Magón and the Mexican Revolution* (Forth Worth: Texas Christian University Press, 1992), 128–33; John M. Hart, *Anarchism and the Mexican Working Class, 1860–1931* (Austin: University of Texas Press, 1987), 88–89, 101–2; Hyman Weintraub, "The IWW in California, 1905–1931" (MA thesis, University of California, Los Angeles, 1947), 49–57; Lowell L. Blaisdell, *The Desert Revolution: Baja California, 1911* (Madison: University of Wisconsin Press, 1962), 41, 47–52; David Struthers, *The World in a City: Multiethnic Radicalism in Early Twentieth-Century Los Angeles* (Urbana: University of Illinois Press, 2019), 127–56.

19 *The Agitator*, 1, 15 April 1911, 15 June 1911; Falk, *Emma Goldman*, 3:107–9, 112–13; Hart, *Anarchism and the Mexican Working Class*, 101–2; Albro, *Always a Rebel*, 117–18; Blaisdell, *Desert Revolution*, 183–84.

20 *The Agitator*, 15 December 1911, 1 March 1912, 1 April 1912, 1 May 1912, 1, 15
    July 1912, 15 August 1912; Blaisdell, *Desert Revolution*, 188–91, 198; Albro, *Always
    a Rebel*, 142; Hart, *Anarchism and the Mexican Working Class*, 111–18; Alan
    Knight, *The Mexican Revolution*, vol. 1, *Porfirians, Liberals, and Peasants*
    (Lincoln: University of Nebraska Press, 1986), 292–94.

21 *The Agitator*, 1 May 1911; John H. M. Laslett, *Sunshine Was Never Enough*
    (Berkeley: University of California Press, 2021), 38; Lew Irwin, *Deadly Times: The
    1910 Bombing of the Los Angeles Times and America's Forgotten Decade of Terror*
    (Guilford, CT: Lyons Press, 2013), 71–72; LeWarne, *Utopias on Puget Sound*,
    203–4; Carr, "Jay Fox," 7; Edward P. Johanningsmeier, *Forging American
    Communism: The Life of William Z. Foster* (Princeton, NJ: University of Prince-
    ton Press, 1994), 74; Wadland, *Trying Home*, 71–78; Burns, *Masked War*, 64, 70.

22 *The Agitator*, 1 November 1911, 15 December 1911, 1 January 1912, 1 February 1912;
    Grace Heilman Stimson, *Rise of the Labor Movement in Los Angeles* (Berkeley:
    University of California Press, 1955), 380; *The Agitator*, 15 January 1912; Falk,
    Emma Goldman, 3:109–10, 468; Goldman, *Living My Life*, 487–88; Avich and
    Avrich, *Sasha and Emma*, 241–42.

23 *The Agitator*, 15 December 1910, 1 July 1911, 15 September 1911, 1 October 1911, 15
    December 1911; Tom Mann, *Tom Mann's Memoirs* (London: MacGibbon & Kee
    Ltd., 1967), 203–7.

24 John H. M. Laslett, *Labor and the Left: A Study of Socialist and Radical
    Influences in the American Labor Movement, 1881–1924* (New York: Basic Books,
    1970), 13–14, 192, 207–9; Julie Greene, *Pure and Simple Politics: The American
    Federation of Labor and Political Activism, 1881–1917* (Cambridge: Cambridge
    University Press, 1998), 37–38; Foner, *History of the Labor Movement*, 2:187; *The
    Agitator*, 1 January 1911, 1 February 1911, 15 December 1911.

25 *The Agitator*, 1 April 1911, 15 May 1911, 15 August 1911, 1 August 1912; Frank
    Bohn, "Is the I.W.W. to Grow?," *International Socialist Review* 12 (July 1911):
    42–44.

26 *The Agitator*, 1 October 1911, 15 January 1912, 1 August 1912, 15 September 1911.

27 *The Agitator*, 1, 15 February 1912, 1, 15 March 1912, 1 April 1912, 1 June 1912;
    Dubofsky, *We Shall Be All*, 227–29, 240–42, 250–53.

28 Jay Fox, "Marriage and Family," "Men, Women, and Morals," and an unpub-
    lished manuscript, in author's possession; *The Agitator*, 1 January 1911, 15
    April 1911, 15 May 1911, 1 October 1911, 1 April 1911, 1 June 1911; Elizabeth Anne
    Payne, *Reform, Labor, and Feminism: Margaret Dreier Robins and the Women's
    Trade Union League* (Urbana: University of Illinois Press, 1988), 70.

29 *The Agitator*, 1 February 1911, 1 March 1911, 15 November 1911, 15 December 1911,
    15 February 1912, 1 June 1912, 1 November 1912; Ashbaugh, *Lucy Parsons*, 174–75,
    226–29; Jones, *Goddess of Anarchy*, 283.

30 *The Agitator,* 15 January 1911, 1 April 1911, 1 May 1911, 1 November 1911, 1 October 1912.

31 *The Agitator,* 15 January 1912, 15 July 1912, 15 October 1912; Avrich, *American Anarchist,* 232–38.

32 Lucy Robins Lang, *Tomorrow Is Beautiful* (New York: Macmillan, 1948), 49–50; Foster, *From Bryan to Stalin,* 36–40, 59; Barrett, *William Z. Foster,* 61–62; Burns, *Masked War,* 68–70, 74–76, 78, 86–89; Hapgood, *Spirit of Labor,* 290–91.

33 *The Agitator,* 1 January 1911, 15 May 1911; Wadland, *Trying Home,* 138; LeWarne, *Utopias on Puget Sound,* 221.

34 *The Agitator,* 15 October 1911, 1 February 1912, 15 March 1912, 15 September 1911.

5. *THE SYNDICALIST* IN CHICAGO

1 *The Agitator,* 15 January 1911; Falk, *Emma Goldman,* 3:121–23, 374; Goyens, *Beer and Revolution,* 189–90, 192–93.

2 *The Agitator,* 1 April 1912; Foster, *From Bryan to Stalin,* 48–51.

3 Foner, *History of the Labor Movement,* 4:415–22; *Solidarity,* 2 April 1910, 1, 11 June 1910, 19 November 1910, 24 December 1910; Mann, *Memoirs,* 203–7; *Solidarity,* 25 March 1911, 25 November 1911, 16 December 1911; *Industrial Worker,* 2, 16 November 1911; Johanningsmeier, *Forging American Communism,* 47–49; Barrett, *William Z. Foster,* 50–52.

4 Dubofsky, *We Shall Be All,* 225; *The Agitator,* 1 May 1912; Jay Fox, "Syndicalism: Its Growth and Decay," Box 1, Folder 18, Fox Papers, Gonzaga; *Industrial Worker,* 9 January 1913.

5 *The Agitator,* 15 May 1912, 1, 15 June 1912, 1, 15 July 1912, 1, 15 August 1912; Foner, *History of the Labor Movement,* 4:422–26.

6 *The Agitator,* 1 July 1912, 15 June 1912, 1 May 1912, 15 September 1912, 15 October 1912; Johanningsmeier, *Forging American Communism,* 61, 71.

7 *The Agitator,* 1 September 1912, 1, 15 October 1912.

8 *The Agitator,* 15 October 1912; Fox, "Syndicalism."

9 Jay Fox to Joseph Labadie, 17 October 1912, Labadie Papers, UM.

10 *The Syndicalist,* 1 January 1913; Ashbaugh, *Lucy Parsons,* 230–31; Jones, *Goddess of Anarchy,* 287–88; Edward Johanningsmeier, "William Z. Foster: Labor Organizer and Communist" (PhD diss., University of Pennsylvania, 1988), 196–97; Barrett, *William Z. Foster,* 61–62; Fox, "Syndicalism."

11 *The Syndicalist,* 1 January 1913.

12 *The Syndicalist,* 1, 15 January 1913, 15 March 1913.

13 *The Syndicalist,* 15 January 1913.

14 Carr, "Jay Fox," 8; Charlton J. Brandt, "William Z. Foster and the Syndicalist League of North America" (MA thesis, Sangamon State University, 1985), 30;

The Syndicalist, 15 March 1913; Jay Fox, "Notes for a Speech in Butte, Montana," transcribed by Sylvia Retherford, in author's possession; *The Syndicalist*, 1 April 1913; David M. Emmons, *The Butte Irish: Class and Ethnicity in an American Mining Town, 1875-1925* (Urbana: University of Illinois Press, 1990), 268-86.

15 Foster, *From Bryan to Stalin*, 57.

16 *The Syndicalist*, 1 March 1913; Johanningsmeier, *Forging American Communism*, 69-71; Ashbaugh, *Lucy Parsons*, 230; Falk, *Emma Goldman*, 3:643-45.

17 Edward P. Johanningsmeier, "William Z. Foster and the Syndicalist League of North America," *Labor History* 30 (Summer 1989): 334; *Mother Earth*, September 1912, 307-8; *Mother Earth*, March 1912, 222; Falk, *Emma Goldman*, 3:404n16; *Mother Earth*, November 1912, 373-78; *Mother Earth*, January 1913, 417-22.

18 Eugene Travaglio to Jo Labadie, 15 January 1913, Labadie Papers, UM; *Why?*, January 1913, 1-4, 9-11; Zimmer, *Immigrants Against the State*, 90-91; Avrich, *Anarchist Voices*, 160-62.

19 Foster, *From Bryan to Stalin*, 58-60; Johanningsmeier, "William Z. Foster and the Syndicalist League of North America," 344; Johanningsmeier, *Forging American Communism*, 71; Barrett, *William Z. Foster*, 58-59.

20 *The Syndicalist*, 1 January 1913; *The Toiler*, November 1913; *The Journeyman Barber*, May 1913, 160; Foster, *From Bryan to Stalin*, 63-64; Earl R. Browder, interview by J. R. Starobin, 11 August 1964, transcript, Oral History Research Office of Columbia University, New York; James G. Ryan, *Earl Browder: The Failure of American Communism* (Tuscaloosa: University of Alabama Press, 1997), 10, 12; Theodore Draper, *The Roots of American Communism* (New York: Viking Press, 1957), 308-9; *Report of Proceedings of the Thirty-Second Annual Convention of the American Federation of Labor* (Washington, DC: Law Reporter Printing Company, 1912), 386; *Report of Proceedings of the Thirty-Third Annual Convention of the American Federation of Labor* (Washington, DC: Law Reporter Printing Company, 1913), 90-91; Philip S. Foner, *History of the Labor Movement in the United States*, vol. 9, *The TUEL to the End of the Gompers Era* (New York: International Publishers, 1991), 87-92; Elizabeth and Kenneth Fones-Wolf, "Trade-Union Evangelism: Religion and the AFL in the Labor Forward Movement, 1912-1916," in *Working-Class America: Essays on Labor, Community, and American Society*, ed. Michael H. Frisch and Daniel J. Walkowitz (Urbana: University of Illinois Press, 1983), 153-84.

21 *The Syndicalist*; 1, 15 March 1913, 1, 15 April 1913, 1 May 1913; *The Agitator*, 15 July 1912; Foster, *From Bryan to Stalin*, 64; *The Unionist*, 13 July 1913, 15 December 1913; Foner, *History of the Labor Movement*, 9:87; Brandt, "William Z. Foster," 36-41; Kerry Segrave, *The Women Who Got America Talking: Early Telephone Operators, 1878-1922* (Jefferson, NC: McFarland, 2017), 178-83.

22 *The Agitator*, 15 May 1912, 1 June 1912; *Solidarity*, 16 December 1911; A. Ross McCormack, *Reformers, Rebels, and Revolutionaries: The Western Canadian Radical Movement, 1899-1919* (Toronto: University of Toronto Press, 1977), 113; *The British Columbia Federationist*, 6 May 1912; *Industrial Worker*, 14, 21 August 1913; Mark Leier, *Where the Fraser River Flows: The Industrial Workers of the World in British Columbia* (Vancouver: New Star Books, 1990), 60.

23 *The Syndicalist*, 1, 15 February 1913, 15 May 1913, 1 June 1913; *Proceedings of the Twelfth Convention of Washington State Labor Federation* (Tacoma: Washington State Labor Federation, 1913), 90.

24 *The Syndicalist*, 1 March 1913; Cloice R. Howd, *Industrial Relations in the West Coast Lumber Industry*, Bulletin of the United Stated Bureau of Labor Statistics 349 (Washington, DC: Government Printing Office, 1924), 55-58; *Report of Proceedings of the Thirty-First Annual Convention of the American Federation of Labor* (Washington, DC: Law Reporter Printing Company, 1911), 333; *Proceedings of the Thirty-Second Annual Convention of the American Federation of Labor*, 114-17, 218, 264-66; Lewis L. Lorwin, *The American Federation of Labor: History, Politics, and Prospects* (1933; repr., Clifton, NJ: Augustus M. Kelley Publishers, 1972), 108, 126; Philip Dreyfus, Toward Industrial Organization: Timber Workers, Unionism and Syndicalism in the Pacific Northwest, 1900-1917" (PhD diss., City University of New York, 1993), 115-18; Maier B. Fox, *United We Stand: The United Mine Workers of America, 1890-1990* (Washington, DC United Mine Workers of America, 1990), 112-14; Norman H. Clark, *Mill Town: A Social History of Everett, Washington, from Its Earliest Beginnings on the Shores of Puget Sound to the Tragic and Infamous Event Known as the Everett Massacre* (Seattle: University of Washington Press, 1970), 144-45; *The Timber Worker*, 1 March 1913, 13 September 1913, 31 January 1914; *The Syndicalist*, 1 March 1913.

25 *The Syndicalist*, 15 January 1913; Philip Foner, *History of the Labor Movement*, vol. 5, *The AFL in the Progressive Era, 1910-1915* (New York: International Publishers, 1980), 258-59; *The Syndicalist*, 1-15 August 1913, 1, 15 April 1913, 1-15 September 1913; *Solidarity*, 15 March 1913; *Industrial Worker*, 17 July 1913; Dubofsky, *We Shall Be All*, 263-90.

26 *The Syndicalist*; 1 July 1913, 1-15 August 1913; Gorn, *Mother Jones*, 169-97; Foner, *History of the Labor*, 5:182-95.

27 *The Syndicalist*, 1 January 1913, 15 April 1913, 1 May 1913; Foner, *History of the Labor Movement*, 4:153, 194-95, 197; *Industrial Worker*, 17 October 1912.

28 *International Socialist Review*, July 1913, 29-31; *The Commonwealth*, 26 June 1913; *The Agitator*, 1 October 1912; *The Syndicalist*, 15 May 1913, 1 June 1913, 1 July 1913, 1-15 August 1913; Émile Pouget, *Sabotage*, trans. Arturo Giovannitti (Chicago: Charles H. Kerr Publishing, 1913), 107; Foner, *History of the Labor*

Movement, 4:161; Earl C. Ford and William Z. Foster, *Syndicalism* (1913; repr., Chicago: Charles H. Kerr, 1990), 19–27.

29 *The Syndicalist*, 1 January 1913, 15 February 1913, 1, 15 March 1913, 1, 15 April 1913; Helen C. Camp, *Iron in Her Soul: Elizabeth Gurley Flynn and the American Left* (Pullman: Washington State University Press, 1995), 16, 18–25, 40; Lara Vapnek, *Elizabeth Gurley Flynn: Modern American Revolutionary* (Boulder, CO: Westview Press, 2015), 26–28; Roger A. Bruns, *The Damndest Radical: The Life and World of Ben Reitmann, Chicago's Celebrated Social Reformer, Hobo King, and Whorehouse Physician* (Urbana: University of Illinois Press, 1987), 230–31.

30 *The Syndicalist*, 1 February 1913, 1, 15 March 1913, 1 April 1913, 1, 15 May 1913, 1 July 1913; Wayne Westergard-Thorpe, "Towards a Syndicalist International: The 1913 London Congress," *International Review of Social History* 23 (1978): 35–36; Mann, *Memoirs*, 230; Chushichi Tsuzuki, *Tom Mann, 1856–1941: The Challenges of Labor* (Oxford: Clarendon Press, 1991), 167.

31 Ross McMullin, *The Light on the Hill: The Australian Labor Party, 1891–1991* (South Melbourne: Oxford University Press, 1991), 53, 65; Mann, *Memoirs*, 199–207, 230–31, 267; Tom Mann, *From Single Tax to Syndicalism* (London: Guy Bowman, 1913), 45–51, 91–95; Joseph White, *Tom Mann* (Manchester: Manchester University Press, 1991), 162, 174–79; Tsuzuki, *Tom Mann*, 150–59; Barrett, *William Z. Foster*, 48; *The Agitator*, 1 May 1912; *The Syndicalist*; 1–15 September 1913; *New York Times*, 15 September 1913; *Cronaca Sovversiva*, 1 November 1913; *Labor Journal*, 10 October 1913; *Bridgeport Evening Farmer*, 5 November 1913; *Seattle Star*, 16 October 1913.

32 *The Syndicalist*, 1 July 1913; Fox, "Syndicalism"; Wayne Westergard-Thorp, "Provisional Agenda of the International Syndicalist Congress, London, 1913," *International Review of Social History* 26 (April 1981): 92–103; Wayne Thorpe, *"The Workers Themselves": Revolutionary Syndicalism and International Labour, 1913–1923* (Dordrecht: Kluwer Academic Publishers, 1989), 320; *The Toiler*, November 1913; Johanningsmeier, *Forging America Communism*, 45–46.

33 *The Toiler*, October 1913, November 1913, January 1914, February 1914; Brandt, "William Z. Foster," 42–43, 51–52.

6. BORING WITHIN

1 Jay Fox, "Organizing Timberworkers," Box 1, Folder 13, Fox Papers, Gonzaga; Foster, *From Bryan to Stalin*, 65; Willian Z. Foster, *More Pages from a Worker's Life* (New York: American Institute for Marxist Studies, 1979), 8; Johanningsmeier, *Forging American Communism*, 77; *Solidarity*, 14 March 1914; Foner, *History of the Labor Movement*, 4:430; *Timber Worker*, 16 August 1913,

20 September 1913, 15, 22, 29 November 1913, 6 December 1913; *The Syndicalist*, 1 March 1913; *Seattle Union Record*, 4 August 1917.

2 Howd, *Industrial Relations*, 19–20; Clark, *Mill Town*, 124; *Timber Worker*, 1 March 1913, 14, 21 June 1913, 27 December 1913; Philip C. Emerson, "The International Shingle Weavers of America," Seattle General Strike Project, University of Washington, n.d., https://depts.washington.edu/labhist/strike/emerson.shtml. Chris Canterbury, "International Union of Timberworkers," Seattle General Strike Project, University of Washington, n.d., https://depts.washington.edu /labhist/strike/canterbury.shtml; *Industrial Worker*, 6 June 1913; Robert Tyler, *Rebels of the Woods: The I.W.W. in the Pacific Northwest* (Eugene: University of Oregon, 1967), 25, 30, 54; IWW Local Unions 1906–1917 (maps), IWW History Project, University of Washington, n.d., https://depts.washington.edu /iww/map_locals.shtml; Foner, *History of the Labor Movement*, 4:219–27; *Proceedings of the Thirty-Third Annual Convention of the American Federation of Labor*, 23.

3 *Timber Worker*, 1, 8, 15, 29 March 1913, 4, 11 October 1913; Dorothy Sue Cobble, *Dishing It Out: Waitresses and Their Unions in the Twentieth Century* (Urbana: University of Illinois Press, 1991), 63, 81.

4 *Timber Worker*, 4, 25 October 1913, 22 November 1913, 6 December 1913; *Labor Journal*, 14 November 1913, 5 December 1913.

5 *Timber Worker*, 31 January 1914, 4 April 1914; *Typographical Journal* 22 (February 1904): 188; *Proceedings of the Twelfth Annual Convention of the Washington State Federation of Labor*, 4.

6 *Timber Worker*, 27 December 1913, 3, 10, 17, 24, 31 January 1914; Philip Dreyfus, "Nature, Militancy, and the Western Worker: Socialist Shingles, Syndicalist Spruce," *Labor: Studies in Working-Class History of the Americas* 1 (Fall 2004): 76–77, 80–81.

7 *Timber Worker*, 24 January 1914, 7, 14, 28 February 1914, 21, 28 March 1914; *Labor Journal*, 6, 13 February 1914; J. G. Brown, "To Whom It May Concern," 17 March 1914, Box 1, Folder 7, Fox Papers, WSU.

8 *Timber Worker*, 7 February 1914, 7 March 1914; Jau Fox, "Organizing Timber-workers," Box 1, Folder 13, Fox Papers, Gonzaga; Howd, *Industrial Relations*, 59; Lester Burrell Shippee, "Washington's First Experiment in Direct Legislation," *Political Science Quarterly* 30 (June 1915): 241–42.

9 *Timber Worker*, 14 February 1914, 11 April 1914, 20 June 1914; Shippee, "Washington's First Experiment in Direct Legislation," 238–41.

10 *Timber Worker*, 24, 31 January 1914; *The Timberman* 15 (January 1914): 25.

11 *Timber Worker*, 28 February 1914, 14 March 1914, 4, 11, 18 April 1914, 20 June 1914, 1 February 1915; *Organized Labor* 11 (16 April 1910): 5; Howd, *Industrial Relations*, 65–68.

12 *Timber Worker*, 11 April 1914, 2, 16 May 1914, 13 June 1914, 11, 18 July 1914; "Organizer and Label Agent Commission" for the American Federation of Labor, 8 April 1914, Box 1, Folder 7, Fox Papers, WSU.

13 Fox, "Organizing Timberworkers"; *The Timber Worker*, 6 December 1913; Ernest Riebe, *"Mr. Block": Twenty-Four IWW Cartoons* (Chicago: Charles H. Kerr Publishing, 1984), 3–8.

14 *Timber Worker*, 3 January 1914.

15 *Timber Worker*, 14 March 1914.

16 *Timber Worker*, 6, 13, 20 June 1914, 18 July 194, 5 September 1914; *Seattle Union Record*, 27 June 1914; Foner, *Labor Movement in the United States*, 2:296–99.

17 *The Syndicalist*, 1 June 1913; *Seattle Star*, 4 July 1914; *Timber Worker*, 4, 18 July 1914.

18 *Timber Worker*, 28 November 1914, 5 December 1914, 2, 9 January 1915.

19 *Timber Worker*, 21 February 1914, 20 June 1914, 18 July 1914, 8 August 1914; *Seattle Star*, 20 January 1914; *The Commonwealth*, 22 January 1914; *Tacoma Times*, 19 January 1914; Albro, *Always a Rebel*, 142–43.

20 *Timber Worker*, 13 June 1914, 4, 11 July 1914, 1, 8, 29 August 1914, 19, 26 September 1914, 14 November 1914, 19 December 1914, 9 January 1915, 1 February 1915; *Labor Journal*, 27 February 1914.

21 *Timber Worker*, 13 June 1914, 8, 22, 29 August 1914, 5 December 1914; *The Toiler*, July 1914, 3, 7–8, 12–13.

22 *Timber Worker*, 25 July 1914, 22 August 1914, 7 November 1914; *The Masses*, January 1913; *Industrial Worker*, 6 June 1913; Falk, *Emma Goldman*, 3:376, 500, 732; van der Walt and Schmidt, *Black Flame*, 135–36; Ralph Darlington, *Radical Unionism: The Rise and Fall of Revolutionary Syndicalism* (Chicago: Haymarket Books, 2013), 41.

23 Hippolyte Havel, ed., *The Revolutionary Almanac 1914* (New York: Rabelais Press, n.d.), 63; Jay Fox to Freedom Group, 27 June 1914, in author's possession; *Timber Worker*, 29 August 1914, 9 January 1915; A. J. Brigati, ed., *The Voltairine de Cleyre Reader* (Oakland: AK Press, 2004), 151–72; Frank H. Brooks, "Ideology, Strategy, and Organization: Dyer Lum and the American Anarchist Movement," *Labor History* 34 (Winter 1993): 79–80.

24 *Timber Worker*, 8 August 1914, 12, 19, 26 September 1914, 3, 24, 31 October 1914, 7, 28 November 1914, 5, 12, 26 December 1914, 2, 9 January 1915; *Labor Journal*, 7 August 1914, 2 October 1914; *Washington Socialist*, 20 August 1914; *Seattle Union Record*, 20 February 1915; Woodcock and Avakumovic, *Anarchist Prince*, 378–84; O'Connor, *Revolution in Seattle*, 81–86; Philip S. Foner, *History of the Labor Movement in the United States*, vol. 7, *Labor and World War I, 1914–1918* (New York: International Publishers, 1987), 41–45; van der Walt and Schmidt, *Black Flame*, 216; Kenyon Zimmer, "At War with Empire: The Anti-Colonial Roots of

American Anarchist Debates During the First World War," in *Anarchism, 1914–1918: Internationalism, Anti-Militarism and War*, ed. Matthew S. Adams and Ruth Kinna (Manchester: Manchester University Press, 2017), 175–98.

25 *Timber Worker*, 18 April 1914, 27 June 1914, 18, 25 July 1914, 1, 15 August 1914, 5 December 1914; *Tacoma Times*, 4 June 1914, 16 July 1914; *The Ranch*, 15 May 1914; *Washington Standard*, 15 May 1914; *Aberdeen Herald*, 7 August 1914; *Labor Journal*, 25 September 1914; *Seattle Post-Intelligencer*, 24 September 1914, 22 October 1914.

26 *Timber Worker*, 12 September 1914, 3 October 1914.

27 *Timber Worker*, 17, 24, 31 October 1914, 1 February 1915; *Seattle Star*, 12 October 1914.

28 *Washington Standard*, 6, 13 November 1914; *Seattle Star*, 4, 6 November 1914; *Seattle Post-Intelligencer*, 4, 5 November 1914; Jonathan Dembo, *Unions and Politics in Washington State* (New York: Garland Publishing, 1983), 110–11; Carlos Schwantes, *Radical Heritage: Labor, Socialism, and Reform in Washington and British Columbia, 1885–1917* (Seattle: University of Washington Press, 1979), 198; Jeffrey A. Johnson, *"They Are All Red Out Here": Socialist Politics in the Pacific Northwest, 1895–1925* (Norman: University of Oklahoma Press, 2008), 103; *Timber Worker*, 14, 21 November 1914.

29 *Timber Worker*, 7, 14, 21, 28 November 1914, 5, 12 December 1914; *Daily Hub*, 1, 11 December 1914.

30 *Timber Worker*, 26 December 1914, 2 January 1915, 15 February 1915; *Seattle Union Record*, 26 December 1914, 9, 23, 30 January 1915, 6, 13 March 1915, 10 April 1915; *Leavenworth Echo*, 8 January 1915; *Anacortes American*, 14 January 1915.

31 *Anacortes American*, 7, 14 January 1915; *Timber Worker*, 1 February 1915; *Seattle Union Record*, 16 January 1915.

32 *Anacortes American*, 7, 14 January 1915; *Timber Worker*, 1 February 1914; *Seattle Union Record*, 16 January 1915.

33 *Timber Worker*, 1, 15 February 1915; *American Federationist*, July 1914, September 1914, February 1915; *Organized Labor*, 24 October 1914, 7 November 1914; *Seattle Union Record*, 26 September 1914, 7, 14 November 1914.

34 *The Toiler*, January 1915; Foster, *From Bryan to Stalin*, 67–68, 73; *Seattle Union Record*, 10 April 1915; William Z. Foster, *Trade Unionism: The Road to Freedom*, (Chicago: International Trade Union Education League, 1915); Fox, "Syndicalism"; Foner, *Labor Movement in the United States*, 9:92–97; Johanningsmeier, *Forging American Communism*, 79–83; Barrett, *William Z. Foster*, 66–68.

35 Howd, *Industrial Relations*, 60; *Seattle Union Record*, 20 March, 3, 24 April 1915, 1, 8, 22 May 1915; *Labor Journal*, 2, 30 April 1915, 7 May 1915; Dembo, *Unions and Politics in Washington State*, 111.

36 *American Federationist*, February 1915, November 1915; *Labor Journal*, 17
September 1915, 4 February 1916; *Seattle Union Record*, 22 January 1916, 26
February 1916, 11 March 1916, 8, 15, 22, 29 April 1916; *Report of the Proceedings
of the Thirty-Fifth Annual Convention of the American Federation of Labor*
(Washington, DC: Law Reporter Printing Company, 1915), 38; Howd, *Industrial
Relations*, 60–61; Canterbury, "International Union of Timberworkers."

7. AN ANARCHO-SYNDICALIST ADRIFT

1 Fox v. Washington, 236 U.S. 273 (1915); "Decision of the Supreme Court (US) in
the Case of Jay Fox v. The State of Washington," Box 1, Folder 25, Fox Papers,
Gonzaga; *Tacoma Times*, 24 February 1915; Hong, "Free Speech," 151; Jay Fox to
Theodore Schroeder, 10 August 1915, Schroeder Papers, SIU; *Central Law
Journal*, 16 April 1915, 289–90.

2 James J. Anderson to Governor Ernst Lister, 15 May 1915, Governor Ernst Lister
to James J. Anderson, 21 May 1915, James J. Anderson to Governor Ernst Lister,
3 June 1915, File 2938 "Jay Fox September 11, 1915, Pierce County Jail Pardon,"
2H-276, Governor Ernst Lister Papers, Washington State Archives, Olympia,
Washington (hereafter File 2938, Gov. Lister Papers, WSA).

3 William O. Chapman to Governor Ernst Lister, 10 June 1915, A. O. Burmeister
to Governor Ernst Lister, 9 June 1915, A. O. Burmeister to Mr. Zeighaus, 9 June
1915, File 2938, Gov. Lister Papers, WSA.

4 Governor Ernst Lister to A. B. Bell, 22 July 1915, Jay G. Brown to Clarence Parker,
3 August 1915, James J. Anderson to Governor Ernst Lister, 3 September 1915,
State of Washington, Executive Department, Olympia, 11 September 1915,
Governor Ernst Lister to James J. Anderson, 11 September 1915, Governor Ernst
Lister to W. O. Chapman, 11 September 1915, File 2938, Gov. Lister Papers,
WSA; *Tacoma Times*, 24 July 1915; *Seattle Star*, 24 July 1915; LeWarne, *Utopias
on Puget Sound*, 219–20; Wadland, *Trying Home*, 103–4.

5 Wadland, *Trying Home*, 104; LeWarne, *Utopias on Puget Sound*, 229; "Organizer and Label Agent Commission" for the American Federation of Labor,
8 April 1915, Box 1, Folder 7 Fox Papers, WSU; *American Federationist*,
March 1916; Jay Fox to Theodore Schroeder, 22 March 1915, Schroeder
Papers, SIU.

6 *Seattle Union Record*, 20 November 1915; Jay Fox to A. B., E. B., and Fitzie, 19
January 1916, in author's possession; Goyens, *Beer and Revolution*, 141, 184–85,
194; Andrew Cornell, *Unruly Equality: U.S. Anarchism in the Twentieth
Century* (Berkeley: University of California Press, 2016), 21–22, 35–36;
Struthers, *World in a City*, 157–83; *Mother Earth*, June 1915, 134–35, Septem-
ber 1915, 238–42; Zimmer, *Immigrants Against the State*, 4–6.

7　*Mother Earth*, January 1916, 363; Theodore Appel to Dear Comrades (*Freedom*, London), 1 September 1916, in author's possession; *The Alarm*, October 1915; *Revolt*, 1 January 1916; *Mother Earth*, January 1916, 372, December 1915, 328–30, January 1915, 369–70; *The Blast*, 15 January 1915.

8　*Mother Earth*, March 1915, 408–10; *The Alarm*, February, August 1916; *Revolt*, 22 January 1916.

9　Jay Fox to A. B., E. B., and Fitzie, 19 January 1916, in author's possession; Jay Fox, "Decline of Anarchism," in author's possession; *Revolt*, 5 February 1916; Falk, *Emma Goldman*, 3:752–53; Jay Fox, untitled manuscript, Box 1, Folder 19, Fox Papers, Gonzaga; Jay Fox, "Why I Joined the Communist Party," Box 1, Folder 2, Fox Papers, Gonzaga.

10　*Mother Earth*, May 1916, 512–13; *Revolt*, 11 March 1916; *The Blast*, 4, 15 March 1916; Theodore Appel to Comrades (*Freedom* London), 1 September 1916; *Alarm*, August 1916; Falk, *Emma Goldman*, 3:725; *Social War*, January 1917.

11　Lumsden, *Black, White, and Red All Over*, 272–73; *Chicago Daily Tribune*, 13 February 1916, 5 February 1925; *The Blast*, 26 February 1916; Paul Avrich, *Sacco and Vanzetti: The Anarchist Background* (Princeton, NJ: Princeton University Press, 1991), 98; Jeffrey A. Johnson, *The 1916 Preparedness Day Bombing: Anarchy and Terrorism in Progressive Era America* (New York: Routledge, 2018), 60–62; Christopher Wellbrook, "Seething with the Ideal: Galleanisti and Class Struggle in Late Nineteenth-Century and Early Twentieth-Century USA," *WorkingUSA: The Journal of Labor and Society* 12 (September 2009): 403–20.

12　Johnson, *1916 Preparedness Day Bombing*, 1–2, 76–88, 134–45, 150; Jay Fox, "Anarchists Leaders Jailed and Deported," in author's possession; Zimmer, *Immigrants Against the State*, 136–38; Avrich and Avrich, *Sasha and Emma*, 255–66; *Tacoma Times*, 30 November 1917; *Seattle Star*, 30 November 1917; LeWarne, *Utopias on Puget Sound*, 223–24; *Communist and Anarchist Deportation Cases* (Washington, DC: Government Printing Office, 1920), 105–6; 121–31; *Investigation Activities of the Department of Justice* (Washington, DC: Government Printing Office, 1919), 81–84; *San Jose Mercury News*, 5 May 1916; *Stockton Independent*, 5 May 1916; *San Francisco Call*, 9 August 1916.

13　*The Blast*, 1 April, 1 May 1916; Radium LaVene, "There Was No Place Like Home," Box 1, Folder 9, CCC, WSHS, Tacoma; Jay Fox, "Off to Home," in author's possession; *Tacoma Times*, 24, 31 August 1915, 19 July 1916, 9 October 1916, 28 March 1917, 10 May 1917; *Seattle Star*, 22 July 1916.

14　Travaglio, "Trials of a Noble Experiment"; J. C. Harrison, "One Picture of Home Colony," Box 2, Folder 2, CCC, WSHS; Mrs. de Crane, "Memoirs of Home," Box 1, Folder 13, CCC, WSHS *Tacoma Times*, 24 August 1916, 27 December 1916, 17, 18, 20 January 1917, 2, 17, 24, 28 February 1917, 1 March 1917, 9 August 1917, 12

April 1918; LeWarne, *Utopias on Puget Sound*, 220–21; Wadland, *Trying Home*, 138–39.

15 Max Dezettel to Jay Fox, 18 August 1917, Box 1, Folder 2, Fox Papers, UW, Seattle; *Chicago Labor News*, 15 September 1916; Foner, *History of the Labor Movement*, 9:96; Johanningsmeier, *Forging American Communism*, 84–85; *Seattle Union Record*, 2 September 1916, 14 October 1916; *Chicago Labor News*, June 1917 and n.d., Unprocessed Collection, Jay Fox Papers, Gonzaga University, Spokane; Ryan Walker, *New Adventures of Henry Dubb: Cartoons* (Chicago: Socialist Party, 1915), n.p.

16 *Chicago Labor News*, n.d., Unprocessed Collection, Fox Papers, Gonzaga.

17 *Seattle Union Record*, 2 September 1916; *Chicago Labor News*, 27 July 1917, Unprocessed Collection, Fox Papers, Gonzaga.

18 *Chicago Labor News*, n.d., Unprocessed Collection, Fox Papers, Gonzaga. In Fox's essay "Men, Women, and Morals," he noted that some African Americans were extremely intelligent but that did not change the "proposition of general racial inferiority of the negro." It is unclear when the essay was written and whether it was ever published or presented as a speech. *Mother Earth*, August 1917, 213–18. For an excellent analysis of Emma Goldman on race and racism, see Kathy E. Ferguson, *Emma Goldman: Political Thinking in the Streets* (Lanham, MD: Rowman and Littlefield, 2011), 211–47; *Revolutionary Age* 2 (23 August 1919): 3.

19 Bekken, "Working-Class Newspapers," 128–74; Jon Bekken, "The Working-Class Press at the Turn of the Century," in *Ruthless Criticism: New Perspectives in U.S. Communication History*, ed. William S. Solomon and Robert W. McChesney (Minneapolis: University of Minnesota Press, 1993), 151–75; *Chicago Labor News*, n.d., Unprocessed Collection, Fox Papers, Gonzaga; *Seattle Union Record*, 27 October 1917, 8, 22 December 1917, 16 March 1918; *Labor World*, 10 March 1916, 26 January 1918; *Paper Makers Journal* 17 (February 1918): 5–6.

20 Foner, *History of the Labor Movement*, 9:92–97; Foster, *From Brian to Stalin*, 90–100; Barrett, *William Z. Foster*, 76–82; Johanningsmeier, *Forging American Communism*, 90–104; *Labor World*, 15 September 1917; *Chicago Labor News*, n.d., Unprocessed Collection, Fox Papers, Gonzaga; *Seattle Union Record*, 8 December 1917; United States Commission on Industrial Relations, *Report of Commission on Industrial Relations*, vol. 4 (Washington, DC: Government Printing Office, 1916), 3486–98.

21 Jay Fox, "The Non-Partisan League" and the League Correspondence Course in Farm Economics, examination paper of student 144 (Jay Fox), Box 1, Folder 32, Fox Papers, Gonzaga; Greg Hall, *Harvest Wobblies: The Industrial Workers of the World and Agricultural Laborers in the American West, 1905–1930* (Corvallis: Oregon State University Press, 2001), 83–85; Lowell K. Dyson, *Red Harvest:*

The Communist Party and American Farmers (Lincoln: University of Nebraska Press, 1982), 7–9; Michael J. Lansing, *Insurgent Democracy: The Nonpartisan League in North American Politics* (Chicago: University of Chicago Press, 2015), 67–69, 92–134.

22 Fox, "Non-Partisan League"; *Non-Partisan Leader*, 25 June 1918; Jay Fox "To the Editor of," six such "letters" in author's possession.

23 *Seattle Union Record*, 6 April 1918, 21, 25 May 1918; *Fargo Forum and Daily Republican*, 21 March 1918; *Labor World*, 23 March 1918; Johanningsmeier, *Forging American Communism*, 156.

24 Johanningsmeier, *Forging American Communism*, 156; Foner, *History of the Labor Movement*, 9:104; Fox, "Non-Partisan League."

25 Carr, "Jay Fox, 9; Foster, *From Brian to Stalin*, 114, 134; *Labor Journal*, 9 April 1920; *Communist and Anarchist Deportation Cases*, 128; *Randi Storch, Red Chicago: American Communism at Its Grassroots, 1928-35* (Urbana: University of Illinois Press, 2007), 16–17; Robert L. Friedheim, *The Seattle General Strike* (Seattle: University of Washington Press, 2018), 57–83; *Seattle Union Record*, 4 January 1919, 3, 6 February 1919.

26 Jay Fox, "Seattle General Strike," in author's possession; *Seattle Union Record*, 5 February 1919; "Minutes of Meetings of the General Strike Committee and Its Executive Committee at Seattle, Washington, February 2–16, 1919," Box 5, Folder "Seattle General Strike," Harry E. B. Ault Papers, Special Collections, University of Washington Libraries, Seattle.

27 Friedheim, *Seattle General Strike*, 129–53; Fox, "Seattle General Strike"; *Minutes of Meetings of the General Strike Committee*; Cal Winslow, *Radical Seattle: The General Strike of 1919* (New York: Monthly Review Press, 2020), 214–18.

28 Jay Fox, "Final Adventures," Box 1, Folder 10, Fox Papers, Gonzaga; *Seattle Star*, 7 December 1918; LeWarne, *Utopias on Puget Sound*, 221–22; Pierce County, Superior Court File 43388, Oscar Engvall et al. v. Anna Haiman et al.; *Reliable Poultry Journal*, September 1921, 590, 592.

8. A COMMUNIST AT HOME

1 Foster, *From Bryan to Stalin*, 132; Jay Fox, "The Russian Revolution," Box 1, Folder 17, Fox Papers, Gonzaga; *Mother Earth Bulletin*, October 1917, 5–6, November 1917, 2–3, December 1917, 1–3; Avrich, *Anarchist Voices*, 47, 56, 61, 199, 242; Draper, *Roots of American Communism*, 121–26; *The Dawn*, February 1922, 10–12; Zimmer, *Immigrants Against the State*, 143; Barrett, *William Z. Foster*, 75, 102; Bryan D. Palmer, *James P. Cannon and the Origins of the American Revolutionary Left, 1890–1928* (Urbana: University of Illinois Press, 2007), 90–94; Darlington, *Revolutionary Unionism*, 185–86.

2 Stanley Shapiro, "Hand and Brain: The Farmer-Labor Party of 1920" (PhD diss., University of California, Berkeley, 1967), 12; Foster, *From Bryan to Stalin*, 138–42, 156–63; V. I. Lenin, *"Left-Wing" Communism: An Infantile Disorder* (Detroit: Marxian Educational Society, 1921), 42–51; *The Federated Press Bulletin*, 2 July 1921, 24 September 1921; Barrett, *William Z. Foster*, 99, 104–9; Johanningsmeier, *Forging American Communism*, 160–70; Foner, *History of the Labor Movement*, 9:108–11; Darlington, *Radical Unionism*, 167–69, 176–77, 189–94.

3 *Federated Press Bulletin*, 22 February 1922; *Labor Herald*, March 1922; Foster, *From Bryan to Stalin*, 164, 167–84; Foner, *History of the Labor Movement*, 9:120, 127–31; Johanningsmeier, *Forging American Communism*, 179–80, 187, 201.

4 *Labor Herald*, April 1922, 6–8, 30; William Z. Foster, *The Railroaders' Next Step—Amalgamation* (Chicago: Trade Union Educational League, 1922); *Labor Herald*, April 1922, 16–17, June 1922, 26–27.

5 Jay Fox, *Amalgamation* (Chicago: Trade Union Educational League, n.d.); leaflet for Fox lecture in San Francisco, 15 November 1923, Box 1, Folder 17, Fox Papers, WSU.

6 *Douglas Island News*, 27 October 1915; *Daily Alaskan*, 2 February 1915; *Iditarod Pioneer*, 14 July 1917; A. B. Callaham to Dear Foxes, 19 August 1922, Box 1, Folder 2, Fox Papers, UW, Seattle; *Seattle Union Record*, 25 May 1919, 11 March 1919; *Labor Herald*, July 1922, 9–10; *Federated Press Bulletin*, 25 March 1922, 1 April 1922; Foner, *History of the Labor Movement*, 9:245–68; *Labor Herald*, April 1923, 16–18.

7 Irving Bernstein, *The Lean Years: A History of the American Worker, 1920–1933* (Baltimore: Penguin, 1960), 84; Montgomery, *Fall of the House of Labor*, 404–10; *Labor Herald*, August 1922, 15–16, January 1923, 20–21; William Z. Foster, *The Bankruptcy of the American Labor Movement* (Chicago: Trade Union Educational League, 1922).

8 *Labor Herald*, December 1923, 20–21, October 1922, 26, November 1922, 20–21, July 1923, 26–27, June 1923, 26–27; *New Majority*, 7, 14 July 1923; *Labor Herald*, August 1923, 3–7, January 1924, 6–8, 26–27; Foner, *History of the Labor Movement*, 9:343–55; Montgomery, *Fall of the House of Labor*, 434–37.

9 *Labor Herald*, January 1924, 21–22, February 1924, 3–5; Bernstein, *Lean Years*, 66; Foner, *History of the Labor Movement*, 9:159–69; Montgomery, *Fall of the House of Labor*, 432–34; Barrett, *William Z. Foster*, 143–44; Foster, *From Bryan to Stalin*, 194–95.

10 Jay Fox, "Final Adventures," Box 1, Folder 10, Fox Papers, Gonzaga; Greg Hall, "'Light Work': Women, Children, and Progressive Era Reform in West Coast Commercial Agriculture and Canning," *Journal of the West* 55 (Winter 2016): 84–86.

11 Storch, *Red Chicago*, 24–25; *The Liberator*, October 1920, 5–11; Fred S. Graham, *Anarchism and the World Revolution: An Answer to Robert Minor* (n.p., 1921);

Road to Freedom, November 1924, 5–6, December 1924, 2–3; Ernesto A. Longa, *Anarchist Periodicals in English Published in the United States (1833–1955) An Annotated Guide* (Lanham, MD: Scarecrow Press, 2021), 230–31; Alexander Berkman to Harry Kelly, 13 February 1933, Alexander Berkman Papers, Microfilm, International Institute of Social History, Amsterdam (hereafter Berkman Papers, IISH); Emma Goldman, *My Further Disillusionment in Russia* (Garden City, NY: Doubleday, Page & Company, 1924), 65–94; Goldman, *Living My Life*, 884–88; *Evening Star*, 13 November 1924; Alice Wexler, *Emma Goldman in Exile: From the Russian Revolution to the Spanish Civil War* (Boston: Beacon Press, 1989), 92–113; Cornell, *Unruly Equality*, 80–110.

12 *Workers' Monthly*, February 1925, 179–81; V. I. Lenin, *The State and Revolution* (New York: International Publishers, 1932), 69–85.

13 *Road to Freedom*, April 1925, 4–7.

14 Jay Fox, "Why I Joined the Communist Party," Box 1, Folder 2, Fox Papers, Gonzaga; Cornell, *Unruly Equality*, 96–100, 129–33; *Mother Earth*, March 1915, 404–7; Harry Kelly to Alexander Berkman, 10 October 1924, and Harry Kelly to Alexander Berkman, 9 June 1925, Berkman Papers, IISH.

15 Johanningsmeier, *Forging American Communism*, 225–27, 234–36; Barrett, *William Z. Foster*, 162, 164, 169, 179; Daeho Ko, "Rough Beginnings," Communism in Washington State, History and Memory Project, University of Washington, n.d., https://depts.washington.edu/labhist/cpproject/ko.shtml; Jay Fox to Theodore Schroeder, 5 June 1929, Schroeder Papers, SIU; United Kingdom Census of England and Wales 1911; United States Census 1930, Home, Washington, and United States Census 1940, Home, Washington.

16 *Daily Worker*, 1 July 1931; "Communist Party Membership in Washington, Oregon, Idaho: 1922–1945," Communism in Washington State, History and Memory Project, University of Washington, n.d., https://depts.washington.edu/labhist/cpproject/maps.shtml; Gordon Black, "Organizing the Unemployed: The Early 1930s," Communism in Washington State, History and Memory Project, University of Washington, n.d. https://depts.washington.edu/labhist/cpproject/black.shtml; Brian Grijalva, "Organizing Unions: The 1930s and 1940s," Communism in Washington State, History and Memory Project, University of Washington, n.d., https://depts.washington.edu/labhist/cpproject/grijalva.shtml; Shelley Pinckney, "Race and Civil Rights: The 1930s and 1940s," Communism in Washington State, History and Memory Project, University of Washington, n.d., https://depts.washington.edu/labhist/cpproject/pinckney.shtml; *Timber Worker*, 9, 16 October 1937, 6 November 1937, 5, 19 February 1938; newspaper clippings from the *Tacoma Daily Ledger*, Box 1, Folder 10, Fox Papers, WSU, Pullman; Communist Political Association Pierce County "Meeting Agenda," Box 1, Folder 22, Fox Papers, Gonzaga.

17 Barrett, *William Z. Foster*, 182–86; Bill Foster to Jay Fox, n.d., photocopy from Edward P. Johanningsmeier to the author.

18 *Daily Worker*, 29 April 1936; *Our World*, 16 February 1951, 3–4; Jay Fox to Theodore Schroeder, 15 May 1939, 15 April 1941, Schroeder Papers, SIU; Ewing C. Baskette to Jay Fox, 5 February 1942, 25 February 1942, 28 February 1942, 12 March 1942, 17 March 1942, 27 March 1943, 28 March 1943, Box 1, Folder 36, Fox Papers, Gonzaga.

19 Jay Fox to Theodore Schroeder, 15 April 1941, 20 July [1941], 25 July 1941, 13 August 1941, 29 November 1951, 11 March 1952, 12 October 1952, Schroeder Papers, SIU; *Our World*, 27 April 1951.

20 *Northwest Enterprise*, 6 August 1931; Stewart Holbrook, "Home Sweet Home: The Anarchists of Joe's Bay," *The Oregonian*, 5, 12, 19 December 1937, newspaper clippings, Box 1, Folder 2, CCC, WSHS; Travaglio, "Trials of a Noble Experiment"; Major Frank Pease to Major George W. Cutting, report, 11 March 1942, photocopy from Edward P. Johanningsmeier to the author; Terry Pettus, "Sixty-Four Years a Union Man," newspaper clipping, Box 1, Folder 21, Fox Papers, WSU; Stewart Holbrook, "There Was No Place Like Home, Wash.," n.d., newspaper clipping, Box 1, Folder 13, CCC, WSHS.

SELECTED READINGS

The primary and secondary literature below have been gleaned from the notes for the book. They are some of the most pertinent and accessible sources for readers interested in learning more about the history and theory of anarchism, labor radicalism, and other events, movements, individuals, and communities covered in the narrative. Scholars and students of history will find all of the documentation for my study of Jay Fox in the book's notes.

Albro, Ward S. *Always a Rebel: Ricardo Flores Magón and the Mexican Revolution.* Fort Worth: Texas Christian University Press, 1992.

Avrich, Paul. *Anarchist Voices: An Oral History of Anarchism in America.* Princeton, NJ: Princeton University, 1995.

———. *The Haymarket Tragedy.* Princeton, NJ: Princeton University Press, 1984.

Antonioli, Maurizio, ed. *The International Anarchist Congress Amsterdam, 1907.* Translated by Nestor McNab. Edmonton: Blackcat Press, 2009.

Avrich, Paul, and Karen Avrich. *Sasha and Emma: The Anarchist Odyssey of Alexander Berkman and Emma Goldman.* Cambridge: Harvard University Press, 2012.

Bantman, Constance, and Bert Altena, eds. *Reassessing the Transnational Turn: Scales of Analysis in Anarchist and Syndicalist Studies.* New York: Routledge, 2015.

Barrett, James R. *William Z. Foster and the Tragedy of American Radicalism.* Urbana: University of Illinois Press, 1999.

Bekken, Jon Everett. "The Working-Class Press at the Turn of the Century." In *Ruthless Criticism: New Perspectives in U.S. Communication History,* edited by William S. Solomon and Robert W. McChesney, 151–75. Minneapolis: University of Minnesota Press, 1993.

Berry, David, and Constance Bantman, eds. *New Perspectives on Anarchism, Labour, and Syndicalism: The Individual, the National and the Transnational.* Newcastle upon Tyne: Cambridge Scholars Publishing, 2010.

Cahm, Caroline. *Kropotkin and the Rise of Revolutionary Anarchism, 1872–1886.* Cambridge: Cambridge University Press, 1989.

Carr, Mary M. "Jay Fox: Anarchist of Home." *Columbia: The Magazine of Northwest History* 4 (Spring 1990): 3–10.

Clark, Norman H. *Mill Town: A Social History of Everett, Washington, from Its Earliest Beginnings on the Shores of Puget Sound to the Tragic and Infamous Event Known as the Everett Massacre.* Seattle: University of Washington Press, 1970.

Cobble, Dorothy Sue. "Pure and Simple Radicalism: Putting the Progressive Era AFL in Its Time." *Labor: Studies in Working-Class History of the Americas* 10 (Winter 2013): 61–87.

Cornell, Andrew. *Unruly Equality: U.S. Anarchism in the Twentieth Century.* Berkeley: University of California Press, 2016.

Crowder, George. *Classical Anarchism: The Political Thought of Godwin, Proudhon, Bakunin, and Kropotkin.* Oxford: Oxford University Press, 1991.

Darlington, Ralph. *Radical Unionism: The Rise and Fall of Revolutionary Syndicalism.* Chicago: Haymarket Books, 2013.

DeLeon, David. *The American as Anarchist: Reflections on Indigenous Radicalism.* Baltimore: Johns Hopkins University Press, 1978.

Dubofsky, Melvyn. *We Shall Be All: A History of the Industrial Workers of the World.* Chicago: Quadrangle Books, 1969.

Ferguson, Kathy E. "Anarchist Printers and Presses: Material Circuits of Politics." *Political Theory* 42 (2014): 391–414.

———. *Emma Goldman: Political Thinking in the Streets.* Lanham, MD: Rowman and Littlefield, 2011.

Ford, Earl C., and William Z. Foster. *Syndicalism.* Chicago: Charles H. Kerr, 1990.

Foster, William Z. *From Bryan to Stalin.* New York: International Publishers, 1937.

Fox, Jay. *Amalgamation.* Chicago: Trade Union Educational League, n.d.

———. *Roosevelt, Czolgosz and Anarchy.* New York: New York Anarchists, n.d.

———. *Trade Unionism and Anarchism: A Letter to a Brother Unionist.* Chicago: Social Science Press, 1908.

Foner, Philip S., ed. *The Autobiographies of the Haymarket Martyrs.* New York: Pathfinder B, 1993.

Free Speech League. *The Free Speech Case of Jay Fox.* New York: Free Speech League, 1912.

Friedheim, Robert L. *The Seattle General Strike.* Seattle: University of Washington Press, 2018.

Goldman, Emma. *Living My Life.* New York: Alfred A. Knopf, 1934.

Goyens, Tom. *Beer and Revolution: The German Anarchist Movement in New York City, 1880–1914.* Urbana: University of Illinois Press, 2007.

Green, James. *Death in the Haymarket: A Story of Chicago, the First Labor Movement and the Bombing that Divided Gilded Age America.* New York: Anchor Books, 2006.

Guerin, Daniel. *Anarchism: From Theory to Practice.* New York: Monthly Review Press, 1970.

Hapgood, Hutchins. *The Spirit of Labor.* Edited by James R. Barrett. Urbana: University of Illinois Press, 2004.

Havel, Hippolyte, ed., *The Revolutionary Almanac 1914.* New York: Rabelais Press, n.d.

Heale, M. J. *American Anticommunism: Combating the Enemy Within, 1830–1970.* Baltimore: Johns Hopkins University Press, 1990.

Hong, Nathaniel Hong. "Free Speech Without an If or a But: The Defense of Free Expression in the Radical Periodicals of Home, Washington, 1897–1912," *American Journalism* 11 (Spring 1994): 139–53.

Johanningsmeier, Edward P. *Forging American Communism: The Life of William Z. Foster.* Princeton, NJ: Princeton University Press, 1994.

Johnson, Jeffrey A. *"They Are All Read Out Here": Socialist Politics in the Pacific Northwest, 1895–1925.* Norman: University of Oklahoma Press, 2008.

Jones, Jacqueline. *Goddess of Anarchy: The Life and Times of Lucy Parsons, American Radical.* New York: Basic Books, 2017.

Joll, James. *The Anarchists.* Boston: Little, Brown, 1964.

Jun, Nathan, and Shane Wahl, eds. *New Perspectives on Anarchism.* New York: Lexington Books, 2010.

Koenig, Brigitte. "Law and Disorder at Home: Free Love, Free Speech, and the Search for an Anarchist Utopia." *Labor History* 45 (May 2004): 199–223.

Kropotkin, Peter. *Conquest of Bread.* New York: G. P. Putman's Sons, 1906.

———. *Mutual Aid: A Factor in Evolution.* Boston: Porter Sargent, 1976.

Lansing, Michael J. *Insurgent Democracy: The Nonpartisan League in North American Politics* Chicago: University of Chicago Press, 2015.

Leeder, Elaine. *The Gentle General: Rose Pesotta: Anarchist and Labor Organizer.* New York: State University of New York Press, 1993.

Lenin, V. I. *"Left-Wing" Communism: An Infantile Disorder.* Detroit: Marxian Educational Society, 1921.

———. *The State and Revolution.* New York: International Publishers, 1932.

LeWarne, Charles Pierce. *Utopias on Puget Sound, 1885–1915.* Seattle: University of Washington Press, 1995.

Loomis, Erik. *Empire of Timber: Labor Unions and the Pacific Northwest Forests.* New York: Cambridge University Press, 2016.

Lumsden, Linda J. *Black, White, and Red All Over: A Cultural History of the Radical Press in Its Heyday, 1900–1917.* Kent, OH: Kent State University Press, 2014.

Mann, Tom. *Tom Mann's Memoirs.* London: MacGibbon and Kee, 1967.

Messer-Kruse, Timothy. *The Haymarket Conspiracy: Transatlantic Anarchist Networks.* Urbana: University of Illinois Press, 2012.

Miller, David. *Anarchism.* London: J. M. Dent & Sons, 1984.

Montgomery, David. *The Fall of the House of Labor: The Workplace, the State, and American Labor Activism, 1865–1925*. New York: Cambridge University Press, 1987.

Nelson, Bruce. *Beyond the Martyrs: A Social History of Chicago Anarchists, 1870–1900*. New Brunswick, NJ: Rutgers University Press, 1988.

O'Connor, Harvey. *Revolution in Seattle: A Memoir*. New York: Monthly Review Press, 1964.

Parsons, A. R. *Anarchism: Its Philosophy and Scientific Basis as Defined by Some of Its Apostles*. Chicago: A. R. Parsons, 1887.

Parsons, Lucy, ed. *Life of Albert R. Parsons: With Brief History of the Labor Movement America: Also, Sketches of the Lives of A. Spies, Geo. Engel, A. Fischer and Louis Lingg*. Chicago: Lucy E. Parsons, Publisher, 1903.

Pernicone, Nunzio. *Carlo Tresca: Portrait of a Rebel*. New York: Palgrave Macmillan, 2005.

Preston, William, Jr. *Aliens and Dissenters: Federal Suppression of Radicals, 1903–1933*. Urbana: University of Illinois Press, 1994.

Renders, Hans, Binne de Haan, and Jonne Harmsma, eds. *The Biographical Turn: Lives in History*. London: Routledge, 2017.

Roediger, Dave, and Franklin Rosemont, eds. *Haymarket Scrapbook*. Chicago: Charles H. Kerr Publishing, 1986.

Roller, Arnold. *The Social General Strike*. Chicago: Debating Club, 1905.

Salerno, Salvatore. *Red November Black November: Culture and Community in the Industrial Workers of the World*. Albany: State University of New York Press, 1989.

Salvatore, Nick. *Eugene V. Debs: Citizen and Socialist*. Urbana: University of Illinois Press, 1982.

Schwantes, Carlos A. *Radical Heritage: Labor, Socialism, and Reform in Washington and British Columbia, 1885–1917*. Seattle: University of Washington Press, 1979.

Smith, Steven Kent. "Abraham Isaak: The History of a Mennonite Radical." *Mennonite Quarterly Review* 65 (October 1991): 449–55.

Struthers, David. *The World in a City: Multiethnic Radicalism in Early Twentieth-Century Los Angeles*. Urbana: University of Illinois Press, 2019.

Thomas, Matthew. *Anarchists Ideas Counter-Cultures in Britain, 1880–1914: Revolutions in Everyday in Everyday Life*. Burlington, UT: Ashgate, 2005.

Tyler, Robert L. *Rebels in the Woods: The I.W.W. in the Pacific Northwest*. Eugene: University of Oregon, 1967.

van der Walt, Lucien, and Michael Schmidt. *Black Flame: The Revolutionary Class Politics of Anarchism and Syndicalism*. Edinburgh: AK Press, 2009.

Wadland, Justin. *Trying Home: The Rise and Fall of an Anarchist Utopia on Puget Sound*. Corvallis: Oregon State University Press, 2014.

Westergard-Thorpe, Wayne. *"The Workers Themselves": Revolutionary Syndicalism and International Labour, 1913–1923*. Dordrecht: Kluwer Academic, 1989.

Winslow, Cal. *Radical Seattle: The General Strike of 1919*. New York: Monthly Review Press, 2020.

Woodcock, George. *Anarchism: A History of Libertarian Ideas and Movements*. Harmondsworth: Penguin, 1975.

Woodcock, George, and Ivan Avakumovic. *The Anarchist Prince: A Biographical Study of Peter Kropotkin*. New York: Schocken Books, 1971.

Zimmer, Kenyon. *Immigrants Against the State: Yiddish and Italian Anarchism in America*. Urbana: University of Illinois Press, 2015.

INDEX

Page numbers in *italics* refer to illustrations.

CPSIA information can be obtained
at www.ICGtesting.com
Printed in the USA
BVHW080755260522
638164BV00004B/6